RAILROADS AND GOVERNMENT

RAILROADS
AND GOVERNMENT

THEIR RELATIONS IN THE UNITED STATES
1910–1921

BY

FRANK HAIGH DIXON, Ph.D.

PROFESSOR OF ECONOMICS, PRINCETON UNIVERSITY

CHARLES SCRIBNER'S SONS
NEW YORK   CHICAGO   BOSTON

THIS BOOK IS AFFECTIONATELY INSCRIBED
TO THE MEMORY OF

HENRY CARTER ADAMS

SCHOLAR, TEACHER, FRIEND
WHOSE CONTRIBUTIONS TO THE SOLUTION OF THE
RAILROAD PROBLEM HAVE PLACED THE
NATION IMMEASURABLY IN HIS DEBT

PREFACE

THE purpose of this book is to take up the story of the federal regulation of railroads in the United States where most of the treatises on transportation have dropped it, at 1910, and bring the history down to the present year. There is no intention to trace from the beginning the development of the fundamental principles of rate regulation upon which present administration relies. This has been admirably done by others. Professor Ripley's two scholarly and exhaustive volumes— *Railroads: Rates and Regulation* and *Railroads: Finance and Organization*—leave little to be said on the period that he covers. And this period will be recalled only so far as is necessary to create a background for the later history. This volume is written by a teacher, with teachers primarily in mind, and it is hoped that it may serve as a supplement to existing texts, in spite of its obvious departure at times from that nice balancing of conflicting points of view which is commonly supposed to be the outstanding characteristic of the academic mind.

But the book has quite another and an equally important object. Effort has been made to relieve the discussion so far as possible of technical features in order to beguile the general reader into at least a hasty perusal. For we have been passing through an extraordinary decade in the relations of railroads and government. More experience and experiment have been crowded into these ten years than into all the remainder of our railroad history of nearly a century.

We have employed our transportation machine as a

war agency to an extent never before experienced, and
for the first time in our history we have ventured upon
government operation. Whether or not this experiment may legitimately be employed as an argument for
or against nationalization of railroads as a permanent
policy, the twenty-six months of federal control demonstrated the soundness and practicability of many projects for more efficient operation under private auspices—
projects that will be a subject of lively discussion until
they are realized in actual practice.

And again the war experiment shook us out of a
lethargic state into which we seemed to have fallen, and
started us with renewed vigor on the task of solving this
perennial railroad problem. Many of the features of
the Transportation Act of 1920 had been long advocated,
but their advocacy had fallen on deaf ears. And suddenly without ostentation and almost naturally they became a part of our regulating statute.

More than this, the railroads are now officially placed
in a new relation to the public, and the regulating body
is imposed with a mandate that requires it to recognize
this relationship. Congress has formally declared that
it is the business of the Government to provide the public with adequate and efficient transportation service
and to assure to private capital the revenue needed to
accomplish the purpose. A new responsibility is placed
upon the Interstate Commerce Commission. But this
very fact emphasizes and enforces the public nature of
the industry with which we are dealing. Railroad executives and railroad labor are warned as never before that
they are administering a public trust, and that the future policy of the nation will be influenced by the character of their stewardship.

We are entering then upon a new phase of the railroad problem, in which knowledge and sound wisdom is
called for from the electorate. It has been the wish of

the author to contribute his mite to an intelligent understanding of the issue.

It is desired to acknowledge the courtesy of the respective editors of the *Quarterly Journal of Economics*,
the publications of the American Economic Association,
and the *Carnegie Economic Studies of the War* for permission to use in condensed form portions of articles
that have appeared under their auspices. The author
rests under especial obligation to Dr. Julius H. Parme-
lee, Director, and Mr. Richard H. Johnston, Librarian, of
the Bureau of Railway Economics, in Washington, who
have placed unreservedly at his disposal their advice
and services, and their unrivalled collection of printed
and manuscript material on railroad problems.

FRANK HAIGH DIXON.

CONTENTS

tory of Section 20 and development of accounting regulations following amendment of 1906—Inspection of accounts—Violations of
accounting regulations—Court cases—Depreciation—Separation of
operating expenses. 6. *Valuation*—The Act of 1914—Work of the
Bureau of Valuation—Valuation theories of the Commission—Importance of the valuation. 7. *Safety measures*—Jurisdiction of the
Commission—Block-signals—Failure of the human element—Trespassing—The automatic stop—Hours of Service Law.

THE WAR PERIOD

THE RETURN TO PRIVATE OPERATION

It demonstrates the reasonableness of the statutory scheme—Earlier attempts at combination untimely—Purpose of consolidation—Competition in service v. competition in rates—Constitutionality—Desirability of consolidation—Pooling permitted—Will this be of importance?—Consolidation of the express companies and the new contract with the railroads—The express company a superfluous agency—*Federal incorporation*—Arguments for and against it—The federal holding company.

APPENDICES

RAILROADS AND GOVERNMENT

CHAPTER I

INTRODUCTION

WITH the creation of the Interstate Commerce Commission, in 1887, the relationship of the federal government to the railroads assumed an importance for the public that it had never before possessed. For the first time a body endowed with executive and judicial functions—what was to be known as an administrative body—was to take a position as an arbiter between the public and our national transportation system. The plan had been tried for a decade or two in some of the states. It was now to be given a wider opportunity and a more critical test.

Why the Commission appeared at this particular time was apparent from the report of the Senate Committee that proposed the bill, and from the spirit of the Act itself. It was primarily to put an end to discriminations and rebates, and it was to protect the public against excessive charges. Naturally such an agency was regarded with hostility by the railroads. In a measure it returned the sentiment in kind. For it looked upon itself as the guardian of the public interests against exploitation by private corporations.

It was in this atmosphere of open hostility and contempt on the one hand, and frank suspicion on the other, that a considerable part of the first two decades of the Commission's history was passed. Little of enduring nature was accomplished by the regulating body during this time, beyond that of acquiring a technical knowl-

edge of the intricacies of the railroad business and laying a foundation of experience in railroad control. The
only legislation of any effectiveness enacted during this
stage was the Elkins Anti-Rebate Act of 1903, passed at
the instance of the railroads themselves.

This sterility of accomplishment had many causes. In
the first place, the country lacked any thorough knowledge of the problem it was attempting to solve. It was a
case of finding one's way step by step and discovering the
right path by the indirect process of following blind leads.
This applied both to the Commission and to Congress.
The statute was quite inadequate to the task set for it,
and its weaknesses revealed themselves as soon as any
reliance was placed upon it. Time after time the Commission sought the aid of the courts in the enforcement of
its powers only to find that the law upon which it leaned
was a broken reed.

While containing at times men of unusual ability, the
Commission included few who had had any previous contact with the railroad problem. And some of the commissioners obviously failed to measure up to their responsibilities. On the whole, however, the Commission grew
in authority and influence, and but for obstacles which
were insurmountable would have shown a considerable
accomplishment for its first twenty years of investigation
and experiment.

Besides the inadequacy of the statute which judicial
decisions exposed, the Commission had to reckon with the
jealousy and the ill-concealed suspicion of the judiciary
itself. This novel administrative body was to assume
functions that had theretofore been from time immemorial
the exclusive possession of the courts. It was natural
that the activities of the upstart should be resented. It
was no mere accident that early in the career of the Commission a federal court should decide that while the
Commission's evidence before the courts must be accepted

as *prima facie*, the courts had the right to consider the case anew from the beginning. Judges were by temperament and training conservative. They did not readily adjust their minds to the introduction of new methods of control and discipline into the field of public-service law. The Supreme Court, in the Texas and Pacific Case in 1896,[1] expressed well the spirit in which the judiciary approached this novel problem: "It must not be overlooked that this legislation is experimental. Even in construing the terms of a statute, courts must take notice of the history of legislation, and out of different possible constructions, select and apply the one that best comports with the genius of our institutions and, therefore, most likely to have been the construction intended by the lawmaking power." But what is the "genius of our institutions" and would the court define this in the same terms as would an Interstate Commerce commissioner?

One of the favorite arguments of the railroads in 1906 against an increase in the Commission's powers was that the Commission had shown itself inefficient and ill adapted to its job, as revealed by the numerous reversals of its decisions sustained at the hands of the Supreme Court. But such argument was wholly disingenuous. Beyond the weakness of the law itself and the hostility of the judiciary already alluded to, there was evident a settled policy on the part of the Commission to arouse public interest in favor of strengthening the law by the device of revealing its weaknesses. It was a shrewd programme which amply justified itself in the amendments of 1906.

It was in 1906 that the railroads fought their fight to a finish against federal regulation. No such reckless publicity campaign was ever known before in the history of railroad control and it is probable that none ever will be again. Backed by President Roosevelt and an aroused

[1] 162 U. S., 218.

public sentiment, Congress revolutionized the Act to Regulate Commerce, and the Commission was now for the first time in position actually to prescribe rates for the future. Moreover, it was at this time that the administrative authority of the Commission was clearly established. Congress made the decisions of the Commission final, except when they came into conflict with the Constitution and with questions of fundamental law. With this series of amendments, the abdication of the courts begins.

But for reasons that will appear later, the statutory structure was not yet complete. In 1910 Congress again enlarged the powers of the Commission, and strengthened weak spots in the law which in the fight of 1906 had been either overlooked or necessarily laid aside until a more convenient season. With the Act of 1910 begins our consideration of the relations of railroads and government.

It is not the purpose of this book to analyze in detail the Interstate Commerce Act or the system of regulation gradually constructed during the first quarter-century of federal railroad control. That task has been well done by others. Here the plan is to consider those significant additions to governmental authority that developed between 1910 and 1916, and to follow this with a critical analysis of the period of federal operation, in which an attempt will be made to discover such features as are of permanent value for our problem of regulation. Finally attention will be given to the Transportation Act of 1920, which returned the roads to their owners and introduced many novel features into our regulating policy.

FEDERAL REGULATION, 1910 TO 1916

CHAPTER II

THE Act of 1910 originated with the Administration. Out of conferences of President Taft with members of Congress and the Interstate Commerce Commission, with railroad officers and others, there appeared a bill drawn by the Attorney-General, which was introduced into both Houses of Congress. In conformity with pledges of the Republican platform upon which the President had been elected, it contained provisions for traffic agreements between paralleling roads and for federal control of capitalization. A considerable portion had to do with the creation of a new court and this, as it turned out, was almost the only portion of the bill that was retained in its original form. For the regulation of security issues there was substituted an investigating commission. The valuable features of the Act originated in Congress and were wrung from the Republican leaders by the "insurgent" element that stood for more effective regulation, assisted in many cases by the votes of the Democrats. In the Act as passed there were but two amendments of fundamental significance, one conferring the power to suspend rates, the other resuscitating the long and short haul clause. These two amendments will be discussed in successive chapters.

Power to suspend rates and pass upon their reasonableness in advance of their effective date was not contemplated in the bill introduced under the ægis of the President. This was one of the fruits of the insurgent movement. It was greatly assisted by the nation-wide move-

7

ment of the railroads for an increase in rates just at the time when the bill was under discussion. The action of the individual carriers in filing schedules of increased rates was so nearly simultaneous as to appear collusive. At any rate, the occasion was seized upon by the Administration to secure an injunction restraining twenty-four carriers from putting into effect higher rates, upon the ground that their action constituted a violation of the Anti-Trust Act. Whether a prosecution was contemplated and whether it would have succeeded if attempted, is beside the point. The carriers withdrew their tariffs, but the popular effect remained, and the suspension clause became law. This amendment to Section 15 provided that whenever there was filed with the Commission any new rate or classification or regulation, the Commission should have power, either upon complaint or on its own initiative and after reasonable notice, but without any formal answer, to enter upon a hearing concerning the propriety of the rate. Pending the hearing, it should have the power, after delivering a statement in writing to the carrier of its reasons therefor, to suspend the rate for 120 days beyond the effective date of the tariff. If the hearing was not completed at the end of this time, the Commission might extend the period of suspension for another six months, but at the end of that time—ten months from the effective date—the tariff went into force if no adverse order had meanwhile been issued by the Commission. Power to make an order concerning these suspended rates was as complete as though the rates had gone into effect, and the Commission were acting in response to the complaint of an injured shipper.

It is of importance to follow the reasoning that led to the adoption of this amendment. Since 1906 the Commission had had the power to prescribe maximum rates upon complaint, but the complaint had to be the result of actual experience of their effects. It was the shipper's business to demonstrate the unreasonableness of the rate. If he succeeded in his demonstration, he could obtain a lower rate for the future and he might be awarded, in addition, reparation for his loss. But if he was a shipper with small capital engaged in a competitive business, he might be on the rocks before help could arrive. Reparation, while of some value as a penalty, is no solution of the problem. Its working is slow, cumbersome, costly. It does not restore to the shipper what he has lost. Sacrifice of business to a competitor who has been profiting by a lower rate is not in any sense compensated for by the return of the excess over what the competitor paid.

Before the passage of this amendment, the shipper at times invoked the aid of the equity courts to restrain advances in rates. But aside from the technical question, much in dispute, whether courts could exercise the power of injunction in rate matters after a federal body had been especially created for the purpose of passing upon rates, injunctions could issue only in favor of the petitioners and only upon the filing of a bond. A decision in favor of the petitioners was of no value in settling the fundamental question at issue, and did not prevent another violation when different parties were involved, and a bond was expensive, in many cases prohibitive. Moreover, the jurisdiction of the court runs only in its own circuit, and there was no assurance of harmony in action among the courts of various contiguous jurisdictions. In a word, the judicial process was ill fitted to handle cases of this character; in fact, the whole system of administrative regulation was a revolt from the earlier processes of the law-courts.

But there was another and more significant aspect of this problem of rate suspension. In the majority of cases, the shipper or the consignee had added the freight charges to the price of his goods, and they had been borne by the ultimate consumer, who was not a party to any action between carrier and shipper and had no standing in court. The extent to which the consumer "pays the freight" cannot be determined with any accuracy. A careful analysis would require knowledge as to the character of the contract between shipper and consignee and the competitive conditions under which producer or shipper was handling his business. But after all, in the long run, transportation costs find their way into price, and, as already intimated, there is no manner in which the final purchaser of goods can recover for the burden of an unreasonable freight charge imposed upon the goods he buys. In any case in most instances the amount is so small for the individual that he would be indifferent to the abuse.

This aggregate of individuals making up the vast consuming public can have no representation in the matter except through the Commission created by law to pass upon the reasonableness of rates, and the degree of protection afforded depends upon whether this official body can determine the justness and reasonableness of rates in advance of their actual inauguration. A rate long in existence is presumptively reasonable, and no serious hardship can arise if a postponement of the new rate is made pending an examination as to its justice. Such was the reasoning that led to the adoption of the suspension clause and has made it, apparently, a permanent part of our regulating machinery. For the changes made in the procedure in 1920, to which reference will be made later, were minor modifications that did not disturb the fundamental principle.

As a logical result of the suspension method, it was provided that thereafter the burden of proof was to be on the carrier to show that the increased rates proposed were just and reasonable. This threw upon the carrier the burden of proving that the new rate *as a whole* was reasonable—not that the *increase* in the rate over the pre-existing rate was a reasonable increase. In this respect the law differed from that in England. There the prevailing rates had by statute been declared reasonable and only the increase had to be justified. Here the whole question of the reasonableness of the fundamental rate could be reopened.[1] The practical result of this necessary interpretation of our law has been an unjustifiable and endless stirring up of our rate structure. Agencies have been established for the sole purpose of securing paid freight bills from shippers with power of attorney to bring complaints. As long as the Commission had power to prescribe only maximum rates, the carrier was free to set a rate at some lower point and thus upset an adjustment to which a group of carriers had agreed. Orders of the Commission formerly held for but two years[2] and unreasonable situations which had been relieved by the Commission's order frequently appeared again immediately upon the expiration of the order. Parties who might be affected by a decision, whether carrier or shipper, refrained from intervening or appearing in a case in order to be free to attack a rate once established or secure a rehearing. By these and many other technical processes, litigation was kept alive, and the plan of regulation resolved itself "largely into a sort of continuous moving around in a circle." Very properly, the Commission protested against the employment by the carrier of its freedom to initiate rates, to disturb adjustments recognized as reasonable and fair by the large majority of shippers and carriers.

This absurd situation in which shippers were at liberty

---

[1] See discussion of English and American practice in Western Advance Rate Case, 20 I. C. C., 310–12.

[2] Under the Act of 1920 orders of the Commission continue in force until further order or for a specified period named in the order. Section 15 (2).

to attack as unreasonable rates long in existence, against which there were only trivial objections, led the Commission to recommend that Congress follow the English Parliament and formally legalize existing rates. After noting that at this time (1916) rates had been open for complaint for ten years before a Commission clothed with rate-making power, and had been subject to suspension for six years, the Commission said: "We are convinced that the best interests of the entire public, of the system of governmental regulation of rates, and of the railroads will be served by the enactment of a statute which as of a specified date fixes the existing interstate rates, fares, classifications, rules, regulations and charges as just and reasonable for the past, and which provides that after that date no change therein may be made except upon order of the Commission. . . . The adoption of such a plan as this would make it possible to apply the energies expended upon rate controversies in the direction of constructive work for the future instead of expending them upon controversies as to reparation for the past, with every probability that in a majority of the cases the one who ultimately bore the charge will never be reached by the reparation."[1] This important proposal has never been acted upon by Congress.

Placing on the carrier the burden of proof as to reasonableness lightened the Commission's task in the extended rate hearings in the summer of 1910, for the Commission had not to decide that the rates filed by the carriers were actually unreasonable, but only that the carriers had failed to establish their reasonableness. It is this negative attitude of the Commission during the years from 1910 to 1916 to which the railroads attribute many of their ills.

At the time the rate-suspension amendment was adopted, there was a determined effort on the part of the

[1] Annual Report, 1916, p. 78.

insurgents to secure the incorporation of a provision that rates should not go into effect without the previous approval of the Commission. They failed in their efforts, securing instead a power of suspension for a ten months' period, within which it was assumed the Commission could determine practically all cases. But in August, 1917, another attempt was made to secure the adoption of this principle. The amendment had a checkered career in the two Houses, and finally was passed in the form of a provision that until January 1, 1920, no increased charge could be filed except after approval by the Commission. This approval could be given without formal hearing, but in such case no subsequent proceeding was to be affected by the approval.[1] The significance of the limiting date, January 1, 1920, was that a joint committee of the two Houses was sitting on railroad affairs, and it was thought that it could by that time work out a permanent plan.

This provision might have resulted in a significant alteration in procedure, with the result of reducing the number of necessary suspensions, and furnishing a method more satisfactory to both shipper and carrier. But within a few months the roads were taken over by the federal government. The Director-General was under no obligation to respect a provision that required permission from the Commission to file increased rates. He not only disregarded it, but ordered all "15th Section applications" for the filing of increased rates withdrawn. No applications of this kind were filed during federal control except by the few unimportant carriers not taken over by the Government. When the roads emerged from Government control, the expiration date of this amendment, January 1, 1920, had been reached, and carriers were now subject to another procedure under the Transportation Act of 1920.

With 1910 begins that co-operation in the handling of

[1] 40 Stat. L., 272.

rate matters before the Commission involving the carriers of widely extended territories, which has been so
characteristic of the last decade. There are many reasons for this abandonment of individual action. Intercorporate relationships had become more intimate and
comprehensive. The carriers were becoming more accustomed to working together. An organization had been
perfected in 1906 to oppose the Hepburn amendments to
the Interstate Commerce Act, and while the extravagance
of its propagandism brought this organization into dis-
repute, and reacted unfavorably upon the cause of the
railroads, yet the carriers gained some experience in co-
operating with one another. In 1910 a national statistical organization, the Bureau of Railway Economics, was
set up to present the facts of the railroad situation to the
public uncolored by the personal bias of any individual
carrier. The railroads felt that their situation was becoming critical, and that a non-partisan presentation of
their situation to the public would win support. Moreover, they wished to have an agency available to prepare
statistical material for presentation to the Commission
on a uniform basis, freed from the confusion that would
arise from a mass of data furnished by individual roads
without any centralized guidance.

Again, there were reasons in the nature of the problem
why roads should associate together for their cases. The
relation between rates and investment was becoming, as
the roads saw it, a serious question, and only by a presentation covering an entire territory could they properly
impress the Commission with its significance. Moreover, the legislation of 1910 had a very direct influence.
The power of the Commission to suspend rates pending
a hearing and to enter upon an investigation, threw the
carriers upon the defensive. The requirement that the
increased rates must be justified necessitated the accumulation of elaborate data covering capitalization, equip-

ment, labor conditions, costs of materials, physical factors of operation—all of which needed to be developed on a territorial scale to make their presentation effective. It is more than likely that the enormous mass of statistical data poured out upon the Commission was in part a waste of effort, but the roads had in view that they must "satisfy the mind of the Commission," and there was no way of foretelling what chance statistical fact might turn the trick.

Two elaborate investigations covering proposed increases in rates were conducted by the Commission in 1910, one in Eastern and one in Western territory,[1] in which the records were stupendous. The plea of the railroads was that they were not earning a fair return upon the value of their property, due to the increased cost of operation, principally increased labor cost. In neither of these cases did the railroads succeed in satisfying the Commission that increases were necessary. The Commission held that operating revenues were increasing sufficiently to absorb the increase in expenses, and that efficient management would take care of the situation without additions to the rates. In view of the present responsibility of the Commission to furnish adequate transportation service as required by the Act of 1920, it is of interest to record the attitude of the Commission ten years earlier.

"We must not regard too seriously, however, the effort of railroad counsel to establish this Commission *in loco parentis* toward the railroads. . . . This country cannot afford to have poor railroads, insufficiently equipped, unsubstantially built, carelessly operated. . . . Nevertheless, it is likewise to be remembered that the Government has not undertaken to become the directing mind in railroad management. We are not the managers of

[1] 20 I. C. C., 243, 307.

the railroads. And no matter what the revenue they may receive, there can be no control placed by us upon its expenditure, no improvements directed, no economies enforced."[1]

But the most significant rate case of the period was the so-called "Five Per Cent Case" of 1914.[2] This controversy attracted wide public notice and contained much that was prophetic of future development. The Commission in its original decision in July, 1914, granted increases in central freight association territory, but denied general increases throughout official classification territory. It conceded that upon the record the net operating income of the carriers was smaller than was demanded in the public interest, amounting in 1913 to 5.36 per cent upon the property investment[3] of thirty-five railroad systems in this territory, but it held that this income could be materially augmented by the introduction of economies and the abandonment of wasteful and unremunerative services. In this position it was in accord with the arguments of Mr. Brandeis, one of the attorneys in the case for the public, who had acquired considerable publicity in 1910 in connection with his advocacy of the introduction of scientific management into railroad operation, and who had estimated a saving to the roads thereby of a million dollars a day.

But the outbreak of the war, with its upset of normal industrial relations, made immediate relief necessary for the carriers. They could not wait upon the leisurely working of the suggested reforms. Upon rehearing, the Commission in October granted, with certain exceptions,

---

[1] 20 I. C. C., 317.

[2] 31 I. C. C., 351.   Rehearing, 32 I. C. C., 325.

[3] Property investment means here the book account, "cost of road and equipment," which has steadily improved in accuracy since the introduction of accounting regulations, July 1, 1907.

a horizontal increase of 5 per cent. It was in this case that for the first time a sharp division of opinion appeared in the Commission concerning the responsibility of that body for the financial condition of the carriers. One view was that the Commission's authority was to be narrowly interpreted, and that it must confine itself to determining whether the proposed increased rates were in themselves reasonable. The other view looked beyond the mere rate to the effect of earnings upon service to the public, and inquired whether the wage that the railroad was getting from the public was a "living wage." This latter point of view, appearing sharply for the first time, is prophetic of the new attitude to be assumed toward the railroad industry after the war as embodied in the Transportation Act of 1920.

As early as 1911 Commissioner Prouty in the Eastern Advance Rate Case said:

"We have no authority, as such, to say what amount these carriers shall earn, nor to establish a schedule of rates which will permit them to earn that amount. Our authority is limited to inquiring into the reasonableness of a particular rate or rates and establishing that rate or practice which is found lawful, in place of the one condemned as unlawful." But he added: "While the authority of this Commission only extends to the passing upon the reasonableness of the rate presented for its consideration, it is not confined to single rates. Any number of rates may be embraced in the same complaint, and the duty of the Commission is to consider and pass upon all those so presented. When, as here, there is involved the propriety of advances which affect the entire rate fabric within this territory, embracing one-half the tonnage and one-half the freight revenues of this whole country, and when that advance is justified mainly upon the ground, not of commercial conditions, but by lack of adequate revenue upon the present rate basis, this Commission must determine the fundamental question."

In the Five Per Cent Case of 1914 Commissioner Clements, in maintaining the strict construction attitude, said: "In my view the foregoing report and decision constitute a new and radical departure and a most serious and portentous step, in that by this step the Commission is shown to deem itself justified in sanctioning these increased rates . . . upon consideration of general financial and operating results, without resorting to other ordinary tests or factors heretofore deemed pertinent and necessary to the determination of the reasonableness of rates. I am not aware of any prior case in which this Commission or any court has held that the need by a carrier of money was of itself proof of the reasonableness of a specific rate. or body of rates, increased to meet such need."

On the other side in the same case may be quoted Commissioner Daniels: "A living wage is as necessary for a railroad as for an individual. A carrier without a sufficient return to cover costs and obtain in addition a margin of profit large enough to attract new capital for extensions and improvements cannot permanently render service commensurate with the needs of the public."

Again in the Western Rate Advance Case of 1915, in which the Commission denied many increases, and granted advances in the case only of a few commodities and in passenger fares, because it was not convinced of the general inadequacy of the carriers' revenues, Commissioner Daniels dissented in an opinion which clearly defines the issue between broad and narrow construction of the Commission's powers.[1]

[1] 35 I. C. C., 654, 679.

"While it is nowhere explicitly stated in the majority report, I am unable to escape the conviction that the reluctance to find that increased rates have been more generally justified is largely rooted in an unwillingness to find that the revenues of the carriers as a whole are smaller than is demanded in the public interest, and also in the belief that the financial exigencies of many of the carriers are traceable to financial maladministration, and that if due economy and integrity had been uniformly observed the difficulty over the attested decline in revenues would have been readily surmounted.

"Among the particular carriers involved in this proceeding the Rock Island and Frisco have recently attained unenviable notoriety by reason of financial mismanagement and other roads parties hereto, such as the Alton, have in the past been wrecked or plundered. There can be no question of these facts. There can be nothing said in extenuation or mitigation of them. And it has therefore resulted that a wide-spread disbelief exists in the general integrity of railroad management and that a skeptical attitude has been assumed by many toward the plea advanced that railroad earnings are inadequate and that increased rates are warranted.

"It would nevertheless appear that, while the severest condemnation of these practices should suffer no particle of abatement, the time had at last come to take a discriminating view of the effect of refusing rate increases otherwise just and reasonable because of a wide-spread resentment at evils perpetrated in the past by dishonest or designing railroad officers or their allied financiers. Such a policy visits in large measure the same penalty upon the proprietors of a railway conducted with integrity and honesty as upon the luckless shareholders of a looted road. In either case those who suffer from its effects are not those who have profited by the wrongs perpetrated in the past. It is therefore suggested that the appropriate remedy is the prosecution and punishment of the individual offenders, not the continued withholding of adequate rates to the carriers as a whole. . . .

"I am individually of opinion that our duty in the present case requires us in frankness to make a finding upon the general issue of the alleged inadequacy of the revenues of the carriers collectively. The carriers, the protestants, and the country are entitled to know the conclusion of the Commission upon this point, and not to be left with a confusing mass of detailed evidence and isolated conclusions upon single matters involved therein. The three previous general rate advance cases have unquestionably held that the Commission may make a finding upon this general question and may employ such a finding to determine, in connection with other relevant testimony, the justice and propriety of permitting particular increased rates to become effective. In the present case the general issue is simply not met, and in passing upon particular rates proposed to be increased a novel doctrine is for the first time invoked to disallow increased rates save where the specific evidence relating thereto makes a refusal manifestly impossible. The failure to follow established premises to their legitimate conclusion only beclouds the principles upon which the Commission may be expected to act in future and leaves nothing certain but uncertainty.

"In the matter of rate regulation and fixation we have reached a point where one of two courses ought deliberately to be chosen and clearly announced. If, despite increased costs not offset by increased revenue, increases in rates are to be denied, except where in individual instances gross injustice would be occasioned by their denial, the carriers ought to be apprised of this policy, so that they may set their house in order, if they can, against such a situation. If, on the other hand, we are to acknowledge in general, what we are perforce compelled to admit in detail, just and reasonable increased rates should be permitted not grudgingly but with such fair measure of allowance as will indicate that the transportation industry is entitled in the interest of the public to earnings sufficient to provide a service commensurate with public needs."

The prospective entrance of this country into the war furnished occasion for another application for increased rates amounting to 15 per cent in the spring of 1917, which involved the carriers in all three territories.[1] The Commission found no country-wide emergency that justified a general increase. It did find that the conditions confronting the Eastern carriers were more serious, and it granted increases in their class rates while denying them to the other two territories. The Eastern carriers succeeded in reopening the case for further hearing in November and obtained an order in March, 1918, granting additional increases on specific commodities and on joint rates into other territories.[2]

These increases throughout the period 1911 to 1916 were secured by the carriers with great labor and toil, and in the face of a very considerable popular opposition. It was difficult for a public that had always been accustomed to falling rates and that had established a Commission to keep rates from rising, to realize that a time might come when the movement would be in the other direction. The pioneer period in which the railroad had unused capacity and in which it was actively bidding for business to fill its tracks and its trains was passing away. Population had grown and had congested the territory in many sections. Traffic was becoming intensified. What was demanded was increased capacity of existing plant rather than extensions into new country, and this in-

---

[1] The Fifteen Per Cent Case. 45 I. C. C., 303.
[2] Ex parte 57.

creased capacity must be acquired in a congested area where expansion was becoming steadily more difficult and costly. Enlarged terminals, yard tracks, sidings, additional main tracks, enlarged platforms and warehouses, heavier equipment, stronger bridges, better ballast, more ties, larger and more ample roundhouses, turntables, machine-shops—and not merely for the present but for a reasonable time ahead, these were the expenditures calling for capital in enormous amounts. Coincident therewith was the steady rise in prices reflected in the cost of materials purchased and in wages paid, so that operating expenses were being increased at the time when the railroads needed to make a favorable showing in the investment market in order to obtain the necessary funds.

A study of the figures for the period 1908 to 1916 tells the story.[1] The direction of physical development is shown by the track-mileage figures. Yard track and siding constructed between 1908 and 1916 kept pace in actual miles with the increase in main-line extensions and nearly equalled the increase in traffic as represented by loaded car miles. This means intensive rather than extensive growth. While efficiency in physical handling of traffic was increasing, as shown by the steady increase in tons per train and per car, and in ton-miles per mile of road, yet operating expenses per ton-mile showed no tendency to decrease. The wages paid per ton-mile remained almost unvarying. Moreover, although gross revenue steadily increased, there was a marked decline in average receipts per ton-mile, from 0.754 cents in 1908 to 0.715 cents in 1916. Investment continued steadily to be made, the total amounting to $4,625,000,000 between 1908 and 1916, but the rate of return in the face of much more attractive investments in other fields was not encouraging. In view of the requirement in the Act of 1920 that the Commission shall fix rates to yield 6 per cent

[1] I. C. C. Annual Rept., 1918, p. 79.

upon property valuation, it is interesting to observe that according to the Commission's calculations the percentage relation of railroad operating income to investment never reached 6 per cent during the period 1908 to 1916 (June 30), and only reached 6.17 per cent in the calendar year 1916. The actual figures are as follows:

PERCENTAGE RELATION RAILWAY OPERATING INCOME
TO PROPERTY INVESTMENT

(All railways except switching and terminal companies)

Year ending June 30, 1908	4.89 per cent
" " " 1909	5.38 "
" " " 1910	5.68 "
" " " 1911	4.92 "
" " " 1912	4.69 "
" " " 1913	5.01 "
" " " 1914	4.12 "
" " " 1915	4.18 "
" " " 1916	5.90 "
" " Dec. 31, 1916	6.17 "

In the Five Per Cent Case in 1914 the Commission found that for the thirty-five railroad systems in Official Classification territory, the ratio of net operating income to property investment for the years 1900 to 1913 ranged from 6.31 per cent in 1906 to 5.19 per cent in 1912, and that the average for the period was 5.64 per cent. It discovered a tendency toward diminishing net operating income and held that the rate of return as a whole was "smaller than is demanded in the interest of both the general public and the railroads." Moreover, the aggregate amount paid in dividends fell off $100,000,000 from the high year of this period (1911), and the average rate on dividend-paying stock which was 8.07 per cent in 1908 was 6.75 per cent in 1916.

Whatever may be one's personal view as to whether this was or was not a satisfactory financial showing for our railroad system, the fact remained that it did not satisfy the investor. Consequently, the sound policy long practised by railroad management of keeping ahead of traffic by providing the necessary facilities for handling it was gradually weakened, and at the time the country entered the war the railroad system was far short of that standard of efficiency which the demands of traffic required. War exigencies perforce aggravated this situation, and when the roads were returned in 1920, their condition of under-maintenance was a factor of grave public concern.

Railroad critics have laid this unfortunate condition at the door of the Commission, and have insisted that the niggardliness and short-sightedness of this body is responsible for the financial condition of the roads. But this explanation of the railroad situation is far too simple. It has the advantage of being able to lay the blame on some specific and tangible object, but it does not reach the heart of the difficulty. The Commission's power was limited to granting increases upon a demonstration of their reasonableness. Railroad income accounts did not always make clear the exigency, and it could only be a matter of judgment as to what the future would bring forth. The fact that earnings fell off sharply in some instances after the Commission had refused increases demonstrated only that it was not an infallible prophet. Railroad credit declined in the half-dozen years before the war, not primarily because of the specific decisions of the Commission, but rather because the Commission had power to decide at all. The long-continued period of declining rates was at an end. Increases were bound to be sought. Whether rates would or would not be increased was now beyond the voluntary determination of the carriers themselves. The investing public for the first time was brought to a sharp realization of the fact that the earning power of the roads was subject to public control. Decline in credit was due to the uncertainty as to what regulating authorities, state and federal, would do when requests for rate increases were brought before them. There is little doubt also that the revelations of financial mismanagement of certain railroad properties during the period had their influence in increasing the timidity of investors.

Any attempt to summarize completely the rate decisions of this period would widely extend this discussion, and would develop few principles or traffic situations not analyzed in the treatises covering the Commission's history before 1910. The long and short haul problem has been deemed of sufficient importance to warrant separate and elaborate analysis. Other types of cases are referred to in their proper context. Beyond this, a few cases may be mentioned that portray interesting features.

A case which has much significance from the standpoint of the future development of traffic handling is that which settled the legal position of the freight forwarder, the agency that solicits less-than-car-load shipments to be combined and forwarded as car-loads. The freight is delivered to the railroad by the forwarder and is accepted at destination by the forwarder's agent, who acts as consignee and who pays the freight charges at car-load rates. The carriers attempted to put a stop to this business by a rule providing that the car-load rate could only be applied when all the merchandise in the car was owned by a single individual. The Commission held that the railroad could not look beyond the physical incidents of the transportation to the ownership of the goods and sustained the position of the forwarders. This opinion was upheld by the Supreme Court.[1] It was the same question that had been fought out through a long series of suits between forwarders and railways in England, and the courts had finally reached the same result as

[1] 220 U. S., 235 (1911); 14 I. C. C., 422, 437 (1908).

was reached here. So far as law could accomplish it, the forwarding business was thereby given a permanent place in our industrial system.

The New York Harbor Case in 1917[1] raised once more the perennial question of the relative rights of the various terminal points on New York harbor. Terminals in the state of New Jersey insisted that they were entitled to lower rates than Manhattan and Brooklyn because they were not subject to the terminal expense involved in lighterage. The Commission admitted that it might have been better had the development of the rate fabric recognized the relative advantages of location and the relative expense of terminal service on the two sides of the harbor, and had adjusted the rates accordingly. A more enduring rate structure would then have been created. But competitors had brought rates generally to a common level. There was no undue discrimination in the existing system, and the benefit to be derived from disturbing it could not compensate for the violence that would be done to the industrial interests involved. In this conclusion the Commission contributed materially to the movement for the unification of the port, which has long been needed and would ere this have been realized but for the interference of political interests.[2]

Two cases before the Supreme Court developed conclusions of significance to the practice of rate making and defined more clearly the limits to the power of public regulation. In the North Dakota Coal Case,[3] the maximum car-load rates on coal established by the state were declared unconstitutional. It was conceded that the state had a broad field for the exercise of its discretion in prescribing reasonable rates, and that carriers were not en-

---

[1] 47 I. C. C., 643.
[2] This opinion is one of the most complete discussions available of the transportation and traffic situation in New York harbor.
[3] 236 U. S., 585 (1915).

titled to the same percentage of profit on every sort of business. Reasonable classification of commodities to be subject to different rates was allowable. But a carrier was entitled to a reasonable reward for the carriage of freight, and the state could not justify on the ground of public interest the selection of a commodity for transportation at less than cost or at merely a nominal compensation. The same principle was enunciated in the Norfolk and Western Passenger Case,[1] decided on the same day, involving a state two-cent passenger law, in which it was held that as the passenger business was one of the main departments of the railroad, the validity of the law was to be determined by its effect upon this class of business considered separately. The principle here laid down is fairly clear. While classification of goods with varying rates is permissible, and while presumably certain commodities might be carried even at less than cost provided the amount of traffic involved does not materially affect the net revenue, nevertheless when the traffic is considerable and the earnings are of importance, the public authority must prescribe rates that are compensating. As Justice Hughes said: "The state does not enjoy the freedom of an owner." What might be done as a matter of public policy under Government ownership and operation is not justifiable when private capital has embarked under a contract which insures it a reasonable return and protection against exploitation.

[1] 236 U. S., 605 (1915).

CHAPTER III

THE LONG AND SHORT HAUL

SECTION 4 of the Interstate Commerce Act, which was intended to put an end to discrimination between places, the so-called long and short haul clause, has had a stormy career. In its original form it provided that it should be unlawful for a carrier to charge under substantially similar circumstances and conditions a greater compensation for a shorter than a longer distance over the same line in the same direction, the shorter being included within the longer distance, but the Commission was authorized to grant exemption from the prohibition, and to determine the extent of the departure therefrom. The clause was intended to destroy the practice under which the roads competed at certain points and recouped themselves by charging higher rates on non-competitive short-haul business. The Commission's interpretation of this clause was called forth at the very beginning of its career in the Louisville and Nashville Case, and with slight modification the position then taken was maintained without change thereafter. It recognized that there were cases in which conditions at the longer-distance point were sufficiently dissimilar to warrant suspension of the section, but these conditions in the main arose out of competition in which one of the competitors was beyond the jurisdiction of the regulating authority—competition of water carriers or of Canadian railroads.

The section lost its effectiveness in 1897 by a ruling of the Supreme Court in the Alabama Midland Case.[1] However vague this opinion may seem to be when taken

[1] 168 U. S., 144.

by itself, its reiteration in succeeding cases[1] leaves no doubt as to the position of the court. Competition that is controlling in traffic and rates produces in and of itself that dissimilarity of circumstances and conditions which the statute had in mind, and when this condition exists a carrier has a right of its own motion to take the situation into account in fixing the competitive rate. In other words, in the only instance in which a carrier would have any desire to violate the distance principle, when it was compelled to meet the competition of another carrier, the prohibition against place discrimination was automatically removed, because the court decided that the conditions at competitive and non-competitive points were under these circumstances substantially dissimilar. Moreover, conditions being dissimilar, no advance permission of the Commission was necessary to take advantage of such dissimilarity. No ruling could have been better calculated to knock the props from under the Commission's authority. Thereafter the Commission could only make suggestions for adjustments to eliminate place discriminations of this character, and whether such suggestions were or were not adopted depended upon whether they appealed to the carriers as in their interest.

No amendment of this section took place in 1906 when the law was first thoroughly overhauled. Attention was primarily centred upon giving the Commission rate-making authority. The long and short haul question was a technical one, not generally understood by the public. The opposition of the railroads and the Eastern jobbing interests seeking to preserve their hold on Southern markets played a part in postponing action. By 1910 the Rocky Mountain congressmen had become alive to the serious discrimination against their section of the country, due to the exaggerated use of the low rate for the long haul to the Pacific coast. They succeeded in

[1] 175 U. S., 648 (1900); 181 U. S., 1 (1901); 190 U. S., 273 (1903).

that year in eliminating from Section 4 the trouble-making clause, "under substantially similar circumstances and conditions." With this gone, the section absolutely forbade lower charges to longer-distance points except after hearing and approval by the Interstate Commerce Commission. At the same time, two important additions were made to the section. One prohibited a greater compensation for a through haul than the aggregate of the intermediate rates. The other aimed to destroy a pernicious type of competition practised by railroads against waterways. It provided that whenever a railroad reduced its freight rates at competitive points in competition with a water route, it could not again increase them unless the Commission decided after hearing that the reasons for the increase rested on altered conditions that were other than the elimination of water competition. Railroads were no longer to be permitted to drive steamboats off the rivers by offering unremunerative rates, and then recoup themselves at their leisure after the disappearance of their rivals. This provision was borrowed from the constitution of the state of California. It was introduced by Senator Burton, the chairman of the National Waterways Commission, which had recommended the provision in its report to Congress.[1]

On its face Section 4 now gave the Commission arbitrary and sweeping powers. But that body realized that such was not the legislative intent and that any attempt to act beyond what was its reasonable authority would be quickly blocked. That its interpretation of its powers was uniformly upheld by the highest court in spite of strenuous corporate opposition, and temporary obstruction by the Commerce Court, was due to the sanity and sound reasonableness with which it interpreted its pow-

[1] For evidence of the manner in which railroads destroyed water lines, read the investigations by the Commission of the practices of the Louisville and Nashville. 24 I. C. C., 228; 31 I. C. C., 281, 301.

ers. It proceeded forthwith, as soon as the amended section was operative, to lay down rules of procedure within which its action was to be circumscribed. The most extensive departures from the distance principle prevailed in the Southeast and in trans-continental traffic. It is not surprising that most of the leading cases in the early years relating to this problem have been Southern railroad cases. Coastwise competition, a potential or what might better be called a plausible competition by numerous rivers for a distance into the interior, the struggle for Southern markets between industries in the East and the Middle West, all these factors brought an irresistible pressure to bear to secure competitive rates at the distant point which were lower than those charged to way stations. This system had become so ingrained that any violent or sudden change would have been industrially disastrous. Accordingly, the Commission sought for a working rule that would remove the unreasonable discriminations and at the same time preserve what was justifiable in the existing situation. Applications for relief poured in by the thousands and from action upon these there evolved a code which later in 1920 was crystallized into statutory form.

In the matter of passenger applications the principle involved was somewhat different from that of freight, because passenger fares are usually constructed on the mileage basis, and freight rates are not, and because the passenger being his own unloader, can, if there is a sufficiently wide discrepancy to warrant it, buy his ticket to the more distant point at the cheaper rate, and unload himself at the intermediate point. The Commission laid down the rule that if a circuitous line exceeded the direct line by at least 15 per cent or by at least six miles, the longer route could meet the passenger rate of the direct line without reference to its intermediate fares. Of wider interest throughout the country was the clause providing that the through rate should not be greater than the aggregate of the intermediate rates subject to the act. The two-cent passenger laws in many states with which the railroads had been obliged to comply created the issue, and carriers had appealed for relief. The Commission felt that the final solution to be arrived at was that state and interstate passenger fares should be on the same basis, but, pending the outcome of litigation on state rates, it permitted the maintenance of the higher interstate charges.

In applications for relief in freight service, very largely from Southern carriers, the Commission laid down the rule that circuitous lines would be permitted to lower their rates to their termini in competition with the direct route and at the expense of intermediate points, only when the long line was manifestly circuitous, when the short line had observed the distance principle at intermediate points, and when the intermediate rates on the long line were apparently reasonable and not subject to attack. It is obvious that if the short line were permitted to violate the distance principle, there would be created exactly the type of railroad competition which the Commission had at the beginning of its history tried to prevent, which the courts had sanctioned in the Alabama Midland Case, and which presumably had been ended by the amendment of 1910.

From New York and New England to South Atlantic and Gulf ports, water competition was influential and necessitated the granting of relief to rail carriers from the effect of the 4th Section. From Ohio River crossings and from St. Louis to New Orleans and other Mississippi River crossings, competition was largely imaginary and had been so for many years. Not since 1890 had there been a through boat service between St. Louis and New Orleans except at rare intervals. In 1914[1] the Com-

[1] 30 I. C. C., 153.

mission, while granting lower rates to river points, recognized that water competition was rapidly dwindling. In 1917[1] it refused to grant lower rates between New Orleans and Kansas City than to intermediate points, because since 1900 rates had been under rail control. In general the policy of the Commission at this time, so far as water competition was concerned, was to grant relief when it was satisfied that, although the competitive rates were subnormal, they yielded some profit above the actual cost of handling, and hence did not burden the intermediate business, and when the intermediate rates were not in themselves unreasonable.[2]

But the South was dotted with so-called "basing-points," wholesale points served by more than one railroad where no water transportation was present, but enjoying rates that put them on an equality with water competitive points. These adjustments were disapproved by the Commission because the rates thus granted created undue preference for these centres at the expense of intermediate points not so favored. There was also market competition arising from the demand of various producing centres, such as lumber-mills located at different points, to be placed on an equality in competitive markets. Here the Commission recognized the force of the argument, but decided that this situation alone was not sufficient ground for relief. In general it may be said that it has been the effort of the Commission to construct a harmonious and properly graded rate structure, freed from the anomalies of the earlier situation, and its orders have compelled on the part of carriers a revision of their entire rate structure from practically all the territory east of the Mississippi into the Southeast.

Of much wider application were the controversies that involved the trans-continental situation—one of those everlasting problems which has persistently dogged the foot-

[1] 44 I. C. C., 727.   [2] 30 I. C. C., 153; 32 I. C. C., 61 (1914).

steps of the Commission. The history of this situation
has been many times described and explained and need
be only summarized here. As a result of a gradual development of water transportation between the Atlantic
and Pacific seaboards, a real competition had sprung up
soon after 1870 between water and rail lines which definitely held the rail rates down. This water competition
through the aid of rail carriers serving the Atlantic seaboard gradually reached inland, and took traffic from
points as far west as Pittsburgh or even farther, and
forced the rail lines carrying traffic westward from these
points to meet the joint rail and water rate eastward.
The result was the gradual spread of a blanket from the
Atlantic seaboard as far west as water-line influence extended, within which the same rate was charged from all
points westward to the coast. This was the beginning
of the blanket-rate system. Under the pretext of water
competition, the blanket was steadily widened to the West,
but the significant influence was not water competition
at all, which obviously became less influential as the distance from the Atlantic seaboard increased, but market
pressure—the demand of Middle-Western manufacturing
and jobbing interests that they be put on an equality
with their competitors farther east. This demand was
favorably received by Western carriers because if the
business originated in the West, they received the entire
revenue from its carriage, whereas if it originated in
the East, they were obliged to divide the receipts with
their Eastern connections. By 1910 this blanket had
been so widened and the sound theory from which it
started so perverted that the same rate was being charged
from Omaha, and in some cases even from Denver, to San
Francisco as from New York. By no process of ingenious reasoning could such an absurd anomaly be defended
except on the ground that it had simply evolved. But
the trouble did not end when Denver was reached, for

the inter-mountain territory between the Rockies and the Sierra Nevadas, in which lie many important industrial centres, was increasingly discriminated against, just to the degree that the blanket rate moved westward. It was the influence of this section through its representatives in Congress that amended the 4th Section, and one of the first important decisions of the Commission following this amendment related to the trans-continental situation.

Recognizing that the system in use had gone far beyond the point where it could be defended on economic grounds, the Commission endeavored to create a rate structure that should bring into full and predominating force the influence of water competition, which was the sole justification for the beginnings of the system and the only sound reason for its continuance. It declared that the intent of the amended law was to make the prohibition of the higher rate for the shorter haul a rule of well-nigh universal application, from which deviation should be permitted only in special cases in order to meet transportation conditions that were beyond the carriers' control.[1] It divided the country into five groups or zones. Zone I extended from the Pacific coast eastward to a line drawn from the Canadian boundary in Lake Superior southwest to Sioux City and thence south to the Gulf. Zone II extended east of Zone I to a line from the Straits of Mackinaw south through Lake Michigan and on to the Gulf. Zone III was east of Zone II, north of the Ohio, and bounded on the east by a line from Buffalo to Pittsburgh. Zone IV included all territory east of Zone III and north of the West Virginia boundary and a line drawn from Tennessee to the Atlantic coast. Zone V, which was not included in the decision, was the remaining territory of the Southeast. Within Zone I there was to be no higher rate to an intermediate point than to Pacific coast termi-

[1] 21 I. C. C., 329 (June, 1911).

nals; in Zones II, III, and IV the intermediate rate was not to exceed the terminal rate by more than 7 per cent, 15 per cent, and 25 per cent respectively. It will be observed that the Commission did not actually fix the rates. It left with the carriers the option of raising the rates to the coast or of lowering the intermediate rates. It simply prescribed the width of the differential.

An appeal was taken by the railroads to the Commerce Court, and the decision of the latter enjoining the Commission's order serves to define the issue. This court held in the first place that the Commission had no power to distinguish between water competition and "market competition," and that the prevalence of competition beyond the carriers' control was sufficient ground for departure from the long and short haul section regardless of the nature of the competition. Again the court held that the Commission was not concerned with the relation of terminal to intermediate rates, provided intermediate rates were not unreasonable, but only with the question whether lower rates could be charged at the terminal point. It had no power to prescribe a differential relationship between the two. The case went to the Supreme Court, and in every respect the Commission was upheld.[1] On the question of the relationship of rates, the court said that the prime object of the transfer to the Commission of power previously lodged in the carriers, through the elimination of the "similar circumstances and conditions" clause, was to vest the Commission with authority to consider competitive conditions and their relation to persons and places. Necessarily there went with this power the right to do that by which alone it could be exerted. The constitutional objection that the 4th Section delegated to the Commission legislative power was held to be without merit.

Following the court's decision, the carriers took steps

[1] 234 U. S., 476, 495 (1914).

to put the zone system of rate-making into effect, but when it came to its application to specific commodities, it was discovered that the situation had materially changed since the original decision of the Commission in 1911, brought about by the opening of the Panama Canal at the time of the outbreak of the European War. Traffic through this waterway in late 1914 and early 1915 was double that ever carried by water in pre-canal days, and in certain kinds of traffic the competition was becoming not only severe but determining as to rates. So far as commodities moving on class rates were concerned, there was no problem. Rates to the Pacific coast were strictly in accord with the long and short haul provision. But with traffic taking commodity rates, handled largely in car-load lots, the situation was quite otherwise. This traffic fell into three classes. The first class contained articles that moved only by rail and in which the long and short haul principle could be and was maintained. A second class was adapted to either rail or water carriage. For many years prior to the opening of the canal, the Commission had authorized lower coast rates because of the decided influence of water-carriage. To these commodities the zone rate structure was to apply. Articles of the third class were produced in Atlantic and Middle-Western territory, were pre-eminently adapted to water-carriage, and normally moved in large volume in that fashion. Such commodities were canned goods, earthen and stone ware, hardware and tools, twine and cordage, hemp, paint, wire, and iron and steel articles. Here the water rate was definitely controlling, not only for commodities produced on or near the seaboard but as far inland as Pittsburgh, Chicago, and the Missouri River, because traffic could not move from these points westward to the Pacific coast except on rates approximately equal to the rates from the Atlantic coast. The Commission recognized the situation by granting further modifications in the existing scheme, as the result of which intermediate rates could exceed Pacific coast rates by a larger differential than originally prescribed, but the maximum intermediate rate was definitely fixed and the terminal rates were made applicable only to those points which were ports of call for Atlantic-Pacific freight steamers.[1] Traffic eastward from California points was likewise affected by the opening of the canal, although rail rates had not been blanketed eastward to the same degree. California products such as fruits, wines, canned goods, and grain were going largely by water. Relief was given the rail carriers by granting them permission to offer car-load rates on certain commodities from Pacific to Atlantic ports lower than the rates from intermediate California points to the same destinations.[2]

But, unfortunately for the Commission, the situation refused to remain stable. Late in 1915 slides closed the canal to traffic, and before it was again operating the demand for ships in the carrying trade for war purposes had diverted most of the coastwise shipping. Intermountain sections thereupon called the Commission's attention to the lack of any further water competition. This led to a reopening of all "4th-Section applications" in which permission had been granted for lower rates to the coast points, both Atlantic and Pacific, than were granted to intermediate points. The Commission found that water competition was now a negligible factor, and ordered a restoration of all trans-continental rates in harmony with the distance principle.[3] In revising their rates the carriers decided to increase certain of their terminal rates instead of lowering their intermediate rates. Again the Commission was called upon by protesting shippers, and again, in January, 1918, it made adjustments approving in part the action of the carriers.

[1] 32 I. C. C., 611 (January, 1915); 34 I. C. C., 13 (April, 1915).
[2] 33 I. C. C., 480 (1915).   [3] 48 I. C. C., 79 (1918).

"Thereby was removed," says the Commission, "a long-standing cause of irritation to the inter-mountain country and a prolific source of complaints to the Commission."

But the unquenchable vitality of a competitive market problem was again demonstrated when in 1921 an association of shippers' organizations and state commissions in inter-mountain territory complained that the Pacific coast was being given unreasonable preference because the commodity rates were not graded to afford intermediate territory the full benefit of its location nearer the East. It was paying the same rates on most traffic from the East as were Pacific coast points. The Commission held that the charge of undue prejudice against inter-mountain territory was not sustained, and that the carriers were warranted, in their discretion, in continuing the existing blanket adjustment.[1] While coastwise shipping was not as abundant as earlier, yet there was ample evidence that it would further develop, and that competition would soon be felt in a serious loss in tonnage, unless the carriers had available appropriate measures to meet the situation. This clearly indicates an expectation on the part of the Commission that in the not distant future it will again be called upon to approve competitive rates to the coast lower than those charged to intermediate points.

These experiments in rate-making in the West, which first developed a blanket system and then a series of zones, raises a fundamental question as to whether we have in this country any conscious and far-sighted system of rate construction, or whether the rates are actually the confused and unscientific and haphazard maze that they appear to be. Is the policy of national growth and non-interference the most enlightened policy for a great territory like ours? In this connection it is helpful to quote the opinion of the late Franklin K. Lane, one of

[1] 61 I. C. C., 226.

the ablest members that the Interstate Commerce Commission ever had.[1]

"This case, when broadly regarded, involves a question of the highest national importance. What is to
be our policy with respect to the movement of traffic?
Shall the country be treated as a whole for commercial
purposes, or shall it be infinitely divided? In our postal
service we deal with the country as a unit. As to our
railroads there is no uniform policy, even upon the same
lines or systems. In some parts of the country rates
are on an almost strictly mileage basis, every 10 miles
that is passed adding to the rate. In other territory
we have a system of small zones or groups which are
placed upon a common basis—a scheme of rate making
that has worked most happily in the country to the
east of the Mississippi River and which, it seems to me,
should be extended westward. The whole continent
for a zone of 2,000 miles is made to serve the Pacific
coast terminal cities at uniform rates, while the states
between the mountains are not given such advantage.
So, too, on California products generally, and not alone
upon citrus fruits, the United States east of the Rockies
is placed in a great zone to which a uniform rate is made.
At the same time, the lumber of the far northwest is not
so treated, nor the wool or hides of the interior.

"Perhaps the United States will one day declare a
policy of its own in this regard. Primarily it is a matter
of national concern and not of railroad policy as to what
system of rate making shall obtain so long as the carriers receive a reasonable return upon the value of their
property. The people may say (1) that railroad rates
shall be made so as to carry all products into all markets
within the four lines of the country; or (2) that after a certain narrow limit is passed the whole of the land shall be

[1] 22 I. C. C., 157–158.

one zone; or (3) a system of rates that will keep producers and consumers as near together as possible and eliminate waste in transportation. These are national questions. They go to the very future of our industrial life. Upon their determination depends the character of the farm products and the nature of the industries in the various sections of the country. The railroad by its rates may make each portion of the country largely independent of the remainder or it may make of the Nation one economic and industrial unit, each portion thereof doing best what nature has fitted it to do best. This is fundamentally the difference in the philosophy which underlies the two methods of making rates which have been given consideration in this case. Without any expression of policy from Congress we accept the policy which the railroads themselves have made, considering that upon the whole the results arising from such policy do not conflict with the provisions of the law. There is no doubt in my mind but that the Commission could not itself prescribe a blanket similar to that obtaining here and which we are approving because neither the carriers nor the shippers wish it destroyed."

One interesting outcome of this long controversy in trans-continental territory was a Supreme Court interpretation of the water-competition clause of the 4th Section. In the readjustment of rates following the disappearance of Panama Canal competition certain rates to the Pacific coast had been increased. This increase was protested by a Seattle corporation as a violation of the clause which provides that when a rail carrier reduces its rates in competition with a water rate, it shall not be permitted to increase such rates unless after hearing by the Commission it shall be found that the proposed increase rests upon changed conditions other than the elimination of water competition. Read by itself, said the Supreme

Court, the clause would be capable of the construction given to it by the complainant, but read in connection with the duties and powers of the Commission as expressed in other clauses of the section and in other sections of the Act, it could have no such narrow application. Obviously if the Commission is intrusted with authority to lower terminal rail rates in order to meet water competition, it cannot be deemed helpless to raise them again if competitive conditions are altered. Any other construction would insure monopoly rather than preserve competition[1] and would make a farce of our whole system of rate regulation.

[1] 249 U. S., 557 (1919).

CHAPTER IV

OF the proposals of the Administration in 1910 for amending the Interstate Commerce Act, the only one of any importance which became law was that creating the ill-fated Commerce Court. This involved no new principle of regulation. It was a device to improve procedure. All suits under the Interstate Commerce and Elkins Acts were to be handled by this special court of five judges, from which direct appeal was to be taken to the Supreme Court. Every effort was made to simplify the process and eliminate delay. It was argued that a body of judges that handled exclusively questions of interstate commerce would be more expert in this highly technical field and that the contrariety of opinion issuing from different circuits would be done away with. But if it were to become genuinely expert, why limit the term of a judge to five years? And why was it not the duty of the Supreme Court to harmonize the conflicting decisions of the different circuits? And was there, after all, a sufficient amount of this litigation to keep such a court occupied?

Technical questions of procedure could hardly have called forth any wide popular interest, and this is doubtless the reason that the proposal for a special court became a law at all. But even then the "insurgents" took a hand to prevent the scheme from becoming too formal and thoroughly enveloping itself in the dignified atmosphere of the court. Although cases were thereafter to be in the hands of the Attorney-General rather than of the Commission, which was no longer to be permitted to be investigator, judge, and prosecutor at the same time, yet the law permitted the intervention of the Interstate

Commerce Commission and all other parties in interest, including communities, associations, corporations, firms, and individuals. Shippers protested that in these complicated cases in which commercial and industrial factors were of more importance than legal principles, there was no assurance that the Department of Justice alone could handle the cases competently and to a successful issue, and there was much experience to justify their protests.

Later during the attacks upon the court by the public and Congress, the Attorney-General came to its defense in his annual reports, recommending at the same time certain modifications in procedure. This liberality in intervention was singled out for particular attack and was consistently opposed by the Department of Justice so long as the court survived. In reply to many criticisms, the Attorney-General showed[1] that the Commerce Court was much more expeditious than the general courts had been previously, that it had upheld the Commission in a larger percentage of cases, and that it had granted injunctions with less frequency. Nevertheless, it had to go, and the reasons therefor are of sufficient significance to warrant careful examination.

While the situation was doubtless seized upon and the mistakes of the Commerce Court exaggerated for political advantage, yet the offense, simply stated, was that the Commerce Court attempted to obstruct the Commission in the exercise of powers granted by law and sustained by the highest court. For two decades the Commission had suffered the irritating delays occasioned by court interference with the exercise of its authority, in which the court had, to be sure, accepted the facts brought before the Commission as *prima facie* evidence, but had declined to be limited to this evidence and had frequently reopened cases from the beginning. This assertion of original jurisdiction by the lower courts

[1] Annual Report, Attorney-General U. S., 1912.

had been frowned upon by the Supreme Court,[1] but there was no way to put a stop to it until the passage of the amendment in 1906 which specifically provided that "if upon such hearing as the court may determine to be necessary, it appears that the order" (of the Commission) "was regularly made and duly served, and that the carrier is in disobedience of the same, the court shall enforce obedience to such order."[2] This clause which was to be the corner-stone of the structure of administrative regulation erected by the Commission, was definitely interpreted by the Supreme Court a few months before the creation of the Commerce Court, and should have been ample notice to that new body as to the limitation of its functions. In this case, which involved a technical question of the distribution of coal-cars in time of shortage, the Supreme Court refused to enter into the merits of the controversy, but contented itself with deciding whether the Commission had acted within the limits prescribed by the statute, and had proceeded constitutionally. This having been decided in favor of the Commission, its action was within its administrative discretion and was not reviewable. This decision marks a turning-point in the career of the Commission, a final recognition of a power in which discretion was given wide range. The significant paragraph of the decision is this:[3]

"Beyond controversy, in determining whether an order of the Commission shall be suspended or set aside, we must consider, a, all relevant questions of constitutional power or right; b, all pertinent questions as to whether the administrative order is within the scope of the delegated authority under which it purports to have been

---

[1] Social Circle Case, 162 U. S., 184 (1896).   [2] Sec. 16.
[3] I. C. C. v. Ills. Cent. R. R. Co., 215 U. S., 452, January, 1910. See also 215 U. S. 481.

made; and, *c*, a proposition which we state independently, although in its essence it may be contained in the previous one, viz., whether, even although the order be in form within the delegated power, nevertheless it must be treated as not embraced therein, because the exertion of authority which is questioned has been manifested in such an unreasonable manner as to cause it, in truth, to be within the elementary rule that the substance, and not the shadow, determines the validity of the exercise of the power. *Postal Telegraph Cable Co. v. Adams, 155 U. S., 688, 698.* Plain as it is that the powers just stated are of the essence of judicial authority, and which, therefore, may not be curtailed, and whose discharge may not be by us in a proper case avoided, it is equally plain that such perennial powers lend no support whatever to the proposition that we may, under the guise of exerting judicial power, usurp merely administrative functions by setting aside a lawful administrative order upon our conception as to whether the administrative power has been wisely exercised. Power to make the order and not the mere expediency or wisdom of having made it, is the question."

In the vast majority of controversies, no constitutional question could arise. It would be virtually impossible for a carrier ordinarily to show that a reduction or the denial of an increase in a rate, or even a schedule of rates, would deprive it of its property without due process. So long as the Commission acted within the limitations imposed by the statute, its authority in the vast majority of instances was to remain thereafter undisturbed. But the Commerce Court, composed of competent jurists, wholly failed to grasp this fact, whether wilfully or not it is impossible to say. Repeatedly it attempted to enter into the merits of the controversy, to review the facts, to pass judgment upon the Commission's interpretations, and in one instance at least to begin the case again in its own court, and with unvarying regularity its position was overruled by the Supreme Court, substantially on the grounds already quoted from the Illinois Central Coal-Car Distribution Case.

A few illustrations will make the controversy clear. An order by the Commission upon water carriers to make reports concerning all their business under Section 20 of the Act, whether the business was under the jurisdiction of the Commission or not, was set aside by the Commerce Court on the ground that the Commission had exceeded its authority. Here the court was clearly within its rights, as its decision involved a legal question simply—the interpretation of the powers of the Commission. But the Supreme Court held that the Commerce Court erred in granting the injunction and that the Commission had authority to require all the information asked for.[1]

The specific nature of the issue between the Commission and the court is well exemplified in the Pacific Coast Switching Cases, in which the Commission, after a long investigation, concluded that the charges imposed by railroads for spotting cars on private-industry tracks were unlawful, and ordered the carriers to cease from imposing them longer. The Commerce Court enjoined the order of the Commission after careful examination of the facts upon which the order rested. This action it defended by the argument that the facts in the case were undisputed, and therefore the court was free to reach a different conclusion concerning them than that reached by the Commission. "Where the facts are undisputed there is no occasion for facts to be found, and the ultimate conclusion of the Commission is a mixed question of law and fact which certainly ought not to be held to

[1] I. C. C. v. Goodrich Transit Co., 224 U. S., 194 (1912). See also 231 U. S., 423 (1913).

be conclusive upon the court." Upon this ingenious argument the Commission commented as follows:

"Before the Commission they were certainly controverted questions of fact upon which volumes of testimony were introduced, and hours of argument expended. It is difficult to imagine an instance in which there could be a more sharply defined question of fact than this very one which was presented to and decided by the Commission. . . . If the Commerce Court is correct in stating that where the facts are admitted, it is for that court to determine whether the rate is unreasonable or the discrimination undue, then ninety-nine one-hundredths of the orders of this Commission can be reviewed upon the question of fact by the courts."

The Supreme Court reversed the Commerce Court and held that the finding of the Commission on the point at issue was not subject to judicial review.[1]

Issue was joined again in a case involving a negative order. The Commission dismissed a complaint against the railroads for levying demurrage upon a loaded private car standing upon the track of its owners, and held that the rule was reasonable and was necessary to prevent discrimination. Thereupon Proctor & Gamble, the complainants, filed a petition in the Commerce Court asking that the order of the Commission be set aside and that the demurrage rule be held unlawful and its operation enjoined. The Commerce Court assumed jurisdiction, and while its conclusion was identical with that of the Commission, it is evident that it could have reached no conclusion at all without reviewing the facts and substituting its own judgment upon them for that of the Commission. Therefore it was for the Supreme Court to say whether a *negative order* of the Commission was

[1] 234 U. S., 294, 315 (1914).

reviewable, whether, in other words, the Commerce Court could acquire jurisdiction sufficient to take up the case from the beginning. The conclusion of the highest court, after a thorough examination of the statute and a review of its history, was that the jurisdiction of the Commerce Court was confined to restraining the operations of the orders of the Commission and that it possessed no affirmative authority to enforce the administrative provisions of the Act.[1]

That this continued controversy between court and Commission did not proceed without friction is evident in the Commission's comments on the Lemon Case. The Commission had, upon complaint of California growers, refused to permit an increase in the rate on lemons. This order of the Commission was enjoined by the Commerce Court because, it was alleged, the Commission had exceeded its authority, in that it was attempting not to establish a reasonable rate but to protect the American grower against the competition of his Sicilian rival. And this because the Commission, in discussing the lemon rate, had devoted a page and a quarter to the facts of foreign competition and but three-quarters of a page to the traffic circumstances of the case. In commenting upon this decision in its Annual Report[2] the Commission took vigorous issue with the court for its insinuations, and denied that the grounds suggested by the court were the grounds of the decision. After stating its position, it concluded as follows:

"The Supreme Court has declared that the making of a transportation rate for the future is a legislative and not a judicial function. It has further apparently declared that this function may be exercised by Congress through the appointment of a commission acting under rules prescribed by it. The rate when fixed is just as

[1] 225 U. S., 282 (1912). [2] 1911, pp. 58, 59.

much legislative when made by a commission as when made directly by the legislature itself.

"That being so, the discretionary power involved in reaching the conclusion that a particular rate is or is not reasonable for the future, or that a particular discrimination is or is not undue, is a legislative discretion which cannot be reviewed by the courts.

"How is the exercise of this judgment in prescribing the future rate any the less legislative because there happens to be no dispute about the facts to which it is applied? Or how, if the conclusion of fact reached by this Commission cannot be reviewed through judicial process, can a court look into the mind of the Commission for the purpose of determining whether that conclusion has been influenced by any improper motive or consideration?"

Within two months of the court's injunction the Commission rendered a second opinion, which left no doubt as to its exhaustiveness or the grounds upon which its conclusions rested, and this time the Commerce Court refused to interfere. In this position it was sustained by the Supreme Court.[1]

Sufficient has been said to render clear the reasons other than political for the demise of the Commerce Court. It performed a valuable service in strengthening the law at many points, and it was by no means always in opposition to the Commission nor favorably inclined to the corporate point of view. It was unfortunate that the court chose to interpret its authority in such fashion as to bring it into conflict with the Commission and to bring down upon it the condemnation of the Supreme Court. Whether this was due to hostility to the Commission, to a desire to create for itself a place

[1] 19 I. C. C., 148 (1910); 22 I. C. C., 149 (1911); 190 Fed. Rep., 591 (1911).

in the judicial system, or to a constitutional inability or unwillingness to surrender final authority in matters of fact, is difficult to say. Probably it was a combination of all three. It is possible that in the absence of a Commerce Court the separate district courts might in the same manner have interfered with the free exercise of authority by the Commission, but the fact that the opposition was concentrated in one body rendered that body conspicuous and drew the fire.

The situation was seized upon for the purpose of manufacturing political capital. By a combination of Democrats and insurgents the court was finally done to death, its life expiring at the end of the year 1913, after two bills providing for its abolition had been vetoed by President Taft. The members of the court were transferred to the circuits and the experiment was at an end. The Attorney-General in 1912, in urging a continuance of the court, had expressed the view that the functions of the two bodies, court and Commission, were not clearly enough defined, and had made suggestions for amendments to the law that would confine the court's review exclusively to questions of law arising in connection with the Commission's opinions and orders. But Congress was not persuaded. The Supreme Court had found a sufficiently clear distinction in the existing statute, and the only method of reform that appealed to Congress was that which wiped the offending agency out of existence.

CHAPTER V

EACH revision of the Act to Regulate Commerce added materially to the administrative functions of the Commission. But beyond this, Congress took occasion from time to time to impose upon this much overworked body duties somewhat alien to the purpose of its creation. It had for a time supervision over the accounts of public utilities in the District of Columbia. Changes in parcel-post rates, weights, and zones were made subject to the consent of the Commission. Its services were invoked to define the time-zones in connection with daylight saving, and it was made the medium for the sifting of evidence and the recommendation to the President of the candidates for medals of honor awarded for "extreme daring" in connection with railroad accidents. These miscellaneous duties are of relatively little importance except that they draw upon the time and energy of the Commission needed for other duties. But a survey of the significant developments of administrative responsibility since 1910 will serve to show the important place that this body now occupies in our governmental system.

Telegraph, telephone, and cable companies were made subject to the Act in 1910, which meant the regulation of their rates, services, and accounts. By a decision of the Supreme Court in 1914[1] the power of the Commission over pipe-lines, granted in 1906, was sustained. The amendment was held to be constitutional and was interpreted to include those oil companies that were common carriers in substance quite as fully as those that were carriers in fact. The practice of the oil companies, the

[1] 234 U. S., 548.

Standard and its subsidiaries, of compelling outsiders to sell to them their oil before transportation, was held not to be conclusive that the transportation itself was not interstate commerce. These oil-transporting companies were required to obey the order of the Commission to file their rates and charges, and accounting regulations have been prescribed applicable to them.

1. *Discrimination*

Violations of law in the form of discriminations and rebates have not ceased. On the contrary, new devices more difficult to detect have been employed, while many of the old practices that were present at the beginning of regulation in 1887 recur with wearisome regularity. False claims for loss and damage, false billing, failure to observe the published tariffs, special services granted to large shippers, concessions resulting from alliances of shipper and carrier, failure to collect demurrage, lease of carrier's property to shipper at nominal rental—these are only illustrations. Shippers apparently still regard railroads as legitimate subjects for exploitation, and we have still a long way to go before the minor railroad official at least will realize that it is beneath the dignity and responsibility of the public-service corporation to resort to the sharp practices of the dishonest trader.

Of the discrimination evils of the decade, the most significant are those concerned with the so-called "tap-lines," and here the policy of the Commission received an unfortunate check from the Supreme Court. These short lines of road were usually owned by industries and employed mainly in transporting the product of the industry to a connection with a trunk line. They were in effect plant facilities. But by incorporating them as common carriers and offering their facilities to a non-existent public, they were able to make traffic arrangements with the trunk lines by which they received such a handsome proportion of the through rate that it amounted to a rebate. The Commission held that the common-carrier function was a mere device. But the Supreme Court said[1] that the Commission had no power so to declare when public policy, as evidenced by legislation, had recognized tap-lines as common carriers; that a tap-line if entitled to a division of the rate on outside business was equally entitled to it on the business of its proprietary industry, and that the question of fixing the division of joint rates so as to prevent discrimination and rebating was entirely in the hands of the Commission. Following this decision, the Commission has examined each tap-line case on its merits, determining first of all whether as a matter of fact it is a common carrier and then fixing a maximum limit to the charge for its services.[2] But even as late as 1918 the Commission was still struggling with the fundamental principles involved. In a case in that year it suggested that in view of the variance of opinion entertained in the Commission and elsewhere upon the many important and difficult questions so frequently arising out of the relations between the trunk-line carriers and the industries with railroads of their own, the rulings in this case which presented conditions that were fairly characteristic "should be reviewed by the courts in order that some definite principle may be judicially established by which we may hereafter be guided in such cases as they arise."[3]

2. Commodities Clause

Through persistent prosecution by the Government and interpretation by the Supreme Court the "com-

[1] 234 U. S., 1, (1914).

[2] In 240 U. S., 294 (1916), the Supreme Court sustained the power of the Commission to prescribe the proportion of the through rate to be enjoyed by the tap-line, incidentally sustaining the power to make joint rates granted to the Commission by the Act of 1910.

[3] 50 I. C. C., 504.

modities clause" of the Act has gradually assumed the form and effectiveness that Congress originally intended. This clause was enacted in 1906, and provided that after May 1, 1908, it should be unlawful for a railroad to transport in interstate commerce any commodity other than timber or its manufactures, which it owned in whole or in part, or in which it had any interest, direct or indirect, except such commodities as were necessary and intended for its use in its business as a common carrier. This legislation was designed primarily to effect a complete separation of coal-mining and transportation, and thus wipe out the close associations out of which sprang unification in management and confusion in accounts, to the detriment of all outside competitors. The relationship took various forms—in some a direct ownership and operation of mines by railroad companies, in others an ownership by the railroads of the stock of the coal companies.

The first test of this clause in 1909 was distinctly disappointing, because the court, taking the legalistic point of view, seemed to consider the preservation of the individuality of the corporate entity of more importance than the public interest as expressed in the statute. It held that when a railroad had stock in a coal company, it did not have a legal interest in the commodity produced, and that the ownership of the stock of a producing corporation did not violate the commodities clause when the corporation was organized in good faith. Moreover, a railroad was not carrying its own coal even though it previously owned and mined it, if it sold the coal to another company at the pit mouth.[1] No more helpful guidance could have been offered by expert counsel to those companies that were seeking a way around the law. Had the court taken the spirit rather than the letter of the statute it would have followed the line laid

[1] 213 U. S., 366 (1909).

down by that sturdy dissenter, Justice Harlan, who declared that the Act when reasonably and properly construed, included a railroad transporting coal if it at the time was the owner legally or equitably of stock—certainly if it owned a majority or all the stock—in the company that mined, manufactured, and then owned the coal which was being transported. Any other view would enable the transporting railroad by one device or another to defeat altogether the purpose that Congress had in mind.[1]

The coal-mining railroad companies proceeded promptly to follow the suggestions of the court, and when necessary, to create corporations for the purpose of effecting technically legal separation. For example, the Delaware, Lackawanna and Western, a corporation unhampered by complicated mortgages and intercorporate relationships, organized a separate coal company and sold its coal to this company at the mine mouth under a closed contract. In view of the later decision of the court, it is to be observed that the stock of the coal company was distributed pro rata and without payment among the Lackawanna stockholders. The Lehigh Valley already had a coal company whose stock it owned, but this stock was pledged under a general mortgage and hence difficult to disturb. Accordingly, it organized a sales company to which the coal company sold the coal at the mine, and which in turn contracted with the railroad for its carriage! There is humor even in corporation finance.

The Lehigh Valley Case reached the Supreme Court in 1911,[2] that of the Lackawanna in 1915.[3] Chief Justice White, who gave the original legalistic opinion in 1909, delivered the opinion in the Lehigh Valley Case.

[1] In the Mann-Elkins Act of 1910 an attempt was made to express more clearly the original intent of Congress by an amendment that would prohibit stock ownership in coal companies by railroads, but the attempt failed.

[2] 220 U. S., 257.　　　　　　　　[3] 238 U. S., 516.

He held that while stock ownership by a railroad in a bona fide corporation irrespective of the extent of this ownership does not preclude a railroad from transporting the commodity produced or owned by the subsidiary corporation, it is still open to the Government to question the right of the railroad to transport such commodity when it uses its power as a stockholder to obliterate all distinctions between the two corporations. The railroad cannot so commingle its affairs with the corporation owned as to cause the two to become one and inseparable. In both this and the Lackawanna case the railroads were held to be in violation of both the Anti-Trust Act and the commodities clause of the Interstate Commerce Act.

This was an encouraging advance by the court upon its earlier position. It still remained to dispose of the corporate arrangement illustrated by the Reading Company, which from the purely legal standpoint seemed to be able to defy the law. The Reading Company was a pure holding company owning all the stock of the Philadelphia and Reading Railway and all the stock of the Philadelphia and Reading Coal and Iron Co., but the railroad had no legal interest whatever in the coal company or in its activities. This case reached the court in 1920[1] and the decision is emphatic. It sweeps aside technicalities and comes directly to the heart of the problem. Having reached the conclusion that the deliberately calculated purchase for control by a holding company of competing railroads and coal companies is a violation of the Anti-Trust Act, it declares that the combination of railroad and coal company through a holding company must cease because it is a violation of the commodities clause. In connection with another phase of the case, the relation of the Central of New Jersey, itself a subsidiary of the Reading, to its coal company,

[1] 253 U. S., 26.

the court goes to the root of the matter in a manner reminiscent of the New York Supreme Court in the Sugar Trust Case back in 1890. It declares that when the ownership of a mining company by a railroad is not for the purpose of normal participation as stockholder, but to make it a mere instrumentality, the courts will look through the form to the realities of the relation as if the corporate agency did not exist. Apparently what the country has needed is not additional legislation but clear vision and courage on the part of the Supreme Court.

In this long-drawn-out court controversy the Commission took no active part, but its influence was constantly in the direction of clarifying the issue, and it had many opportunities to express its view in cases before it. In the investigation of the relations of railroads and coal mines in Illinois made at the instance of Congress in 1914,[1] it reached the conclusion that public and private business should be clearly separated, that credit should not be extended by railroads to private industry, and that the commodities clause should be enforced and extended to all traffic. In 1915 in an investigation of anthracite coal rates[2] it laid stress upon the inherent unlawfulness of rates and practices that were the outgrowth of past conditions in which carriers were producers, shippers, transporters, and venders of coal. Again in the same year the Commission investigated the rates governing the transportation of railroad fuel and other coal.[3] After laying down the principle that the carrier was entitled as shipper to the same consideration as any commercial shipper, but to no more, even when the shipment moved partly over its own rails, the Commission called attention to the fact that some carriers had not complied with this often-reiterated principle, and announced that the next case of this sort would proceed under the criminal provisions of the Act.

[1] 31 I. C. C., 193.   [2] 35 I. C. C., 220.   [3] 36 I. C. C., 1.

3. *Express Rates*

In response to repeated and wide-spread complaints, the Commission in 1912 undertook a comprehensive survey of the rates and practices of the express companies. It found that their practices were unjustifiable, that their methods of doing business were archaic, and that their rates were discriminating and unreasonable. It thoroughly overhauled and reformed express company methods. It established for the first time through routes and joint rates and eliminated the through charge that had been constructed out of the sum of the local rates. It put a stop to the criminal practice of the double collection of charges. Moreover, it worked a complete revolution in the methods of rate computation by dividing the country into zones and blocks and devising a system of class rates in connection therewith. This system of rate making, which simplifies the tariffs for both the companies and the public, may be set down as the most important piece of constructive rate making that the Commission has accomplished.[1] It has now been adopted for intra-state traffic by practically all the states[2] and is being gradually extended to include commodity tariffs as well as class rates.

4. *Mail Pay*

Later, the Commission had thrust upon it the duty of determining the proper payment for the carriage of the mails. This is a question which has from time to time occupied the political stage. Rates of pay based upon weight of mail and distance carried and upon equipment furnished in the form of mail cars, had been prescribed

[1] 24 I. C. C., 380; 28 I. C. C., 131.
[2] Effective January 1, 1919, the Director-General adopted the block system for the three states that had not theretofore adopted it. (General Order No. 56.)

by Congress as far back as 1873. Reductions in these rates had taken place by Congressional action in 1876, 1878, and in 1907, and from time to time through change in administrative regulation and interpretation.

Intermittently, the question of pay arose in Congress. It was the contention of the railroads that not only were the rates not exorbitant, but, because pay was based upon the results of weighings that took place but once in four years, the railroads, due to the increase in mail matter, were actually carrying before the succeeding weighing more weight than they were being paid for. Congressional investigations followed one another and resulted in the accumulation of much interesting data but in little or no action. The situation had from the first been rendered more difficult because of the ammunition that the subject provided for the political orator, and because various postmasters-general found it of advantage to attempt to balance their accounts and avoid a deficit by cutting off something from the railroad compensation.

With the introduction of the parcel post in 1913 the problem became more complicated and the issue was brought to a head. The weight basis of payment seemed now no longer to meet the situation satisfactorily and it was clear that the compensation to the railroads was inadequate. The joint Congressional committee that reported in 1914 (the Bourne committee) held that the railroads were entitled to an increase in compensation but recommended a shift to the space basis of payment. The railroads desired to continue the weight basis with annual weighings. By the Act of July 28, 1916, the Interstate Commerce Commission was directed to prescribe the basis and amount of compensation for mail carriage and the services to be performed in connection therewith. The Postmaster-General was authorized, with the consent of the Commission, to put into effect experimentally, to the extent he deemed necessary, the space-basis system of pay at the rates provided in the Act of Congress. Reports were to be made and hearings conducted following the experiment. Accordingly, on November 1, 1916, the Postmaster-General introduced the space basis on practically all roads in the country. Following the experiment and the hearings, the Commission rendered its opinion on December 23, 1919,[1] in which it approved the space basis of payment and required its introduction on all mail routes after March 1, 1920. It prescribed rates for the different classes of service, increasing the rates then in effect,[2] discontinued certain terminal allowances, and required that certain auxiliary services should be paid for separately at cost. It is to be hoped that this thorny question has at last been eliminated from politics, and that mail rates, like all other transportation rates, may hereafter be a matter solely of administrative regulation.

5. *Accounting*

Section 20 of the Act to Regulate Commerce, under which the statistical and accounting activities of the Commission have been developed, has attracted relatively little public interest, and its importance and influence in the problems of regulation has been largely overlooked. In fact, for many years the Commission itself set little store by the work of its statistical division, and it is only within the last decade that the significance of accounts and statistics has been adequately appreciated within the offices of the Commission itself.

This is in part to be explained by the slowness with which uniform statistics and accounts have been developed, the delay being due in the first instance to the in-

[1] 56 I. C. C., 1.
[2] The average rate increase for 1918 and subsequent periods over the rates prescribed by Congress in 1916 was 65 per cent.

adequacy of the legislation, and, when this was corrected, to the gigantic size of the job—the necessity of working out detailed accounting regulations and classifications for all the varied transportation agencies subject to the Act. It was only when these preliminary tasks were completed and the results began to come in that the Commission, and later the public, began to be aware of their value from the regulation standpoint. To cite but one instance: The contracts under which the Government took over the roads during the war would have been greatly delayed and seriously complicated but for the uniform accounting system which made it a relatively simple matter to determine for each road its "average annual railway operating income for the three years ending June 30, 1917."

In the original Act of 1887 carriers were required to file annual reports with the Commission and the items were specified. Blanks were provided and classifications of certain general accounts were issued in co-operation with the roads, in the hope that this might aid in the promotion of uniformity. But these classifications could not be ordered into force. The carriers were merely requested to adopt them. Accordingly, while the statistical compilations made from these reports steadily improved in content and quality, they did not inspire confidence with respect to significant items, because the carriers were free to report or not as they saw fit. An attempt on the part of the Commission to compel answers to certain questions led to a ruling by the Supreme Court that in view of the lack of penalties and of enforcement provisions, no suit could be maintained to compel the furnishing of information refused in the annual reports.[1]

This situation was corrected by the amendments of 1906, which required reports under oath, prescribed penalties for the violation of the Commission's regulations,

[1] 197 U. S., 536, (1905).

and established a mandamus process for enforcing its orders. The original Act had provided that the Commission might in its discretion prescribe a uniform system of accounts for all carriers subject to its jurisdiction. It was now furnished with a force of examiners having authority to inspect the accounts and records of the carriers. Immediately upon the passage of these amendments, the Commission, in co-operation with accounting officers of the carriers, began the formulation of systems of accounts for the various transportation agencies, beginning with steam railroads. Three classifications—those of operating expenses, operating revenues, and road and equipment expenditures for steam roads—were completed and put into effect on July 1, 1907. By 1915 uniform systems of accounts had been prescribed for each class of carriers subject to the Act, and it was the opinion of the Commission that no extensive revision of these classifications would be required for some years to come. These prescribed accounts covered steam and electric roads, water carriers, express, pipe-line, sleeping car, telephone, and telegraph companies. The importance of uniformity in accounting in these public-service industries and the increased value of reports based upon uniform accounting can hardly be overestimated. Whether looked at from the standpoint of investor, of shipper, of regulating authority, of the general public, publicity of uniform, intelligible, comparable information is invaluable.

But in order to perfect the value of this service a thorough and continuous inspection was absolutely necessary. Rules and regulations were capable of honest misconception. The exercise of individual judgment might destroy the uniformity sought for. There were abundant opportunities for deliberate misstatement of earnings and expenses or for a manipulation of property accounts if the books were not personally inspected by agents of the Government. While cases of flagrant violation of accounting regulations have been rare and most of the roads have readily complied with requirements, yet the perfection desired is not attainable without adequate inspection. It is more than likely that many of the cases of mismanagement of transportation companies in the past would have been impossible had the accounting system with its corps of examiners been working with complete efficiency. Such inspection has never yet been completely satisfactory, due to the fact that the various special investigations which the Commission has felt called upon to make either on its own initiative or on that of Congress have drafted the services of examiners, and diverted them from the specific object of their appointment.

Two types of deliberate violation of accounting rules may be mentioned as the most important and most frequently recurring offenses. The one has to do with the overstatement or understatement of operating expense, which can usually be accomplished in connection with maintenance. An overstatement makes the net earnings appear smaller than they actually are, and thus creates a secret reserve of property value which appears nowhere on the books, but which may be dragged forth at a favorable moment for speculative purposes. An understatement of operating expense develops fictitious earnings and a fictitious surplus which furnish an excuse for additional securities. In such cases accounting is no longer a record of financial transactions but merely a reflection of corporate policy.

But it is in the property account that the greatest manipulation has taken place, in the item of "cost of road and equipment." A clear-cut distinction between operating expenditures and expenditures for property was recognized by the Commission as fundamental. In its classification of expenditures for road and equipment in 1907, it laid down the rule that all entries under this head must be in terms of cash, thus showing what the investment actually cost. There have been frequent severe criticisms of the property accounts of the carriers, some of which have gone to the extreme of declaring them to be worthless. These criticisms are in many instances well founded so far as the accounts previous to 1907 are concerned. Items carried on the books as investments or specifically included in the term "cost of road," when subjected to close analysis, reveal such doubtful elements as "vest-pocket" construction charges, cost of preliminary and imaginary surveys, promotion expenses, valuations hoped for but not yet realized, securities of subsidiary corporations which are often only evidences of possession but are carried on the books at par. Since 1907, if the regulations of the Commission have been observed, all entries have represented cash expenditure, and the railroads are justified in pointing to this fact as evidence that their property accounts are growing steadily more acceptable, and that they now contain a large element of investment that has been officially approved.

But here again, in order that this contention should be wholly acceptable, it is necessary either that the carriers should universally and voluntarily obey the regulations of the Commission, or that the Commission's system of inspection should be perfect. And neither alternative is wholly true. Some unfortunate and glaring instances of violation of accounting regulations have been uncovered from time to time. Heretofore, however, departures from the regulations have been corrected as far as possible by correspondence. Only two questions have been taken to the courts, and in both of them the Commission has been sustained. The one involved the right of the Commission to require reports from water carriers and to exercise accounting jurisdiction over them.[1]

[1] I. C. C. v. Goodrich Transit Co., 224 U. S., 194 (1912).

This case was significant because the court at the same time sustained the constitutionality of Section 20, and thereby rendered secure the authority of the Commission over accounts and reports. The other case involved technical questions of accounting,[1] the recording of transactions in connection with the abandonment of property and the substitution of improvements. It is a significant recognition of the finality of the administrative power of the Commission that the court in this case refused to interfere with the Commission's regulations notwithstanding the fact that it was strongly impressed by the arguments of railroad counsel. The court refused to set its judgment above that of the Commission.

In its discussion of the accounting delinquencies of the Puget Sound Railway[2] in 1914 the Commission admitted that it had been lenient with the carriers during the formative period. But now that the accounting system was complete and the various questions involved in its introduction largely disposed of, the Commission proposed thereafter to invoke the penalties of the law for infraction, and to hold the chief accounting officer strictly responsible for his signature under oath attached to the report to the Commission. Moreover, said the Commission: "We shall not hesitate to call to account with even greater severity anyone above the accounting officer in authority who may share in the responsibility for any violations of the accounting rules and regulations which have been prescribed for the use of the carriers that are subject to the Act."

Among the unsettled accounting problems the most important is that of depreciation. It is obvious that net earnings are not correctly stated if adequate charges are not made in the operating expense accounts to cover

[1] Kansas City Southern Ry. v. U. S., 231 U. S., 423 (1913).
[2] St. Paul and Puget Sound Accounts, 29 I. C. C., 508 (1914).

depreciation of property. There has been much discussion as to whether and to what extent depreciation actually obtains in the railroad business, many insisting that an adequate scheme of renewals renders reserves for depreciation altogether unnecessary. It is not the purpose to enter upon this technical discussion here. It is clear that the Commission's accountants never took that position, for provision was made in the classification of operating expenses in 1907 for depreciation on equipment. No experience was available upon which to base depreciation rates, neither was the Commission clear as to its power definitely to prescribe rates. Accordingly, the roads were required to charge the actual depreciation, the rate being left to the determination of the individual carrier. The practice varied all the way from charging nothing up to a charge of 7 per cent, the variations being due not to actual differences in physical depreciation but rather to differences in financial policy. Many roads, as already stated, felt that depreciation was adequately covered by renewals. Many made undercharges or overcharges with larger financial policies in mind. The regulations of the Commission served merely to reveal the corporate practices of the carriers and developed no uniformity in depreciation accounting.

In the revised classifications of 1914 provision was made for depreciation of fixed property as well as equipment. By 1916 the Commission was becoming more insistent that some rate of depreciation should be employed, and was ordering corrections when rates appeared excessive or inadequate. But up to the passage of the Act of 1920 no specific rate was required. The Commission contented itself with ordering that each carrier should charge a rate based upon its own experience which it should be prepared to justify.

The practicability of applying the methods of cost accounting to railroad operations has been a subject of much discussion inside and outside the Commission. In the railroad industry it takes the special form of the separation of operating expenses, mainly between the two services of freight and passenger. It has been the commonly accepted view that railroad services were in a sense the product of joint cost, that the one plant served its various uses, and that any attempt to assign expenses to specific services could be accomplished only in so arbitrary and crude a fashion that the results would be valueless. Certain expenses might of course be definitely assigned, those specifically relating to train operation, but maintenance of way and general expenses were practically unassignable. And the theory of rates based upon this survey of conditions was that of charging according to the value of the service, each shipment to contribute to joint costs roughly in proportion to its ability.

On the other hand, those who lean in the direction of the more extensive application of the cost basis of rate making have argued that there is no reason why the developments in the science of cost accounting should not be applied to railroads as well as to other industries, that from 60 to 70 per cent of the operating expenses can be assigned in a fairly satisfactory manner, and that this result would be of distinct assistance to the Commission in adjudicating rate problems, by helping to determine the cost of specific services, and to study intelligently comparative costs on different railroads. Roads should be in position to know, at least in a general way, what traffic was producing the largest profits and what traffic was being carried below cost. To the contention of this group that a large number of roads were already making this separation for their own purposes, and so would not be burdened seriously if required to do it for the Commission, the railroad accountants replied that so long as the basis of separation was the same from year to year and the results reached were used only for comparative purposes, the separation, however arbitrary, might be useful to a road for operating purposes. But it would not stand the test of scientific analysis and should have no official recognition.

Separation had been attempted at the very beginning of the Commission's history but was abandoned in 1894, because largely arbitrary and useless. The question was resurrected in 1914 and, following elaborate hearings, the Commission decided that all Class I roads (those having annual gross earnings of over $1,000,000) should separate their operating expenses according to certain prescribed bases.[1] By an order effective July 1, 1915, separation was required of all expenses except certain items of maintenance of way. However, the war came before the system had reached a stage of effectiveness, and the necessity of reducing accounting work to the minimum, because of shortage of labor, led to the suspension in 1917 of all requirements for the apportionment of expenses.

6. *Valuation*

This second decade of the twentieth century will be significant in railroad history because of the inauguration of one of the most important surveys ever undertaken in this country, that of the valuation of the railroads. While the decade has not seen its consummation, it has witnessed all the preliminary and underlying investigations and the settlement of fundamental principles upon which the structure is being speedily erected. When the idea of a sweeping federal valuation was first suggested, it met with terrified opposition from the railroads. It was declared to be prohibitive in cost. It would be out of date long before its completion, and in any case it was an absurd waste of time and money be-

[1] In the matter of the Separation of Operating Expenses. 30 I. C. C. 676 (1914).

cause valuation had no relation to rate making. Yet
as railroad managers considered the question more carefully, their instinctive opposition disappeared and they
saw many advantages to be gained from a definitive,
officially indorsed property valuation. For one thing,
the bogie of overcapitalization would be laid once for
all, for they were confident that a valuation would reveal
property value in excess of outstanding securities. Moreover, for their own uses there was much to be gained
from a thorough overhauling of their domestic accounts.
It was a costly process, but it needed to be done, and this
would provide the stimulus. Accordingly, when the
Valuation Act was finally put through in 1913, there was
practically no opposition from railroad men. Executives confined their activities to suggestions for making
the valuation as comprehensive and as thorough as possible.

There is not opportunity here to treat this question
thoroughly. It involves technical considerations that
demand a separate handling. It will be sufficient to
summarize the law and the procedure of the Commission
thereunder and make clear its position in the present
scheme of regulation. By the Valuation Act[1] the Commission was required to report the value of all property
owned or used by every common carrier subject to the
Interstate Commerce Act. It was to report for each
piece of property the original cost to date, the cost of
reproduction new, the cost of reproduction less depreciation, and "other values and elements of value, if
any." Lands were to be reported separately, and the
amount and value of land grants or donations were to
be ascertained as well as the benefits derived from their
sale. Railroads were required to aid the Commission
by furnishing maps, profiles, contracts, and any other
pertinent documents and to co-operate in any way de-

[1] Interstate Commerce Act, Sec. 19a, March 1, 1913.

sired in the undertaking. Provision was to be made by accounting regulations and reports for revision and correction of the valuation to keep it up to date. After a tentative valuation had been completed, notice was to be given to the Attorney-General of the United States, to the Governor of any state involved, and to the carrier, and if no protest was made within thirty days, the valuation was to become final. If protested, hearings were to be held before final valuation was announced. All final valuations were to be *prima facie* evidence of the value of the property in all proceedings under the Act.

The Commission proceeded promptly to the organization of its Bureau of Valuation, placing at its head Judge Charles A. Prouty, whose long and brilliant career as a member of the Commission had qualified him admirably for this intricate and path-breaking task. The work fell naturally into three divisions: the field survey, the accounting and statistical computations, and the land value section. The first was largely an engineering problem, having to do with a census of standardized units. The second accumulated price data and applied it to the results of the field survey. Likewise it was concerned with values derived from records as distinct from those obtained by observation. The land question had a sufficient number of knotty problems to warrant its assignment to a separate division. Alongside the Commission organization, which was national in scope, went the valuation departments of the individual roads that accumulated the data and documentary material required by the Commission and assisted and checked the results of the Commission's engineers. In this way a physical appraisal could be agreed upon that would materially expedite the process of reaching a final valuation.

The Commission began its work by selecting a few roads in different sections of the country which were small and possessed of varying characteristics, and in which the records were available, in order to uncover and dispose of the various controversial points at the beginning, and thereby be enabled to apply a standardized practice to the carriers as a whole. Gradually the forces were increased and efficiency developed until the survey division was covering a little over 50,000 miles of road annually. Field work is now practically completed and the field forces have been disbanded. The latest figures (of September 1921) show 150 tentative valuations served upon carriers. In the case of several of these properties, all preliminary reports have been published but the Commission has not yet fixed a single sum as the final value for any one of the properties. Action in this direction was suspended and delayed by an adverse decision of the Supreme Court that required the Commission to take into account certain matters relating to condemnation costs which the Commission had omitted.[1]

The decision of the Commission to find a single sum as a final value for each road compels it to reach a final conclusion on the many complex questions involved and to find the truth in the many conflicting theories. Having found original cost to date, the actual investment, the cost of reproduction new and less depreciation, the Commission must in the end announce *the value*, and it is the reasoning upon which this value will be based that will be of the greatest public interest. It is obvious that there is no rule by which such a value can be determined. It must in the end be a matter of expert judgment.

In the matter of land values, which perhaps possesses the greatest interest for the economic student, the Commission is required to find the original cost and the present value. Its rule for finding present value of common-carrier lands has been to follow Justice Hughes in the Minnesota Rate Case, and to estimate it from the present fair average market value of adjoining lands, allowance

[1] Kans. City Southern Case, 252 U. S., 178, March 8, 1920.

being made for any peculiar adaptability of the land to railroad use, but nothing being added for expense of acquisition or for severance damages. The reproduction cost of carrier lands has not been estimated nor the present cost of condemnation and damages, or of purchase. It was this last omission which the Supreme Court held to be contrary to the mandate of the statute.

The valuations issued by the Commission and still considered as "tentative" report a "final value." This seems in most cases to be the cost of reproduction less depreciation for the depreciable property, together with the present value of common-carrier lands and the working capital, including materials and supplies. It is the claim of the carriers that the method adopted to determine depreciation—the straight-line method with the assignment of different service lives to the constituent items of a carrier's physical property—does not determine the actual existing depreciation on any property, but only the estimated expiration of service life at the date of the inventory. Hence the valuations reported contain an excessive depreciation, which reduces the value found below the actual investment value. Again, it is insisted, the cost of reproduction new is based on certain theoretical assumptions, and many items of cost, actually incurred in the construction of the property and charged on the books, have been omitted. Moreover, this value is limited to the cost of bringing the property into existence and ready for operation, and includes nothing for later development of property or traffic. Nothing seems specifically to be included for the excess cost of carrier lands, for appreciation of property or for the element of which the railroad counsel took much account, going-concern value. In view of the fact that the Commission has omitted much in the way of intangible elements that the railroads claim, the problem of valuation is not likely to be disposed of promptly. It will simply be transferred to the courts.

Yet it would not be surprising to find the court influenced to a considerable degree by the findings of the Commission, and somewhat disinclined to set up its own judgment against that of an expert administrative body. It is more than likely to indorse the opinion it has repeatedly expressed that in matters within its administrative discretion, the Commission's judgment is final.

Has this gigantic undertaking been worth while? What place will the results occupy in the field of regulation? We hear less to-day than formerly that there is no relation whatever between value of property and rates, that the railroad must charge what the traffic will bear, and that whether there is anything left as a return on property is a matter to be determined by the Board of Directors when the annual report is made up, but does not primarily concern the traffic department. This form of argument never was true except to a limited degree. Individual rates are, no doubt, made frequently with little consideration for their ultimate effect upon net revenues, although the traffic manager must always have this consideration in the background. But when an entire schedule of rates is under consideration, the one outstanding question is that of an adequate return upon railroad investment. The tendency to advance this argument to the fore increased steadily after the decision in Smyth v. Ames in 1898, in which the court declared that what the carrier was entitled to was a reasonable return upon the fair value of the property devoted to public use. As the carriers, beginning with 1910, undertook in co-operation with one another to increase entire schedules of rates covering extended territories, their most effective argument was not a demonstration of the intrinsic reasonableness of specific rates, but rather the fact that these general increases were necessary to give them that reasonable return on their investment which was assured by law. These tactics had the advantage

which they did not overlook, of disposing of the cry
that the railroads were seeking dividends on an inflated
capitalization. They no longer asked for dividends.
They asked for the fair return on their property. This
obtained, dividends would come or not, dependent upon
the nature and extent of their capital securities. This
point has been dwelt upon because it illustrates the growing importance of the property-value concept in railroad
regulation, and hence the importance of the valuation
survey now nearing completion. The law of 1913 was
passed none too soon and its results as fast as available
are to be incorporated into the structure of our federal
machinery. This is evident from a reading of the Transportation Act of 1920. Smyth v. Ames had prescribed
a minimum return to the carrier, a reasonable return
upon a fair value, below which confiscation would apparently begin. The Act of 1920 prescribes a maximum
return beyond which recapture by the Government is to
begin. In determining what rates will provide the return on property prescribed by this statute, the Commission is to utilize the results of the valuation so far as
they are available, and where final value has been ascertained, this is to be taken by the Commission as the
value upon which the carrier is entitled to earn.[1] To
the utter confusion of those who assert that there is no
connection between value of property and rates, Congress
makes property value the sole guide in determining their
reasonableness.

Again the consolidation clause of the Act of 1920 provides that the capitalization shall not exceed the value
of the combined properties as ascertained by the Commission under its valuation procedure.[2] While no specific mention is made of valuation in connection with
the authority granted over capitalization, yet the discretion granted the Commission in determining the sound-

[1] I. C. C. Act, Sec. 15a (4).   [2] I. C. C. Act, Sec. 5 (6b).

ness of the application will lead it without doubt to consult its valuation records.

Property value officially determined has been transformed from the dream of a few idealists into the corner-stone of our regulation policy. It constitutes the ultimate determinant of rates. It sets the limits to the financial policy of consolidation and dampens the ardor of the financial juggler. It will be a substantial aid in all future capitalization. Finally its influence upon railroad accounting should be healthy and far-reaching. In the accounting problems of the present, such for example as depreciation, an accurate valuation of property with all the historical confusion of accounts eliminated, and a systematic method of keeping this valuation abreast of the times should be of enormous utility. Anything that contributes to the soundness and scientific exactitude of accounting increases the efficiency of public regulation.

7. *Safety Measures*

Deserving of more than passing mention is the work of the Commission in the interest of safe travel. It takes a wide range, including such varied functions as the awarding of life-saving medals, the prescribing of rules for the safe transportation of explosives, the enforcement of the limited hours of service of employees and the use of the various standardized devices in train equipment.

The development of the original safety appliances and their introduction belong to the first decade of the Commission's life. By 1900 cars and locomotives were almost universally equipped with air-brakes and automatic couplers. Since that time one device after another has been standardized and introduced, such as grab-irons, handholds, side steps, running-boards, and ash-pans. In 1910 the Commission was required by statute to designate the number, dimensions, location, and manner of application to cars of the various appliances provided for by previous legislation, which indirectly increased its power over the enforcement of the laws. As an aid to enforcement monthly reports of accidents were required. In the same year, Congress conferred upon the Commission authority to investigate all collisions, derailments, or other accidents resulting in serious injury to persons or property. Obviously it could not investigate all accidents. It interpreted the law as a mandate to inquire into the more serious cases, with the object of studying causes and devising measures of relief. Its investigations covering a decade may be briefly summarized.

The block-signal system, both automatic and manual, has been slowly extended, by no means as rapidly as conditions of service have demanded. At the end of 1920, 38,000 miles of line were equipped with automatic block signals and 64,000 miles with non-automatic, which means that considerably more than half of the mileage of the country has no block signals at all. The Commission has from time to time urged compulsory legislation but the expense of installation, combined with the interferences of the war period, has resulted in leaving the matter to the voluntary determination of the individual carrier.

The failure of the human element to measure up to its responsibilities is the most serious factor in the safety of railroad operation to-day. The Commission has recommended that the operating rules be standarized nationally by legislation. This would remove danger due to confusion of rules on different railroads and misunderstandings arising therefrom. Of course obedience to the rules would not follow automatically. To accomplish this, reliance must be placed upon the development of a proper spirit upon each road. And in fact the decline in the number of collisions up to 1916 was due not so much to the introduction of automatic devices to prevent them as to the setting up of safety committees that have performed a very substantial service in the development of a greater degree of responsibility on the part of the personnel.

The alarming increase in the number of accidents due to derailments, an increase from 6,697 in 1911 to 22,477 in 1920, has led the Commission to the conclusion that size and weight of equipment has outrun the physical condition of track and roadway and that efforts must be directed to restoring the balance. In the matter of equipment, the Commission has recommended that steel cars be required in passenger service. It is doubtful whether legislation would in any way alter the prevailing policy, at least of the larger roads, which are substituting steel for wooden equipment as rapidly as circumstances permit. It might arouse the smaller and more impecunious carriers and it might jog the others to a livelier pace.

It is of interest to observe that the Commission in its last report (1920) asks Congress to consider the advisability of prohibiting by statute trespassing on trains and tracks. This abuse, which is responsible for 40 per cent of the deaths in railroad accidents, has been neglected in national legislation, probably because it was considered to fall within the police powers of the states. But we are moving rapidly away from the separation of powers in its application to railroad transportation. Decisions under the safety-appliance acts which have sustained the federal power are evidence of the trend. Certain it is that, having emerged from our pioneer stage of nation-building, we are no longer justified in continuing on our happy-go-lucky way and permitting this enormous abuse to continue.

Failure to obey signals even in automatic-block-signal territory has developed an interest in inventions that provide for automatic stops and train control. Under a congressional resolution of 1906 a Block Signal and Train Control Board was appointed which conducted investigations extending over a period of four years. As a result it reached the conclusion that automatic train stops, if properly installed and maintained, would contribute to safety, that these were urgently needed in many situations, and that appliances were available to meet the need. However, it was not prepared at that time (1911) to recommend a legislative requirement for the use of automatic stops. This action, it held, should come only in case the railroads failed to show diligence in developing this aid to safety. From that time on nothing was done by the steam railroads beyond occasional experimenting. The automatic stop is in use only in subway operation. By the Transportation Act of 1920 the Commission is given power after investigation to order any railroad to install automatic or train-control devices, *or other safety devices* upon any part of its railroad, two years' notice being given. A broad interpretation of "other devices" would seem to give the Commission authority with respect to every type of safety provision which might be introduced into railroad operation. In conformity with the purpose of this section, and at the request of the Commission, a joint committee on automatic train-control has been appointed by the American Railway Association, consisting of representatives of the operating, engineering, signal, and mechanical divisions, which is co-operating with the Bureau of Safety in more extended service tests of automatic devices than have heretofore been conducted. Inspection and observation has thus far been confined to short stretches of track on three railroads, the Chicago and Eastern Illinois, the Chesapeake and Ohio, and the Chicago, Rock Island and Pacific. The committee will make no recommendations until a device has stood the test of winter conditions.

The requirement laid down by the Commission in 1909

that the railroads should make monthly reports of violations of the Hours of Service Act[1] was contested by the roads but upheld by the Supreme Court.[2] As a consequence the Commission has been in position to analyze in detail the causes which have led to longer hours than the law permits in the case of train service employees and train despatchers and operators, and through such publicity to eliminate many unnecessary situations. However, prosecutions in small number still continue, and the law is constantly subject to examination and interpretation by the courts.

[1] Act of March 4, 1907, 34 Stat. L., 1415.
[2] 221 U. S. 612 (1911).

CHAPTER VI

RELATIONS OF RAIL AND WATER LINES

THE jurisdiction of the Commission over water lines has always been reached by indirection, through its power to regulate other agencies. There has been a widespread conviction that water transportation in general could be trusted to take care of itself without any injury to the public. If the highway were free to all vessels, competitors would force the rates down to a reasonable level. It is curious how persistently and how universally the theory has held in the face of conditions that were just the reverse of competitive. Ownership of docks and wharves by railroad or other corporate interests, ownership of boat lines by railroad companies, singly or in combination, has, so far at least as coastwise and lake transportation is concerned, reduced competition between water and rail in large degree to mere theory. Water rates have been fixed at a level lower than rail, but the differential has served merely to express the difference in service. This adjustment has been modified from time to time by the appearance of independent water lines but the altered relationship scarcely ever lasted long. Sooner or later these lines either disappeared or "conformed."

What should have been done at the very beginning of transportation regulation was to place the waterways directly under the control of the Interstate Commerce Commission. To be sure, such regulation could have been only partially effective so long as the Commission had no power to prescribe minimum rates, and so could not stabilize the rate structure. But much nevertheless would have been accomplished. Instead the Congress has clung desperately to the theory of competition, and has left the water agencies untouched directly, in the confidence that they voluntarily would serve as a check upon the actions of their railroad rivals.

The original Act of 1887 gave the Commission jurisdiction over common carriers engaged in the transportation of passengers or property, partly by railroad and partly by water, when both were used "under a common control, management or arrangement for a continuous carriage or shipment." This covered joint water and rail rates, applied to through billing. The Commission's interpretation of this power is found in a decision in 1909 in which it held, three members dissenting, that water carriers were subject to the Act *only* in respect to such traffic as was handled under a common arrangement. Otherwise they were free of all jurisdiction.[1] The dissenting commissioners took the position that once a water carrier had entered into a common arrangement with a rail carrier *all* of its business was subject to control. They regarded the decision of the majority as a virtual invitation to rail carriers to provide themselves with water connections and use them as agencies to defeat the purpose of the law. It is to be noted that in 1912 the Supreme Court of the United States took the view of the minority, so far as it applied to the accounting section of the Act. In 1910 the Commission had sent out a circular calling for statistics from every water carrier within the jurisdiction of the Commission, as a basis for the determination of the proper form of annual report for water carriers. Certain water carriers refused to answer as to that portion of the report that did not concern joint business with railroads. The Supreme Court in the case already cited,[2] required complete compliance on the general ground that information concern-

[1] 15 I. C. C., 205.   [2] See p. 65.

ing all the transactions of these carriers was necessary if the Commission was properly to regulate matters within its jurisdiction, that Section 20 of the Act conferred this authority, and that the power then granted did not exceed the constitutional authority of Congress. Following this opinion, water lines generally complied with the Commission's request and expressed willingness to co-operate in working out the details of an accounting system and an annual report.

A very definite step was taken to increase the jurisdiction of the Commission in connection with the passage of the Panama Canal Act in 1912.[1] While this Act, so far as railroads were concerned, had in mind primarily the problem of competition between the two coasts, it went farther and attempted to solve once and for all the question of intercorporate relationships between rail and water carriers. It provided that after July 1, 1914, it should be unlawful for any railroad to own, lease, operate, or control or have any interest whatsoever through stockholding or community of management, in any water carrier operating through the Panama Canal. Neither was any such relationship to continue elsewhere than through the Canal in cases where the railroad did or might compete with the water line for traffic. It was a definite attempt to force competition by legislative edict.

But this provision, while apparently satisfactory in its application to the canal, required some leeway when applied to other situations. Accordingly it was further provided that if the Commission should be of the opinion that any existing water service *other than through the Panama Canal* was being operated in the public interest, and was of advantage to the convenience and commerce of the people, and that it did not exclude, prevent, or reduce competition, it might permit the intercorporate

[1] 37 Stat. L., 566.

relationship between the rail and water lines to continue. But in every such case the "rates schedules and practices" of the water carrier were to be filed with the Commission, and were subject to the Act to the same extent as were those of the controlling railroad.[1] Thereby the authority of the Commission was extended to cover all water carriers that were retained under the control of railroads. This left entirely free from control water carriers operating through the Panama Canal, and all other independent water carriers that refrained from participating in joint business with railroads.

The prevailing relationship between water and rail carriers at the time of the passage of the Panama Canal Act is shown by a report of the Commission on the relations between carriers by water and rail prepared in response to a Senate resolution.[2] This report showed that 27 railroad systems were interested either directly or through subsidiaries in transportation of freight by water, and 121 railroads were associated with 86 water carriers through some form of intercorporate relationship, stockholding, joint directorate, or joint management. The total gross tonnage of vessels represented in these two categories was 3,000,000. Of the gross tonnage of the first class, that of actual ownership and operation, amounting to 1,058,000 tons, the Southern Pacific Company accounted for 260,000 tons and the New Haven Railroad for 162,000 tons. The remainder was widely scattered among a large number of companies, about 200,000 tons being found on the Great Lakes.

By 1914 the Commission had received fifty-eight applications for continuance of joint rail and water relationship, the petitioners including seventy-nine water lines. Many of the adverse decisions of the Commission were bitterly contested. But the Commission fell back upon the clear mandate of the law. It held that the compe-

[1] I. C. C. Act., Sec. 5 (9–11).   [2] 39 I. C., 1 (1916).

tition referred to in the section was not "a vague indefinite or remotely possible competition, but something real and substantial." When this kind of competition prevailed, it had no power, so it said, to abate the prohibition against common ownership without clear evidence that a continuance would not prevent or reduce such competition. Testimony of shipping interests that the water service was essential and was in the public interest, which were factors that were required by the statute to be given consideration, was not sufficient to bring from the Commission a ruling permitting a continuance of rail control unless it could be shown that competition was negligible. The Commission appreciated the situation in which commercial interests were placed, but it felt that the wording of the statute was specific and that relief must be sought at the hands of Congress. In fact, in its 1917 annual report, it recommended that the Commission be empowered to permit a continuance of railroad ownership of water lines when such continuance was in the interest and for the convenience of the public, even though such ownership might reduce competition on the water route.

As a consequence of this strict interpretation of law, there took place a very considerable unscrambling of intercorporate relationships. At the same time, continuance of ownership was granted in many instances where a casual examination would have predicted a contrary outcome. The Central of Georgia was permitted to retain its ownership of the Ocean Steamship Company[1] and the New Haven was left in undisturbed possession of its steamship lines on Long Island Sound.[2] In the case of the Old Dominion Steamship Company, owned by five railroads, four of the owners, the Southern, Chesapeake and Ohio, Seaboard, and Atlantic Coast Line, were held not to offend the law and were left in

[1] 37 I. C. C., 422.   [2] 50 I. C. C., 634.

possession, but the Norfolk and Western was compelled to dispose of its share.[1] In the instance of the Morgan line operating between Galveston and New Orleans and New York, retention of ownership by the Southern Pacific Company was permitted after the steamship company had corrected certain discriminations against New Orleans and made certain changes in its rate policy.[2]

But the most serious upset in existing relationships took place on the Great Lakes where railroads succeeded in retaining little except their car ferries. The roads that were compelled to dispose of their lake lines were the Pennsylvania, Lehigh Valley, New York Central, Rutland, Erie, Grand Trunk, and the Lackawanna. The Commission found that not only did the amendment forbid continuance of possession when the railroad actually paralleled the water line, but also when the owning road was a party to through all-rail tariffs, or was a member of a fast freight line or of an association of railroads owning boat lines, the function of which was to keep the operation of its boat lines from interfering with rail operations. This was the issue in the Lehigh Valley case in which the carrier contended that its geographical location made it impossible for it to compete with a water line. But the Commission's dissolution order was upheld by both district and Supreme Court.[3] It was the intent of Congress in enacting the clause to restore the conditions that prevailed when railroads had no interest in and exercised no control over the boat lines plying the country's water routes.

There is another phase of water-line regulation created by the Panama Canal amendment to which relatively little public attention has been thus far directed, but which will command an increasing share of public interest as the legislation of 1920 becomes operative. It

[1] 41 I. C. C., 285.　　　　[2] 43 I. C. C., 168; 45 I. C. C., 505.
[3] 234 Fed. Rep., 682; 243 U. S., 412 (1917).

was provided[1] that when property was transported by rail and water either through the Panama Canal or elsewhere, the Commission should have jurisdiction to require suitable physical connection between the rail line and the dock whenever such connection could be safely made, was reasonably practicable, and was justified financially by the amount of business involved. To the Commission was given authority to determine the terms on which this connecting track should be operated, and this authority extended over owners of docks that were not carriers. It was given authority to establish through routes and maximum joint rates over the rail and water lines thus connected; to establish maximum proportional rail rates that should apply to and from the port on joint water and rail traffic, and to determine to what traffic and vessels and under what conditions these proportional rates should apply; to require any rail carrier that entered into arrangements with a water carrier for handling through business from an interior point in the United States to a foreign country to enter into similar arrangements with any other steamship line from the same port.[2] The purpose of this amendment is obvious on its face— to break down prevailing port and dock monopolies and exclusive traffic agreements between specific rail and water lines, and to throw open this joint business in the interest of a larger public.

That this situation needs thorough overhauling and vigorous handling will be evident to any one who gives it careful examination. In 1911 the Commission re-

---

[1] Sec. 6 (13).

[2] This section was modified in the Act of 1920 by providing that construction of connecting tracks should be subject to the same findings of public convenience and necessity as were required in the case of new construction under Sec. 1; by eliminating the control over docks owned by other parties than the carriers; and by extending authority in the case of proportional rail rates to minimum as well as maximum rates.

ported[1] indictments against a series of railroads which
had been leasing their docks and valuable terminal facilities to favored shippers, the lease contract giving the
shipper control of the dock and granting him certain
allowances for operating it which amounted to discriminations and rebates.   This relation prevailed not only
at lake ports but at gulf and ocean ports as well.   The
purpose of the carriers was to relieve themselves of the
operation of the terminals and take them out from under
the jurisdiction of the Commission.   On the theory that
the terminals are private property, they have sometimes
denied the facilities altogether to some shippers while
granting them to others.[2]   The fundamental principles
here at issue will be discussed later when the whole subject of the future water-transportation policy is under
consideration.

[1] Annual Report, 1911, p. 10.
[2] See Louisville and Nashville policy in 33 I. C. C., 213, and 27 I. C. C.,
252.

CHAPTER VII

THE LABOR PROBLEM

At the time the railroads were taken over by the Government, it is probable that not much over one-third of the employees were organized into unions. Of the organized employees, the four brotherhoods comprising the men in train service were the most powerful and had developed the principle of collective bargaining to the greatest degree. By 1910 "concerted" movements among employees in train service had become common. For many years previously, negotiations had been conducted on the individual road by representatives of the "local," and the gains then acquired had been used as a lever for securing similar concessions on a rival line. But although this accomplished much, it was an arduous and slow-moving process. It was evident that more could be accomplished by combined effort over an extended territory.

Meanwhile the roads were associating themselves together more closely for various purposes. Whether this grouping came in response to the growing power of labor, or whether the larger labor organization was rendered necessary by the growth in railroad co-operation, is a question that cannot be definitely answered. Neither party seems desirous of claiming priority. But certain it is that by 1910 federations of employees in train service were facing federations of general managers, not nationally but over wide territories, coincident with the three classification territories of the country.

National legislation on the wage problem goes back to the Erdman Act of 1898, which did not, however, become an active influence in wage controversies until the end of 1906. It was confined to employees engaged in train service. Its main function proved to be to provide machinery for mediation. It designated two federal officials, the Commissioner of Labor and the chairman of the Interstate Commerce Commission, as mediators, who, in case of a controversy interrupting the business of a common carrier, were at the request of either party to endeavor to effect a settlement. In case of failure, a board of arbitration of three might be appointed, one member by each of the parties and the third by the two appointees. It was to be stipulated in the signed agreement to arbitrate that employees dissatisfied with the award could not quit the service, nor could employers discharge their men before the expiration of three months, without thirty days' notice. The award was to be final unless set aside for errors of law, and was to continue in force for a year.

Procedure under the act was purely voluntary. Neither side was compelled to resort to it, and neither side was obliged to accept the offer of mediation after it had been made. Furthermore, the mediators had no power to intervene until invited by one of the contestants. Yet, in spite of the strict legal limitations of the statute, the imperative necessity for uninterrupted transportation and the power of the public to bring its will to bear made appearance of "free will" in large degree illusory. Railroad managements, faced with the problem of suspension of service, realized its heavy cost to them financially and likewise fully appreciated the fact that an inconvenienced public would be deaf to any appeal on the merits of the controversy, and would visit its wrath upon the delinquent corporation. Therefore it is not surprising to find that the railroads as a rule were the ones to appeal to the mediators, and it indicates the brotherhoods' sensitiveness to public opinion that with very few exceptions they agreed to mediation, even though in most

cases they possessed the strategic advantage in the controversy. It has been stated that the mediators were not
empowered by the Erdman Act to intervene of their own
initiative, yet they did so more than once at the request
of the President of the United States. What appears to
be only voluntary "getting together" becomes practically
compulsory when the head of the nation, representing
the whole people, sends his "mediators" to the scene of
impending conflict.

As controversies assumed larger dimensions and the
concerted movement became a regular and apparently a
permanent method of negotiation, it was realized that a
board of three members, in which the decision lay with
one man alone, was too small a body to which to intrust
issues of such magnitude. This was the motive for replacing the Erdman Act in 1913 with the so-called Newlands Act. At this time negotiations were being conducted
between the railroads and the conductors and trainmen
in Eastern territory. Both sides realized the desirability of a larger board and pressed for immediate legislation. Certain changes in the form of procedure long
recognized as needed were also urged and adopted. The
Newlands Act provided first for mediation by a Board of
Mediation and Conciliation, consisting of a permanent
commissioner and two other government officials. They
were given the power not possessed by the former mediators of proffering their services. In case the controversy
went to arbitration, the board might consist of six members rather than three if the parties preferred, two representing each side and two intermediaries chosen by a
majority vote of the four. A majority might make a
binding award. The board was to confine itself in its
decision to questions specifically submitted or to matters
directly bearing thereon, and misunderstandings concerning the interpretation of the award were to be referred
back to the board.

This machinery differed from that of the Erdman Act in certain fundamental particulars. It provided for a permanent Commissioner of Mediation, thereby making it more probable that the work of the mediator would be informed and expert, and hence more acceptable to both sides. To be sure, the working of the old Act had been effective because of the skill and experience acquired by the two federal officials, who fortunately had retained their official positions during the life of the statute. Had the occupants of these positions changed frequently— the chairmanship of the Interstate Commerce Commission now shifts annually—no such satisfactory results would have been accomplished. Another significant amendment to the procedure introduced in the Newlands Act was the reference of misunderstandings concerning the award of arbitration back to the board for interpretation. One of the evils that grew out of the voluntary arbitrations in 1912 and 1913 was that awards made by inexperienced neutral arbitrators were difficult to understand and were left for interpretation to local railroad officials. The employees charged that interpretation had deprived them of much that arbitration had granted. Again arbitrations were thereafter to be confined to the evidence formally submitted to the board. One of the criticisms passed upon the board by the labor group in the engineers' case in 1912 was that it had gone outside the evidence and reached its conclusions from data independently assembled.

Wage controversies of wide territorial extent followed one another rapidly between 1910 and 1916. In 1910 increased cost of living, through the rapid rise of prices, was bearing heavily upon the employees. The mediations of this year resulted invariably in increases, and standardization of conditions was spreading throughout the Eastern district. An elaborate arbitration on the New York Central furnished guidance for the settlement of disputes on many other roads. In 1912 occurred the most important labor dispute that had arisen in the country since the anthracite strike in 1902. It involved the Brotherhood of Locomotive Engineers on fifty-two roads in the Eastern district. It was adjusted by a voluntary arbitration board of seven members, five representing the public. The demand of the engineers was for a higher wage due to increased cost of living and for standardization of pay on all the roads, with a minimum rate. The roads opposed it on the ground of inability to pay, and the fact that an increase would disturb the differential between the engineers and other classes; in other words, it would result in demands from other classes for a restoration of the balance. The board granted substantial increases in pay and established the principle of the minimum wage for the district. It recommended the creation of federal and state wage commissions similar to the public service commissions, which was dissented to by the representative of the employees on the ground that it would amount to a form of compulsory arbitration.

What the railroads had feared now promptly took place. One organization after another came forward with demands. The firemen in Eastern territory settled their controversy in 1913 with an arbitration board of three, appointed under the Erdman Act. Further controversies appearing on the horizon, the Act was amended, as already described, by the passage of the Newlands Act, and the conductors and trainmen of the Eastern district submitted their grievances to a board of six under the amended law. This was followed by arbitrations in Western territory in 1915.

It was evident to close observers that while these negotiated settlements were accepted by both sides, they were, after all, merely truces. The ideal machinery of adjustment had not yet been discovered. Mediation by its own confession settled nothing. It was the mediator's business to keep the wheels moving, and he had done his job when he had found out what one side was willing to give and what the other was willing to take, and had brought them together. Whether there is any fundamentally just wage is a good deal of a question, but, at any rate, the mediator did not hunt for it. As for arbitration, its unsatisfactory results were due to the fact that the neutral arbitrator, or arbitrators, by the very nature of the case, knew absolutely nothing of the controversy. That was their highest recommendation. They were chosen like the man for the jury-box. They could not in the limited time of a hearing become intelligently familiar with the intricacies of railroad wage schedules. Their inclination was to seek middle ground, and in their innocence they made settlements capable of misunderstanding and double meaning, and consequently at the mercy of interpretation by individual railroad managers and groups of employees. When this was stopped by requiring in the Newlands Act the reference of doubtful points back to the board, controversies dragged and settlements were delayed.

But the decisions of the arbitration boards were not more unsatisfactory than the reasoning upon which they were based. The arbitrators for the firemen in 1913 shrewdly gave no reasons at all, merely publishing their award without comment. In the conductors' and trainmen's case, the first under the Newlands Act, the award leaves the impression upon the mind of the reader that the decision was first arrived at and the reasoning to support it later supplied. In the engineers' case in 1912, in which five neutral arbitrators did duty, an elaborate discussion was interjected as to what constitutes a reasonable wage. But the board got nowhere. By the use of questionable statistics, it merely reached the conclusion that wages should bear some relation to those in other industries and in the same industry in other parts of the country.

The somewhat heated comment upon the award, by Mr. Stone, chief of the engineers' brotherhood, is worth quoting, because it uncovers the real difficulties of this arbitration method.

"They selected five men of international reputation, very learned men in their professions, but who knew absolutely nothing about the A B C of railroading or the fundamental principles underlying a wage scale. They would not have known a box car from a freight-car, or a passenger-engine from a freight-engine, if they had met them coming down the street. They started in to make a wage scale for 32,000 men, with the local conditions underlying the 54 railroads, and the result was that they stayed together as a unit, and if reports are correct these five men representing the public, for fear they might become contaminated with the other members of the board, held meetings of their own, which, if true, was an offense absolutely inexcusable, in my opinion. The result was that when the full board did meet the steamroller worked overtime and they had their own way. We got what they called an award. Nobody knows yet what that award really means.

"On the 29th day of April, 1912, we signed a contract to arbitrate. It was to be binding for one year from that date—May 1. It expired on May 1 of this year. On the 28th day of November they handed down the first draft of their award. On the 16th day of February they handed down a subdraft of the report, or rather an additional explanatory draft of what the original draft really did mean. And now we are back to them trying to find out what the last award they handed down really means. And now that the time limit has expired—on May 1 of this year—only 19 roads of the 54 have put it into operation, and we are still trying to get the rest, and we hope at least that our grandchildren will get the benefit of the award . . . They were very learned gentlemen in their particular class. One man has an international reputation as a geologist. He wrote a part of some 80 or 90 pages of this report, on political economy and sociology, and arbitrated a number of questions that no one dreamed would ever be arbitrated. That was the unfortunate feature of it."[1]

The substitution of arbitration for mediation had resulted in no enduring gains. It had deprived the wage controversy of the aid of expert mediators. It had substituted the forms of judicial procedure, but the verdicts were in every case compromises emerging from the struggle of conflicting interests. Neither was this arbitration method employed by the contestants as an ideal system should be, to discover if possible the proper basis for a reasonable wage. It was used, as always has been the case and perchance always will be, as a source from which certain results were to be extracted by the particular process which at the time seemed most effective. Cost of living was usually advanced as an argument because prices were continuously rising. The preservation of the differential between different classes and between the same classes in different parts of the country was strongly urged. Perhaps the most picturesque argument was that employees should share in the productive efficiency of the plant and organization of which they were a part, an argument of which little is heard in these days when the plant is no longer productive. The railroads in the main fell back upon their inability to pay and presented statistics which revealed to the boards their uncertain financial condition. But this again was an argument which could have little weight if the board of arbi-

[1] Testimony before Senate Com. on Interstate Commerce, 1913.

tration were genuinely seeking for a reasonable wage. This having been determined, it would be the business of the railroad to find the money with which to pay it.

In 1916 occurred the first nation-wide labor movement in the railroad field, a movement the results of which have been profoundly influential upon all the relations of capital and labor in this industry. This was the movement for the eight-hour day in train service. It followed upon several years of labor controversy and adjustment which, as already indicated, had not been satisfactory to labor. The year 1916 was an unusually restless one. There was the general activity of industry due to the European War, and the unusually favorable position of labor brought about by the extraordinary demand for its services, and by the scarcity of labor resulting from diminished immigration. Cost of living was rising rapidly. Employees everywhere were demanding higher wages, shorter hours, union recognition. It was in this atmosphere that the chiefs of the four brotherhoods representing 400,000 men made a demand upon the managers of 200,000 miles of railroad for a "basic" eight-hour day with time and one-half for overtime. The railroads replied that under the guise of securing a shorter working-day, the men were employing a new method to secure increased wages, that the working-day could not be shortened to eight hours, that the men would receive for eight hours what they were before receiving for ten, and that the additional two hours would be overtime, to be paid for at penalty rates. It was estimated that the daily pay would be increased by 25 per cent and the overtime pay by 87½ per cent, and that this would amount to $100,000,000 per year;[1] that it was a demand on the part of 18 per cent of the employees, who were already receiving 28 per cent of the

[1] Compare estimate of Eight Hour Commission, page 103.

total pay-roll. Conferences and efforts at mediation failed. Arbitration was favored by the carriers but refused by the men, who held that the question was not arbitrable. President Wilson took a hand and proposed the adoption of the eight-hour day without punitive overtime. He also promised to use his influence for the creation of a federal commission that should investigate the situation and report measures of relief. This was favored by the brotherhoods but flatly rejected by the managers. The issue was drawn and each side prepared for a fight to a finish.[1] Notwithstanding the public suffering likely to follow, each felt convinced that the issue had to be fought out sooner or later in the public interest. A country-wide strike was called for September 4 in the midst of the negotiations, and, when the President requested the withdrawal of the strike order, he was informed that the convention of brotherhood chairmen which had called the strike and dispersed on August 27 was the only body empowered to withdraw it, and that it was too late to reassemble the convention. It was a piece of cold-blooded strategy which showed discourtesy

---

[1] J. P. Tumulty, in his "Woodrow Wilson as I Know Him," makes the following reference to the President's conciliatory efforts: "I remember what he said to me as he left the Green Room at the conclusion of his final conference with the heads of the brotherhoods. Shaking his head in a despairing way, he said: 'I was not able to make the slightest impression upon those men. They feel so strongly the justice of their cause that they are blind to all the consequences of their action in declaring and prosecuting a strike. I was shocked to find a peculiar stiffness and hardness about these men. When I pictured to them the distress of our people in case this strike became a reality, they sat unmoved and apparently indifferent to the seriousness of the whole bad business. I am at the end of my tether, and I do not know what further to do.'

"His conferences with the managers were equally unproductive of result. Gathered about him in a semi-circle in his office, they were grim and determined men, some of them even resentful of the President's attempt to suggest a settlement of any kind to prevent the strike."

to the President and a cynical indifference to the public
consequences that should have lost the brotherhoods all
public support. But they were now on the war-path.
On August 29 the President sent a special message to
Congress asking for legislation that would avert the
impending catastrophe and would provide against any
future recurrence. In his message, after relating the
circumstances leading up to the crisis, and explaining
his proposal for settlement, he said:

"The representatives of the brotherhoods accepted
the plan, but the representatives of the railroads declined to accept it in the face of what I cannot but
regard as the practical certainty that they will be ultimately obliged to accept the eight-hour day, by the concerted action of organized labor, backed by the favorable
judgment of society. The representatives of the railway
management have felt justified in declining a peaceful
settlement which would engage all the forces of justice,
public and private, on their side to take care of the
event. . . . The railway managers based their decision
to reject my counsel in this matter upon their conviction
that they must at any cost to themselves or to the country stand firm for the principle of arbitration, which the
men had rejected. I based my counsel upon the indis-
putable fact that there was no means of obtaining arbitration. The law supplied none; earnest efforts at mediation had failed to influence the men in the least. To
stand firm for the principle of arbitration and yet not get
arbitration seemed to me futile, and something more
than futile, because it involved incalculable distress to
the country and consequences in some respects worse
than those of war, and that in the midst of peace. . . .
Having failed to bring the parties to this critical controversy to an accommodation, therefore, I turn to you,
deeming it clearly our duty as public servants to leave

nothing undone that we can do to safeguard the life and interests of the nation."

Among the specific proposals of his message were the eight-hour day for all train employees, a commission to study the effects of the law upon railroad operation, an expression from Congress whether or not the Interstate Commerce Commission would be justified in increasing freight rates to cover the additional costs of the shorter day, a law making all railroad strikes unlawful until after official investigation, and a grant of power to the President to draft railroad employees into service when required by military necessity.

On September 2 Congress hastily passed the eight-hour law, which provided that eight hours was to be deemed a day's work "and the measure or standard of a day's work for the purpose of reckoning the compensation for services." For all "necessary time" in excess of eight hours the pay was to be not less than pro rata. A commission of three was to be appointed to observe for a period of from six to nine months the operation and effects of the law and to make a report to the President and to Congress. Beginning with January 1, 1917, and until thirty days after the report of the investigating commission, compensation for a standard eight-hour work-day was not to be reduced below the existing standard day's wages.

None of the other proposals of the President was considered. All amendments were rejected, not on their merits but because they would require time for consideration. The sole object was to pass something that would avert a strike, and from this standpoint the legislation was entirely successful. The strike order was withdrawn. But labor had for the first time tasted victory to the full. For the first time in any significant way it had seen the

legislative machinery employed in its interest.[1] Instead
of shunning political activity and confining itself strictly
to the economic field of collective bargaining, it was from
now on to take a close personal interest in the doings of
Congress. Three of the four brotherhood leaders had
always been opposed to Government ownership. Following this experience and that of the war period, they
became ardent converts, not on altruistic grounds, but
because they saw in this relationship of Government and
employees advantages that could not be secured from
private negotiation.

Following the passage of the Act, controversy continued for another six months, which centred about the question of the constitutionality of the law. The railroads
took prompt steps to test this question, and succeeded
in getting a decision in November from a United States
District Court declaring the law unconstitutional, from
which appeal was taken to the highest court. Meanwhile the question which troubled the brotherhoods
was whether the eight-hour day would become effective
on January 1, or only in case of a favorable decision of
the Supreme Court. The railroads had entered into an
understanding with the Attorney-General to continue
on a ten-hour basis, but to give the men back pay from
January 1 in case the law should be upheld. But as
time passed without a decision, as it became clearer that
we must soon enter the war, labor became more and more
restive. It felt the imperative necessity of clinching
this congressional gift before something might happen,
whether from the direction of the court or elsewhere,
to rob them of it. Accordingly, a national strike was

[1] A forerunner of this form of settlement is found in the conductors'
and trainmen's dispute in 1913 in which a threatened strike was averted
by the influence of President Wilson in hastening the passage of the
Newlands Act. Congress put to one side amendments that gave
promise of procedure that was superior to the proposals of the bill because of the pressure for immediate passage.

called for the 17th of March to compel the railroads to put in the eight-hour day without awaiting the court's decision and regardless of the constitutionality of the law. Members of the cabinet and of the Council of National Defense effected a postponement of the strike date to March 19, a court "decision day." Meanwhile the managers, because of the acute political situation and under the spur of patriotism, yielded to the men and put the eight-hour day into effect without waiting for the court. On March 19 the court upheld the law.[1]

Four justices dissented on the ground that the law was in fact not a regulation of the length of the day but a scheme for determining conditions of work and pay, and therefore an interference with freedom of contract. But Chief Justice White, who delivered the opinion, held that the statute was clearly within the power of Congress under the commerce clause as a means of meeting a national emergency. When a nation-wide dispute between railroads and their train operatives is likely to result in a general strike with grave loss and suffering to the country, Congress has power to prescribe a standard of minimum wages not confiscating in its effects but obligatory on both parties, to be in force for a reasonable time in order that the calamity may be averted and opportunity afforded the parties to substitute a standard of their own. Of significance in connection with the present-day discussion of compulsory arbitration as a permanent solution of the wage problem, the opinion says that the Act amounts to an exertion of the power of Congress to arbitrate compulsorily the dispute between the parties, a power susceptible of exercise by direct legislation as well as by enactment of other appropriate means. It does not invade private rights of employees, since their rights to demand wages and to have employment individually or in concert *are not such as they might*

[1] Wilson v. New et al., 243 U. S. 332 (1917).

be if the employment were in private business, but are necessarily subject to limitation by Congress, the employment accepted being in a business charged with a public interest, which Congress may regulate under the commerce power.

The Eight Hour Commission made its report on December 29, 1917. It found that a complete elimination of overtime was not practicable; in other words, that work performed in ten hours before the passage of the law could not now be compressed into eight. To what extent it would be practicable ultimately to limit the hours of train employees to eight per day its limited investigation did not permit it to determine. It examined proposals such as that made by the brotherhoods that trains should be speeded to an average of twelve and one-half miles per hour instead of being operated at an average of ten miles, and concluded from available information that it would be more economical to continue the existing methods of operation with overtime than to increase the speed of trains by cutting the tonnage. Neither was it possible to relocate terminals. Some minor delays could be eliminated, and suggestions were made to that end, but they were not numerous or fundamental. It estimated the increase in wages due to the Adamson Eight Hour Act as follows:

ESTIMATED ANNUAL INCREASE IN WAGES
OVER 1916 (CLASS I ROADS)

	AMOUNT	PER CENT
Passenger service.............	$ 2,532,000	2.73
Freight service...............	31,669,000	15.03
Yard service.................	27,333,000	24.60
Hostlers.....................	1,875,000	25.00
	$63,409,000	

THE WAR PERIOD

CHAPTER VIII

THE RAILROADS' WAR BOARD

WHEN this country finally realized that participation in the war in Europe was inevitable, it found little valuable experience and less statutory authority upon which to build a war administration of the railroads. Great Britain had had a statute since 1871 that provided a method of railroad management in case of war, and since 1896 there had been an organization of railroad executives which could be converted into a war board. The Spanish War had taught us what to avoid. We had suffered the consequences of a decentralized military administration in which co-operation with the railroad authorities was wholly absent.

When the troubles on .the Mexican border arose, the Quartermaster-General suggested to the Secretary of War in the fall of 1915 that the American Railway Association, composed of the operating officers of the different railroads, establish a committee on military transportation with which the department could co-operate in the transportation of troops and supplies. The committee was appointed, a plan of co-operation of War Department and railroads was drawn up, and when the state militia were mobilized in June 1916, the plan was made effective. By means of a scheme earlier arranged between the Quartermaster-General and the Master Car Builders' Association placards were placed on car-load shipments of Government property, which gave it priority and prevented congestion. Mobilization of troops and supplies was handled with thorough efficiency. Out of this experience grew the organization that was to handle the railroads during the first months of war.

In the Army Appropriation Act of August 29, 1916, was a provision establishing a Council of National Defense "for the co-ordination of industries and resources for the national security and welfare." It was to consist of six cabinet officers who were to nominate "an Advisory Commission consisting of not more than seven persons, each of whom shall have special knowledge of some industry, public utility or the development of some national resource, or be otherwise specially qualified" to perform the duties assigned. President Willard, of the Baltimore and Ohio, was appointed to this Advisory Commission as transportation expert. The duty of the council, so far as transportation was concerned, was "the location of railroads with reference to the frontier of the United States so as to render possible expeditious concentration of troops and supplies to points of defense; the co-ordination of military, industrial, and commercial purposes in the location of extensive highways and branch lines of railroad; the utilization of waterways."

In February 1917, the executive committee of the American Railway Association met and elaborated plans for a more thorough co-operation with the Government, enlarging their committee of five, which had served in connection with Mexican troubles, to eighteen, under the same chairmanship, that of President Fairfax Harrison, of the Southern Railway. This committee took steps at once to enlist the support of the railroads in a national plan of voluntary co-operation. The declaration of war on April 6, 1917 led the Council of National Defense to seek for more definite assurances of support from the railroads, and they requested Mr. Willard to call upon the railroads "to so organize their business as to lead to the greatest expedition in the movement of freight." In response thereto, an epoch-making meeting was held in Washington, at which nearly 700 railroad executives attached their signatures to the following resolution:

"*Resolved*, That the railroads of the United States, acting through their chief executive officers here and now assembled, and stirred by a high sense of their opportunity to be of the greatest service to their country in the present national crisis, do hereby pledge themselves, with the government of the United States, with the governments of the several states, and with one another, that during the present war they will co-ordinate their operations in a continental railway system, merging during such period all their merely individual and competitive activities in the effort to produce a maximum of national transportation efficiency. To this end they hereby agree to create an organization which shall have general authority to formulate in detail and from time to time a policy of operation of all or any of the railways, which policy, when and as announced by such temporary organization, shall be accepted and earnestly made effective by the several managements of the individual railroad companies here represented."

The special committee on national defense of the American Railway Association was enlarged to thirty-three members, distributed geographically, and the executive authority was placed in the hands of a subcommittee of five, thereafter known as the Railroads' War Board.[1] Mr. Willard, as ex-officio member of the executive com-

[1] The membership of this committee was Fairfax Harrison, president of the Southern Railway, chairman; Samuel Rea, president of the Pennsylvania Railroad; Howard Elliott, chairman of Committee on Intercorporate Relations, New York, New Haven and Hartford Railroad Company, and chairman of executive committee, Northern Pacific Railway; Julius Kruttschnitt, chairman of the Southern Pacific Co.; and Hale Holden, president of the Chicago, Burlington and Quincy Railroad.

mittee, established its relations with the Council of National Defense, and Mr. Edgar E. Clark, of the Interstate Commerce Commission, performed the same function with reference to that body. To the War Board reported various subcommittees to which were assigned such functions as car-service, equipment, materials and supplies, tariffs and accounting.

Before summarizing the activities of the Railroads' War Board it is necessary to create the background by describing the legislation that was on the statute-books at the time this country entered the war, and that which Congress found it necessary to pass during the year. Among the amendments to the Interstate Commerce Act in 1906 was one that provided (Section 6) that, in time of war or threatened war, preference should upon the demand of the President be given over all other traffic to the transportation of troops and material of war, and carriers should adopt every means within their control to expedite the military traffic. In August 1916, at a time of severe congestion in railroad traffic, a clause was inserted in the Naval Appropriation Act providing that in time of peace shipments consigned to the United States should be exempt from any embargo. The 1906 clause covered only military traffic. The 1916 provision, while comprising commercial traffic, merely expedited movement. The only other statutory power applicable to the situation was that conferred upon the President by the Army Appropriation Act of 1916, which gave him authority in time of war to take possession of any system of transportation and to utilize it for the transfer of troops and war material to the exclusion, as far as necessary, of all other traffic, and for such other purposes as the emergency might require. This gave the President a power which he could bring into play whenever the voluntary organization of the railroads failed of accomplishment.

It early became apparent that the war was to be fought not only with troops and military supplies but also with food and fuel and with the many raw materials and manufactured goods that indirectly sustain the nation's fighting strength. It was not a time when new equipment could be supplied to the railroads nor were the railroads in position to pay for it could it have been furnished. The task of the War Board was to get the utmost possible service in the interest of the nation out of the existing plant and equipment. Accordingly, the problem in its simplest form was one in the efficient use of cars. Centralized management of car-service had been in existence for some time before we went into the war. Acute congestion in 1916 had led to the location in Washington of the standing committee of the American Railway Association on car efficiency, which had acted in co-operation with the Interstate Commerce Commission. This was reorganized in December 1916, and was given greater authority to act in behalf of the roads, apparently with the purpose of staving off drastic recommendations of the Commission for an increase in its powers, recommendations that resulted from the apparent inability of the carriers to secure adequate co-operation among themselves. This Commission became later a subcommittee of the Railroads' War Board. On May 29, 1917, Congress passed the Esch bill, amending the Interstate Commerce Act[1] substantially in the form recommended by the Commission. This gave to the Commission the power, after hearing, to establish car-service rules covering the movement, distribution, exchange, and return of cars, and payment for their use. Whenever in its judgment an emergency existed, the Commission might at once without formal notice suspend the operation of the rules and substitute others. It might also require the carriers to file their car-service

[1] Sec. 1 (10–17).

rules and regulations as a part of their tariffs. This statute was merely permissive, and while the Commission organized its division of car-service, it did not assume the powers granted, but preferred for the time to hold them in reserve and to co-operate with the committee of the carriers.

It has already been stated that military supplies and troops were not the only traffic essential to the war. Yet no formal power existed to control the selection of traffic and to insure the uninterrupted movement of that which was essential. Accordingly, on August 10, 1917, Congress passed the Priority Act, under which the President was authorized during the war to direct carriers to give preference in transportation to such traffic as in his judgment was essential to the national defense. In their compliance with orders, carriers were to be relieved from penalty for the violation of any existing law. This presumably referred to the discrimination sections of the Interstate Commerce Act. Robert S. Lovett, chairman of the executive committee of the Union Pacific Railroad, was appointed director of priority shipments. It was his policy to interfere as little as possible with the independent operation of the roads, and up to the middle of November he had issued but two priority orders, the first relating to the handling of bituminous coal to Lake Erie ports, the second reserving the use of open-top cars for certain specific commodities necessary for national defense. It should be emphasized, therefore, that during the first nine months of the war, April to December 1917, the Government interfered scarcely at all with railroad operation. Power hovered in the background, power to control the distribution and use of cars, even to take possession of the railroad properties themselves, but it was not exercised. Even the power which appeared to be so essential at the time it was granted, that of discriminating between different sorts of traffic, was exercised but sparingly. The railroads were given every opportunity to work out the problem for themselves.

Much valuable service was performed by the various subcommittees of the War Board, which did not attract public attention, but which assisted in smoothing out the difficulties of mobilization and transportation. These cannot be detailed here. But it should be especially noted that the spirit of co-operation among railroads and the various Government agencies connected with the war was highly developed and steadily sustained. There was apparent none of the disorganization that had characterized our Spanish War administration.

However, the important task of the railroads was that of operation, the employment of every available car and locomotive to its utmost extent. Car-service and operating efficiency were the problems to which the War Board gave the larger share of its attention. Its activities in behalf of these objects took two forms: first, instructions to the individual carriers concerning interchange and routing, the allocation of special kinds of equipment to specific uses, and the granting of preferential service to certain commodities. Pooling of coal regardless of ownership was ordered at lake and coastwise ports, thus avoiding the delays attendant upon the handling of consignments individually for specific shippers. Box cars were ordered pooled regardless of ownership and despatched in train-loads of empties to sections where they were needed. Passenger-train service was ordered reduced to conserve fuel, economize power, and free the rails for freight traffic, and it was estimated by the War Board that between May and September there was a reduction equivalent to 25,000,000 train-miles annually.

A second form of activity of the War Board was the drive for a more intensive loading of cars and trains. It is a well-known fact that because of many conditions under which traffic is handled, the load per car in normal times has not been up to the capacity of the car nor have locomotives hauled trains that on the average approached their registered tractive power.[1] The nature of the commodities hauled, the physical conditions under which they are handled, the competition which compels the granting of favors to shippers in the matter of loading requirements, these among other reasons have prevented a showing of greater efficiency. The War Board started a campaign for a load not only to the marked capacity of the car but to 10 per cent in excess of this capacity— the maximum load that cars are constructed to sustain. Under the patriotic stimulus shippers were induced to abandon privileges of long standing and to load to capacity. Doubtless they were encouraged to take this course by the lack of equipment and the fear of being deprived of even that which they had. But not only was the campaign directed to saving space but also to saving time. The railroads' business is not tons but ton-miles. Its cars are vehicles, not warehouses. Time spent in loading and unloading is just so much waste to be avoided if possible. It delays movement and it employs track room. In placement of cars for loading, in inspection and repairs, in furnishing of the billing for shipment, in the reduction of demurrage accumulations, and in numerous other ways, with the co-operation of the shipping public, time was saved and car-service increased. The War Board's record for the seven months of its service is one which it may well regard with satisfaction. If the experiment failed to meet fully the war exigency, it was not because of a lack of efficiency in the board, nor because of a failure to grasp the ends to be achieved or the means of reaching them. Uncontrollable factors determined the ultimate course of events.

[1] The per cent of car capacity utilized by loads declined from 59.9 per cent in 1904 to 55.4 per cent in 1916, and was as low as 53.3 per cent in 1911.

The most dramatic achievement of the War Board was the handling of troops and military supplies. In October the War Board announced that the railroads had moved approximately 720,000 soldiers from their homes to training-camps or embarkation points. All but 32,500 men in the first 5 per cent of the National Army required special train service, involving 13,500 passenger-cars, including 1,500 Pullman and tourist sleepers, 2,000 baggage-cars, and 4,500 freight-cars. In the handling of the National Army, the longest haul was from Yuma, Arizona, to Fort Riley, Kansas—1,514 miles, consuming 48 hours; the shortest that of the District of Columbia unit to Camp Meade, Maryland—less than 25 miles. The National Guard movements were mostly of great length, the longest being a battalion of engineers from San Francisco to the Atlantic coast. Although nearly 90 per cent of the mileage of American railroads is single track, all this was accomplished without serious derangement of passenger schedules, notwithstanding that the railroads were at the same time handling large amounts of Government material in freight-trains and absorbing an enormous additional commercial traffic as a result of the war. By December the troop movement amounted to a total of 1,867,248 men.

In the handling of materials for camp construction, the railroads showed the same efficiency. Within thirty days from the date that the Government placed its first order for cantonment materials, there had been delivered more than 12,000 car-loads of lumber and other building materials to the 16 cantonments, and many miles of extra trackage had been built by the railroads at their own expense for the local handling of government freight. Shipments of food and materials continued uninterruptedly, the number of cars of material of all kinds arriving at army camps having reached by December a total of 128,350.

A study of the statistics of operating efficiency as presented in the table herewith reveals some interesting facts.

OPERATING EFFICIENCY, 1917–1919, BY MONTHS [1]

Month	CAR MILES PER DAY			TONS PER CAR (REVENUE AND NON-REVENUE)		
	1917	1918	1919	1917	1918	1919
January............	25.3	18.3	21.4	26.4	29.6	29.0
February...........	23.9	22.0	20.3	26.1	28.4	27.7
March.............	25.6	24.9	20.4	26.4	28.1	27.6
April..............	27.4	25.9	21.0	25.6	29.4	27.3
May...............	29.0	26.4	22.8	26.7	27.7	27.7
June..............	28.4	26.8	23.0	27.8	28.3	27.5
July..............	28.3	26.5	24.1	27.1	30.1	27.8
August............	27.1	26.0	24.2	27.9	30.1	28.0
September.........	26.6	26.8	26.5	27.0	29.7	28.3
October...........	26.3	26.2	27.3	27.7	29.7	28.0
November.........	26.2	24.6	23.3	27.2	29.5	26.2
December.........	21.3	22.8	22.3	29.2	29.8	27.7
Average	26.1	24.9	23.1	27.0	29.1	27.8

[1] Bureau of Railway Economics summary.

Car miles per day and tons per car showed a general tendency to increase during the War Board's administration in 1917. It should be noted, however, that this increase was partly seasonal, for the same phenomena may be observed in the succeeding years. Comparing car miles for the year 1917 with those of the two succeeding years of federal operation, we find the same general tendency toward improvement from the beginning of the year until September, with a falling off thereafter. In tons per car, the increase is very marked from April to December 1917, a gain which the Railroad Administration retained throughout 1918 and to a lesser degree in 1919. The average load for the two years of federal control, which was higher than the War Board accomplished, was the direct result of the pioneer work of that organization.

But in spite of every effort put forth in the drive for operating efficiency, the War Board began to realize in November that the results were not wholly satisfactory, or, what is more probable, it gave utterance at that time to a conviction which it must have long entertained. Industries were speeding up to a higher and higher pitch, creating an abnormal demand for fuel and raw materials and for transportation for the finished products. The concentration of these industries in one section of the country constituted a problem that the railroads of other sections were unable to relieve. But of more serious import to the fate of voluntary co-operation was the fact that while the railroads had submitted themselves to the orders of the War Board, each railroad still handled, so far as possible, the business that normally belonged to it. Each executive still dealt with his own customers. While he endeavored to carry out the orders from Washington, he did it in his own way subject to no restrictions. There were some departures from this method, notably in the pooling of box-car equipment, but as a rule the independent identity of the individual railroad was maintained. It was perhaps natural that the War Board should proceed slowly in exercising real authority. Anything in the way of unified action might have brought the roads under the condemnation of existing statutes, the Anti-Trust Act and the Interstate Commerce Act.

And yet when it is recalled that the railroads had organized for co-operative action at the suggestion of the Council of National Defense, and that they had pledged themselves on April 11 to merge "their merely individual and competitive activities in the effort to produce a maximum of national transportation efficiency," it is amazing that not until November 24, when the emergency became too acute to be longer disregarded, did the board adopt "revolutionary measures" to relieve congestion on the Eastern railroads. It then directed that all available facilities be pooled and that the railroads be operated as a unit "regardless of their ownership and individual interests." Doubtless the War Board moved as rapidly as support from the railroads warranted, but there could be no clearer evidence needed of the fact that co-operation in any genuine sense for war purposes was not to be accomplished under private management. A local committee of executives was appointed for this Eastern district which promptly put out drastic orders, including embargoes, diversions, and suspensions of passenger service. But it all came too late. The Government at Washington was convinced that more drastic action was required and, in the words of Commissioner McChord, that "the strong arm of governmental authority is essential if the transportation situation is to be radically improved."

CHAPTER IX

On December 26, 1917, the President of the United States took possession by proclamation of all the railroads and waterways of the country under the war powers already described. There will always be controversy as to whether this step was necessary or desirable. Most students of the question, however, have concluded that it was not only an inevitable step, but from the standpoint of the public exigency was justifiable and wise. The traffic situation at the time was alarming. In the Eastern and Northeastern section of the country, traffic was being created rapidly for export, and into and through this congested section was moving from farther west the food and munitions for overseas consumption, the raw materials and coal for the manufacturing sections, the building materials for cantonment use. Traffic for export was being routed to the usual outlets without any attempt at distribution to different ports, because coöperation with the shipping interests had not yet been sufficiently perfected to make any other policy possible. The situation was greatly aggravated by the abuse by governmental departments of the priority privilege. The priority shipping-tag seemed to be freely at the disposal of any Government official however humble, and the extent of its use depended upon the temperament of the official. The consequence was that at times over 80 per cent of the freight on the rails was travelling under priority orders, and serious congestion resulted. What was necessary was a central controlling agency with final power to direct the movement of traffic from its point of origin, and such a plan was being initiated by the Railroads' War Board at the time the railroads were taken over by the President.

There were other operating troubles in this section of the country that aggravated the situation. Motive power had been kept long in service with little opportunity for thorough overhauling and was crippled and inefficient. The burden was enhanced by the confiscation of many coastwise vessels by the Army and Navy Departments, thus throwing additional traffic upon an overloaded railroad system. Added to all this was a winter of unprecedented severity that blocked the marine terminals and stopped for a time the flow of traffic.

This operating problem was confined almost wholly to the East; there was no traffic congestion west of Chicago. It is possible that from the operating side alone, in spite of their conflicting interests, the railroads could have handled the situation with a fair degree of success, if they had been encouraged in their efforts toward cooperation. There is no reason, for example, why Congress under the stress of war should not have suspended for a time the application to the railroads of the Anti-Trust Act, thus permitting them freely to co-operate for the common good. But, on the contrary, the Department of Justice kept watch on the policy of the roads during 1917, and made some inquiries as to the extent of their agreements in common, and no governmental agency until the very end of the year took any steps to make the path of the railroads easier.

Railroads had been brought up in a competitive atmosphere, in which all attempts at common understanding had been definitely discouraged. All our legislation up to the war had been in the direction of the preservation of competition. Faced with penalties if they made any move to divide earnings from competitive traffic, the roads naturally were not eager to have their traffic diverted without compensation to a rival route that might be less congested. It was this feeling that led some executives even in the face of the agreement for voluntary co-operation to place the interests of their roads first and thereby to prevent the wholly effective working of the voluntary plan.

In the statement accompanying the proclamation of the President may be found the reasons that influenced him to take possession of the roads. His first reason, that they were being deprived of earnings for which there was no compensation under the restrictions of existing law, has already been noted, and could have been met by a suspension of the operation of the Anti-Trust Act and the anti-pooling section of the Interstate Commerce Act. But the other reasons were more potent. The financial needs of the railroads and of the Government could not at the same time be met unless they were brought under a common direction. The railroads were facing a serious financial situation. They had come into the war with their equipment and physical facilities in none too good condition, and with little or no surplus to meet expansion in traffic. They were now faced in the Eastern section of the country with an unprecedented traffic and a need for rapid enlargement. Their earnings were not sufficient to attract investors readily. They had had little success in getting increased rates from regulating bodies, and the process of getting increased rates, even if ultimately successful, was too slow to be relied upon in this emergency. Even had they been granted the increases, they could not have met their capital needs out of their surplus earnings. Capital had to be lured from the investor, who was being appealed to by the Government to turn all his savings into war loans. Without direct Government aid, there was no power to get prior claims upon steel and other materials needed for plant and equipment, nor even upon cars and locomotives which were going abroad for war service. And added to all this were the demands of labor for the increases in wages that the increasing cost of living made necessary, and that were being granted in competitive industry. It seemed clear that the Government alone could keep labor satisfied and prevent strikes. It was a time for a close partnership between the railroads and the Government. The Government was ready to back the railroads in their war service, but it must have the responsibility for their operation and the sole direction of their financial management. This was the price of its aid. The programme of the partners was to be the use of existing facilities and equipment to their utmost capacity regardless of individual ownership.

The conditions under which the roads were taken over and operated are to be found in three documents. In the presidential proclamation the fundamental principles were laid down upon which all further legislation and negotiation were based. An Act of Congress being required for the appropriation of the necessary funds to make nationalization effective and to guarantee the compensation to the carriers for the use of their property, the Federal Control Act was passed on March 21, 1918. Finally a contract in the nature of a lease was drawn up between the Government and each railroad corporation, applying in detail the principles laid down in the proclamation and the statute. Under this contract, the specific property was to be conveyed in legal form with due protection of the rights of the owners.

The proclamation assumed control of every system of transportation located within the boundaries of the United States, including coastwise and inland water transportation, terminals, sleeping-, parlor-, and private-car lines, elevators, warehouses, telegraph and telephone lines, but excepting street electric passenger railways and interurbans. It was declared that so far as exclusive use for war purposes should not be necessary or desirable, such systems should be operated to serve other national interests and to perform the usual duties of common carriers. William G. McAdoo, the Secretary of the Treasury, was appointed Director-General, and he was authorized to enter upon negotiations with the individual companies for agreements as to compensation on the basis of an annual guarantee, equivalent to the average of the net operating income for the three-year period ending June 30, 1917. Rights of stockholders and creditors were to be preserved, dividends and interest were to be continued until the Director-General ruled otherwise. Statutes and orders of state commissions and the Interstate Commerce Commission were to be in effect so long as the Director should determine, but any subsequent orders of the Director were to have paramount authority. The President reserved the right to relinquish in whole or in part any railroad or other transportation system of which he had taken possession.

The Federal Control Act enacted formally the terms of the presidential proclamation and authorized the President to make an agreement with and to guarantee to any carrier as just compensation an annual sum not exceeding the average annual railway operating income for the three years ending June 30, 1917.[1] This annual railway operating income was to be ascertained and certified to by the Interstate Commerce Commission and its certificate was to be conclusive. Any income accruing in excess of the guaranteed amount was to remain the property of the United States. War taxes were to

[1] The terminology of the law and the contract follows the accounting terminology of the Interstate Commerce Commission. "Railway operating income" is derived by deducting from total operating revenues the operating expenses and tax accruals, and by deducting or adding the debit or credit balance of rents for the use of equipment and of joint facilities.

be paid by the corporation, but all other taxes were to be covered into operating expense. During federal control dividends were to be limited to the regular rates of the three test years, unless the President approved of an increase. If no dividends had been paid, the President might determine the rate. Every contract was to contain adequate provision for maintenance and depreciation of the property and for necessary reserves, to the end that the property of the carrier might be returned in substantially as good condition as it was at the beginning, due consideration being given to the amounts expended for maintenance during the three "test years" of 1915 to 1917. Provision was to be made in the contract for the reimbursement of the United States for the cost of additions and betterments, not properly chargeable to the Government. The President might make or order any carrier to make additions, betterments, and extensions, and provide terminals, motive power, cars, and other equipment necessary for war purposes, or in the public interest. He might advance any part of the expense, such advances to be charged to the carrier and to bear interest at a rate determined by the President. Expenditures of this kind made at the expense of the carrier with the approval of the Government were to earn a reasonable rate of return for the carrier, to be added to the fixed amount of the annual compensation.

Should a carrier decline to sign an agreement with the Government in accordance with the terms outlined in this statute, the President might pay to the carrier 90 per cent of the estimated annual compensation. The balance was to be adjusted by submission of the matter to a board of three referees appointed by the Interstate Commerce Commission. If the report of the board was unsatisfactory, petition might be filed by either party in the Court of Claims.

A sum of $500,000,000 was appropriated, which, with

any surplus over the operating income guaranteed to the carriers, was to constitute a revolving fund for the purpose of paying the expenses of federal control and the deficits in the guaranteed income of carriers, and of providing terminal facilities and equipment. Moreover, in order to provide funds to cover maturing obligations, to reorganize bankrupt roads, and "for other legal and proper expenditures," carriers might issue securities approved by the President. These might be purchased by the Government from the proceeds of the revolving fund at a price not exceeding par, and sold by the Government at a price not less than cost. From the revolving fund the President might also make expenditures for the utilization and operation of canals, and for purchase, construction, and operation of marine equipment, and might make such contracts for water transportation as were in the public interest.

The time limit upon the period of federal control was fixed at twenty-one months after the proclamation of the treaty of peace, but the President might relinquish control of any system of transportation not deemed needful or desirable prior to July 1, 1918, and by agreement with the owners release any system at any time. Furthermore, he might relinquish all the railroads under federal control at any time he considered such a step to be desirable. The Act was expressly declared to be war emergency legislation, and was not to be construed as expressing or prejudicing the future policy of the Government concerning the ownership and control of carriers or the methods or basis of capitalization.[1]

With the statute as a guide, negotiations were begun for a uniform contract in which the interests of both sides should be adequately protected. With conferences well-

---

[1] Other provisions of the Act relating to rates and the relation of the federal and state commissions to the Government will be considered under their appropriate headings.

nigh continuous, the final draft of the "standard contract" was not issued until late in October 1918, and so varied were the conditions upon different roads and so numerous the claims for special consideration that many of the roads never signed contracts at all. The standard contract necessarily followed the instructions of the statute, in many respects being merely a transcription of provisions of the Act. It listed the property taken over, which included in general everything from which the revenues were derived that made up what was known as the "standard return," that is, the officially determined "railway net operating income." Each company reserved the benefit of all leases, the revenues from which were classified as miscellaneous income, but each company gave the Director-General the right to terminate leases of any part of the right of way or yards when the properties were required for operating purposes.

With property transferred to the Railroad Administration went all materials and supplies on hand at midnight of December 31, 1917, and all "net balances receivable from agents and conductors." Federal operation, so far as accounting was concerned, was to begin at midnight of December 31, 1917. All expenditures incurred by the companies during federal control which related to the maintenance of their corporate organizations or of properties not taken over by the Government, were to be borne by the companies. But the expenses of the valuation then under way, to the extent deemed necessary by the Director-General, were to be included in operating expenses. The companies were to have the right at all reasonable times to inspect the books and accounts of the Director-General relating to their own properties, and the Director-General was required to furnish the companies with operating reports of their properties, and annually with a complete list of their equipment.

Inasmuch as the question of maintenance has been one of much controversy, it is of interest to note carefully the provisions for "upkeep" embodied in the standard contract, which were designed to make effective the requirements in the Federal Control Act that the property should be returned to its owners in substantially as good condition as when received. Section 5 of the standard contract required the Director-General, in order to accomplish the purpose just stated, to expend or charge to operating expense proper sums for maintenance, repairs, renewal, retirement, and depreciation. It was provided that a full compliance with this covenant would be accomplished if the annual charges for such purposes during the period of federal control were equal to the average of the three years preceding (1915–1917), less the cost of fire insurance which the Government abolished. Moreover, where the safe operation of the property necessitated, the Director-General might expend additional sums on the basis of a use similar to that of the "test period," which should not enhance maintenance costs over the normal standard of railroads of like character and business. In this case such excess expenditures were to be made good by the companies. But of particular significance in relation to the later controversy was the provision taking account of the shifting price level, which was already a serious factor when the contract was drawn up. It was agreed that in comparing amounts expended during federal control with those of the test period, allowance should be made for any difference that might exist in the cost of labor and materials, and between the amount of property taken over and the average of the test period, and for any difference in use in the two periods which in the opinion of the Commission was substantial enough to be considered, so that the result should be, as nearly as practicable, *the same relative amount, character, and durability of physical reparation.*

Compensation in its general terms had already been provided for, first in the President's proclamation, and then in the Federal Control Act. The contract embodied the specific sum found by the Commission and arranged the details of payment. It was provided that deductions by the Government from the guaranteed return, to cover excess maintenance or additions and betterments not chargeable to the United States, should not be effected to such a degree as to prevent the companies from making reasonable expenditures for the support of their corporate organizations, from keeping up sinking funds, and from paying taxes and interest. No deductions were to be made for additions and betterments made for war purposes which were not for the normal development of the properties, nor for road extensions. It was further stipulated that the power to make deductions from the guaranteed return to cover the cost of additions and betterments not chargeable to the United States was an emergency power, to be used only when no other reasonable means of reimbursement could be found, and that it would be the policy of the Director-General to so use his power of deduction as not to interrupt unnecessarily the dividend policy pursued by the companies during the test period. Without prior approval of the Director-General, companies could not issue securities or enter into contracts or agree to pay higher interest or rentals than prevailed when the roads were taken over.

Another clause of the contract with which controversy is associated was that which provided (Section 8 (f)) that the Director-General should not acquire any motive power or equipment at the expense or on the credit of the companies in excess of what in his judgment was necessary to provide for traffic requirements of their particular systems. But such equipment once acquired might be used by the Director-General on any line operated by him.

Protracted negotiations took place before the railroads finally accepted the clauses relative to the right of the Government to restore deferred maintenance, and to deduct from the compensation under certain conditions what was owed to the Government. But the most insistent contention of the carriers, which was finally denied, was the right to litigation at the end of federal control on the issue whether they had suffered damage by reason of diversion of business. It was held by the Director-General, upon advice of the Solicitor-General, that the roads having been taken over for war purposes, Congress intended that the authorized compensation should cover this element.

At the end of federal control, contracts had been signed by 161 Class I roads that called for an annual compensation of $812,500,000. Fifty-seven Class I roads and large terminal companies signed no contracts. This list of refusals includes the Southern, Chicago and Alton, Chicago and Eastern Illinois, Long Island, Missouri, Kansas and Texas, New York, Chicago and St. Louis, and Western Maryland. In addition to the Class I roads, contracts were made with 110 roads of Classes II and III (with annual operating revenues of less than $1,000,-000), and with 174 switching and terminal companies.

The aggregate rental payments, including all facilities taken over whether under contract or not, approximated $945,000,000. This compensation was considered by many to be extraordinarily liberal and much denunciation of the Government ensued. But the railroads maintained, and in individual instances certainly were justified in maintaining, that the compensation was not adequate. For example, in the case of the Southern Railway, which declined to sign a contract, a thoroughgoing policy of betterments had been instituted, the results of which did not appear in net earnings in the "test period," and hence would not be provided for in the contract. Yet they were realized upon during the period of federal control, the Southern being in consequence one of the few roads that consistently earned the standard return. The question whether the average earnings of the "test period" constituted a fair compensation is really a question as to whether the years 1915–1917 were normal years. Leaving out of consideration the year 1914, which was nearly identical with 1915, it would be necessary to go back to 1908 to find as low an aggregate of net operating income as 1915 revealed, and 1908 was an abnormally low year, suffering the consequences of the 1907 panic. On the other hand, 1916 surpassed any previous year in railroad history in the aggregate of net operating income, being $300,000,000 greater than 1915, and 1917 was less than 1916 by only $100,000,000. Had the railroads enjoyed the same contract as the British railways, which were guaranteed the net income of the last complete year before assumption by the Government, they would have received almost exactly what their contracts called for. When everything is considered, the bargain must be adjudged a fair one, equitable from the standpoint of both Government and carriers.

A special contract was drawn up to cover the situation of the so-called "short lines." These were small roads independently owned, which relied almost wholly for their solvency upon business furnished them by their larger connections, and which were not in most cases essential to the prosecution of the war.[1] It was evident to their owners, however, that unless their interests were carefully safeguarded, the war policy of railroad operation would leave them stranded. The presidential proclama-

[1] The total number of short-line railroads, including interurbans but not street-railways, was approximately 2,500, of which 229 competed for traffic with lines operated by the federal government. Six hundred operated as common carriers but were non-competing, and the rest were industrial railroads, plant facilities, tap-lines, and terminal and switching companies.

tion was all-inclusive. It took possession of "each and every system of transportation" located wholly or in part within the continental boundaries of the United States, except street and interurban railways, plant facilities and industrial roads, which were excluded under the limitations of the war powers granted in 1916. The Federal Control Act provided that every independently owned railroad which had competed with a railroad then under federal control, or which connected with such railroad, should be considered as within "federal control," and necessary for the prosecution of the war. But the Act likewise provided that any road not needed might be relinquished prior to July 1, 1918. In accordance with this section, on June 29, 1918, there were relinquished from federal control 2,161 short-line railroads, including standard railroads, plant facilities, electric lines, and switching and terminal roads. By restoration and further relinquishment under agreement, the net number relinquished stood on January 1, 1919, at 2,110.

A contract was drawn up for the protection of these relinquished roads which was open to voluntary signature. It guaranteed a fair division of joint rates, that such division should not be reduced below that prevailing on January 1, 1918, and that whenever joint rates were increased, the amount allotted to the short line should be increased proportionately. An equitable allotment of cars and, where possible, of motive power in the possession of the Director-General was guaranteed. The Director-General might take over the road at any time for war purposes, in which case it came under the standard contract. Meanwhile it agreed to obey all orders affecting the movement of troops or war-supplies. If the short line were a road that formerly had enjoyed competitive traffic with roads taken over by the Government, it was to furnish a statement of its competitive traffic and revenue during the test period and of the traffic diverted under the operation of the Director-General. If the statement justified the company's contention as to diversion, the company was to receive in cash the difference between the total revenue on competitive freight traffic for the seven months of 1918 (April 1 to October 31) and the average for the corresponding months of the test period, less 33⅓ per cent of the revenue, retained to cover out-of-pocket cost to the lines that had handled the diverted traffic. From November 1, 1918, arrangements were to be made for routing over the company's line a sufficient amount of competitive traffic to bring the total up to that of the test period. A limited number of short lines, amounting at the end of 1919 to 134 out of a total of 800, signed the co-operative contract, but the large majority declined to do so because they felt that it had serious legal defects and could not be enforced against the Government.

CHAPTER X

FEDERAL OPERATION

It has been made clear that the fundamental purpose in taking the railroads under federal control was a military one,—to utilize our national transportation resources, without regard to individual corporate interests, in assembling men for training and in transporting supplies and munitions and men overseas. In examining critically the operations of the railroads under Government direction this purpose should be kept constantly in mind. The situation was unprecedented. The purpose to be achieved had no relation whatever to the normal objects of a transportation service. To attempt to draw conclusions, except in a most general way, as to the desirability or undesirability of permanent Government operation of our railroad system is either stupidly to overlook altogether the inevitable requirements and limitations of a war machine, or wilfully to deal in fallacious arguments in the hope of deceiving that portion of the public that does not think for itself. As the purpose of this book is to trace the development of federal regulation throughout the decade, the war period will be treated only in such detail as is sufficient to fulfil this object, and the policies pursued under federal operation will be examined primarily with regard to their value as permanent features of a transportation policy in time of peace.

The administrative organization for war purposes need not be dwelt upon. Its more significant phases will appear as the discussion proceeds. Suffice it here to say that the Director-General divided the country into regions for operating purposes, over each of which he placed an experienced railroad executive as Director. Each of these had his own staff. Federal managers in charge of the more important single railroads, or groups of less important lines, were as a rule selected from the operating staffs of the roads of which they were to take charge. In many cases the president of the road was made federal manager, but in some instances the president was passed over for one of his subordinates whose duties had not brought him as much in touch with the broader corporate problems, and whose loyalty could, from the Administration point of view, be counted upon more surely. The working organizations of the railroads were left unimpaired, and only such alterations took place therein as resulted from voluntary withdrawal. The central administration in Washington was split into divisions with a Director at the head of each. Of the functions thus emphasized, the most important were finance and purchases, capital expenditures, operation, traffic, labor, and public service and accounting. Walker D. Hines was appointed Assistant Director-General, and succeeded Mr. McAdoo as Director-General upon the latter's retirement at the end of 1918. With a few exceptions the directors of the divisions and their subordinates were drafted from the railroad service. They were all required, as were the regional executives, to sever their railroad connections and become Government employees. They one and all performed their tasks with unwavering fidelity to the public interest and most of them with extraordinary efficiency. Whatever criticisms may be passed upon Mr. McAdoo's administration, he must be given full credit for his sound judgment in intrusting the operation of the roads to men of the highest standing in the railroad field and eliminating political influences. Those who have been impatient with federal operation usually overlook the fact that it was in the hands of the same men who are again active in railroad affairs now that the roads have been returned to their stockholders.

Spokesmen for the Federal Railroad Administration, and especially the Director-General himself, made glowing predictions as to the economies that would result from unified operation of the railroads. There is a strong appeal in the argument for a larger degree of co-operation in the handling of our transportation facilities. We have grown up under competitive conditions. Yet, while clinging blindly to competition as our safeguard against oppression, and resisting every proposal that looked to agreements of any kind, we have nevertheless been slowly awakening to a realization of the enormous wastes of the competitive process, particularly when applied to industries of this nature. It will be profitable, therefore, to gather whatever lessons are available from the experience of the Government in its attempts at co-operation, although we must always remind ourselves that the situation was abnormal and that we were fighting a war and not trying out economic experiments on their merits.

Of the many policies inaugurated for securing economies in service, those which, according to the estimates of the Administration, realized the largest financial return were the elimination of passenger service, the unification of terminals, and the reduction in size and expense of the organizations of the individual railroads. That there was ample justification for elimination of passenger service as a war measure needs little demonstration. Even before the war, there was much unfavorable comment upon the duplicate passenger service out of the large cities, particularly those of the Middle West, like Chicago, St. Louis, and St. Paul. And now when every available locomotive and car was needed either for the handling of food or munitions or in transporting troops to the camps and the embarkation points, and when track room at the inadequate terminals was at a premium, the Administration was well within its rights in introducing somewhat ruthlessly a severe cut in service. The saving appears to have been largest in the West and Northwest, where passenger accommodations had been the most liberal, and in the Eastern region where the traffic was heaviest. The method followed was to eliminate duplicate service, and in many cases to lengthen the schedules of limited trains and impose upon them the duty of handling local traffic. The hours of trains on parallel lines were "staggered," and railroad-tickets were honored by alternative routes. Some trains with light earnings were discontinued altogether. In the case of transcontinental traffic, the fastest service was assigned to the most direct route, the others being used for local traffic. Sleeping-car service was much restricted and many Pullman facilities were abandoned. It was a genuine attempt to discourage travel. The Director-General estimated the annual saving in passenger train-miles as 67,291,000, or a little over 10 per cent of the annual total for the country. Some of the regional directors computed the saving at one dollar per mile. The reduction in service offered did not, as was hoped, reduce passenger travel, which was 8 per cent greater in 1918 than in 1917, and was continuing to increase in 1919.

That the policy resulted in very appreciable inconvenience and discomfort to the travelling public was evident, although such consequences were insignificant when compared with those suffered in England and on the Continent. They were borne generally with cheerfulness as a war measure. That the Administration was fully alive to the situation is shown by the fact that upon the signing of the armistice the restoration of passenger service began, and by the end of June 1919, there had been restored 11,462,000 of the train-miles of which the people had previously been deprived. By the end of 1920, service had returned virtually to the pre-war basis, and the old rivalry of speed, the cutting down of running time, had begun to show itself again on many roads.

It is necessary under either system of control, whether Government or private, that the public should be served adequately with a comfortable and convenient passenger service. It is politically necessary. This form of service touches the individual personally as the freight service does not, and governments owning railroads have recognized the strategic importance of low rates and good service in the passenger department. But this does not require that offerings of service be carried to the extreme that is found in the United States, where in many sections the competition to meet the desires of the traveller is so great that the operations in many cases produce no profit at all. In such cases a part of the burden of expense is actually thrown upon the freight service. It has been commonly maintained that any agreement between roads to adjust passenger schedules would be a violation of the Anti-Trust Act. There is doubt whether the Supreme Court, in view of its recent decisions as to what constitutes restraint of trade, would so hold. But even if the court did not interfere, it is not at all clear that the roads would take advantage of the opportunity to cut down their passenger-train service. Each desires to enjoy the advertising value that comes from scheduling a train at the popular hour of the day and would not, except in times of great economic necessity, be inclined to yield this advantage readily to a rival. Yet in this regard as in respect to other co-operative policies to be discussed, the public is vitally interested in seeing to it that it pays only for that service which is socially desirable.

In the unification of terminal facilities, the opportunities for radical economies were not so abundant as in the reduction of passenger service. While many of the competitive practices were done away with, the physical bar-

riers to a thorough unification could not be removed.
The growth in population and the increase in land values
have intensified a situation which was essentially uneco-
nomic and unscientific from the beginning, and which is
due to the competitive and individualistic character of
our railroad development. On the side of passenger service, the most striking case of unification was the opening of the Pennsylvania terminal in New York to the
use of the Baltimore and Ohio and the Lehigh Valley
Railroads, a step which amply justified itself, and which
has been continued to the present time.

For the control of freight traffic, terminal managers
were appointed at all important points. While the actual physical reconstruction of terminals was of course
impossible, there was opportunity for saving in switching costs, and consequently in time consumed in handling.
Efforts were made to route traffic so as to insure delivery
with the minimum of switching, and when switching
was required, to confine the service to as few carriers as
possible. It was found, for example, that in some cases
in the Chicago terminal as many as nineteen different
railroads were serving one plant or district solely as a
result of competition. Not only was switching saved,
but also economies were made through the unification
of inspection and repair forces. Better organization of
the terminals materially increased the capacity of the
roads using them, for it lessened congestion, reduced delays, facilitated interchange, reduced empty-car mileage,
and increased the car-supply.

Detailed estimates of the saving made by regional
directors must be accepted with caution. For such savings can be only roughly approximated, and they were
made upon a bald money basis without any regard to
the *cost* of the savings in the disservice suffered by shippers. This latter consideration would necessarily have
weight in any plan for permanent unification of terminal

operation. With the return of the roads to their owners most of the joint terminal operations created by the Government were abandoned.

The weakest point in our present operating machine is found in the state of the terminal facilities, a condition growing rapidly more serious with the increase in population and the lack of available space. It is a comparatively simple problem to increase trackage on the line, but the benefit of such increase is altogether neutralized if cars cannot be handled expeditiously at terminals. It may happen that additional business is taken on at an actual loss because this additional traffic slows up the entire service and creates congestion and stagnation. The result of the pressure of competition among traffic men has been to speed up the loading of cars, the getting of business on to the rails, without regard to the question of prompt delivery. The accent both in law and practice has been upon the acceptance of freight for transport by the common carrier rather than upon its final delivery. Hence, cars have been pushed forward to connections and into terminals with little regard to the ability of the terminal to receive and handle them with despatch. The only relief heretofore has been the resort by terminal roads to the crude and unsatisfactory method of embargoes, which have simply forced the congestion back along the line, and have produced wave-like movements of traffic difficult to handle. This situation was greatly aggravated during the war by the fact that shippers on foreign contract usually received the proceeds of their sale as soon as the goods were loaded on cars for shipment.

Under federal operation, the so-called "permit system" was introduced. At first it was made applicable only to traffic essential for the war. Later it was extended more widely. Under this system a carrier could not accept traffic without a permit from the Car Service Bureau, and the issuance of the permit was dependent upon the ability of the consignee to accept and unload the freight without car delay. This system, in the management of which all Government departments co-operated, alone made possible the handling of the immense war traffic without congestion. All War and Navy Department shipments were handled on a permit basis. All export traffic via Atlantic, Gulf, and Pacific ports was handled in this manner, and the system was applied during the war to domestic shipments to Philadelphia, New York, and Baltimore. Wheat and hog shipments to primary markets were thus stabilized. The U. S. Railroad Administration declared that the operation of the permit system made it possible to keep the heavy export business moving through the ports, keep the coal for tidewater and lake trans-shipment under control, move the heavy grain crop in an orderly manner, and at the same time handle a maximum volume of other business, through the avoidance of congestion and the freeing for other loading of cars, power, and facilities which would not otherwise have been available. Such a device might well become a part of our normal operating system. Its value has been recognized by railroad executives but, naturally enough, it has not met with the enthusiastic indorsement of shippers. They regard it as only an embargo under another name and an opportunity for serious discrimination. They take the position that it is the business of the railroad to transport and deliver, and that inability to do this at any particular time should not work to deprive the shipper of the right to ship.

The Administration also undertook to co-ordinate the marine departments of the different railroads, and to use all piers regardless of ownership. An Exports Control Committee was set up with power to determine the ports to which traffic should be hauled, and the permit system was employed to prevent the shipment of goods to any port until there was a practical certainty that ships would be promptly available. The war did not last long enough to give this committee the opportunity to make its influence felt in any large way on the traffic of the country. But its efforts point the direction in which we should now move. We are not making the best use of our port and steamship facilities; congestion and blockade are all too familiar phenomena in normal times. The whole problem of port facilities and their relationship to inland transportation has received too little attention.

The third "economy" upon which Director-General McAdoo laid stress was that of the elimination of high-salaried executives, which was to bring about an annual saving of $4,600,000. This had a wide popular appeal, and seems to have been put in the foreground of the programme largely because of that fact. The greater part of the officers released by the Railroad Administration from active operating duties retained their salaried relationships with their own corporations, and the aggregate administrative expense continued as before. So far it was a matter of bookkeeping only. But it later developed that if efficiency in executive positions was to be obtained, salaries somewhat approaching those paid in other fields must be offered. A report of January 1, 1919, showed that five of the seven regional directors were receiving $50,000 annual salary and the other two $40,000, and that in addition to the regional directors seventeen operating officials were receiving $20,000 or more. Even at these salaries, the officials assumed their positions at large financial sacrifice and wholly for patriotic reasons. The entire estimated saving in any case was not over one-tenth of 1 per cent of the operating expenses, and would have been hardly worthy of mention but for the political use to which it was put.

The other operating policies of the Railroad Administration upon which less stress was laid may be disposed of in more summary fashion. Short-routing of freight to avoid unnecessary mileage was urged from the beginning, and was attempted in all regions. General Order No. 1 of the Federal Railroad Administration instructed railroad managers to disregard shippers' routing of freight whenever speed and efficiency would be promoted thereby, thus setting aside a privilege which had been granted to shippers by law. Traffic agreements among carriers were not to be permitted to interfere with expedition. Shippers whose interest was in the shortest distance between points, now that traffic solicitors had disappeared, assisted the campaign. In fact, in some regions the savings by voluntary action of the shippers were greater than those made by the railroads themselves. But the result in many cases, especially in the East, was to congest the direct lines and compel the diversion of traffic to the more roundabout routes. In some cases where paralleling lines existed, all of the traffic of a certain kind, such as coal, was routed over a specific line, thus promoting efficiency in handling by reducing variety. Routing was also worked out to take advantage of ruling grades and to avoid congested population centres. No satisfactory estimate of the savings can be or was made. Such figures as were presented by the operating officials were so crudely approximate as to be practically worthless. Moreover, even accepting the aggregate saving in car miles as estimated, it represented in any particular region but a fraction of 1 per cent of the total car miles travelled.

The "sailing-day plan," under which less-than-car-load freight was assembled in solid cars and despatched without transfer to destination, was widely introduced, but not without protests from shippers in some sections, who felt that their privileges were being curtailed. They protested against being obliged to bring their traffic to the freight-station on designated days only, and to ship it only by designated routes, and they insisted that in some centres it worked to discriminate against them and in favor of competitors who were not subject to these limitations. Better loading of cars and trains, begun under the Railroads' War Board, was continued with the invaluable aid of the various Government agencies. Shippers contributed to this campaign not alone from patriotic motives but because they felt the necessity of making full use of their limited supply of cars. Solid trains were routed direct from origin to destination, expediting traffic and saving yard expense. The service was applied most extensively to traffic in flour and grain, lumber, fruit, packing-house products, live stock, cotton, and oil. However, the statistics of loading, particularly for the Eastern region, were materially affected by the extent of empty-car mileage westbound, which the war exigencies forced upon the management. So far as was possible, the "permit system" was used as a weapon to enforce full return loads. These two methods of economizing operation—the solid train-load and the sailing-day plan—had long been recognized by railroad managements as desirable, and some of them had put the practices into effect before the war. But it is evident that under competitive conditions and under the pressure that can be brought to bear by shippers, it is impossible in normal times to introduce such practices to any satisfactory degree, except on roads whose traffic is large and assured. No road is willing to see its traffic drift away to a rival while it is waiting for a full load. It is not surprising, therefore, that this operating economy should have largely disappeared with the end of federal control. In fact, the sailing-day plan as a federal policy went by the board as early as April 1919.

Unification of facilities for war purposes had its best exemplification in the matter of equipment. The car and locomotive supply was located and relocated with entire disregard of ownership, payments for the use of foreign cars were eliminated, and equipment of all kinds was repaired in the most accessible and least congested shop. From the very beginning of through traffic in the sixties and seventies of the nineteenth century, freight-cars had moved freely from road to road in order, so far as possible, to carry their load to destination without transfer. But the system had never worked with entire satisfaction to all managements, and various devices had been tried in the way of penalties to induce prompt return of cars to the home road. There have been many advocates of the pooling plan, under which each road would contribute a certain number of cars of a non-specialized type for through traffic to a common supply, or under which the car-supply for through traffic would be handled by a separate organization, as in the case of sleeping-car equipment. Such plans have more than once nearly reached a realization, but have in each case been defeated by the individualistic attitude of a few roads. So far as locomotives are concerned, it has never been the practice to send them beyond their own lines. The necessity for frequent overhauling and constant inspection, and the fact that they have been designed to meet physical conditions on their own roads, have made pooling of locomotives impracticable. The results of the extreme application of the pooling system forced by the war emergency were observable as the period of federal operation drew toward its close. Equipment needed by Eastern roads for their specific kind of traffic, such as coal-cars, was largely in the West, and the box-car equipment that Western grain roads required was on the Eastern lines. Moreover, maintenance adequate for normal times was possible only when equipment was handled by the owner in the home shop. Three months before the end of federal control, the Director-General ordered the return of cars to the home road, and this movement then begun continued as rapidly as conditions permitted. The normal proportion of cars on home roads is about 50 per cent. After a year of federal operation it had fallen to a little over 25 per cent. By the end of 1920 it had recovered to 33 per cent. There is no evidence that the railroads have any desire to continue the pooling plan, and there is no compulsion upon them to do so except in times of "shortage of equipment, congestion of traffic or other emergency," when the Commission, under the recent legislation, has power to disregard ownership of equipment, and make such directions with respect to car-service as will best promote the public interest.

The coal-zoning plan, introduced primarily to meet the fuel shortage, was effective in eliminating a large waste in transportation, although it necessitated a serious readjustment in markets that were accustomed to certain grades of coal, and were by this plan now obliged to resort to substitutes. This was abolished February 1, 1919. An increase in demurrage rates, almost to a prohibitive point, was put into force to speed up the unloading of cars. Through interline way-billing was extended beyond anything in use before, and reconsignment and similar privileges that cause delay were largely eliminated. A system of store-door delivery of package freight was introduced in New York and Philadelphia to relieve the terminal congestion. The Car Service Section secured to some degree in the summer months of 1918 the advance movement of important raw materials to avoid a possible congestion in the fall, but the unfavorable business situation of the following year brought this programme to an end. Finally, as factors contributing in an indirect way to the campaign for economical freight operation, there may be mentioned the steps taken to consolidate and simplify freight tariffs, and the completion of the huge job long under way before the war, of a uniform freight classification which was submitted to the Commission, but did not reach the point of practical application.

In the passenger field the project which was looked upon with the greatest satisfaction by the Administration was that of the consolidated ticket office. The number of these was 108 at the end of 1919, replacing between 500 and 600 offices previously in existence. It was claimed that the convenience to travellers in the combination of Pullman and ticket offices, and in the opportunity to decide between alternative routes with a minimum of inconvenience, constituted a service that the public would demand as a permanent feature. All that can be said for it at present is that it has persisted longer than almost any other of the war innovations. Once old leases have been disposed of, it means a very tangible saving in expense through reduction in rental. Whether the savings are sufficient to offset the loss of individuality and the advertising value of a separate establishment is a question that each road is deciding for itself. At the beginning of 1921, the consolidated office was in operation in whole or in part in a considerable number of the larger cities. In Chicago, three out of twenty-two roads had withdrawn to set up separate agencies. Where the union office still prevails, there is a tendency to resurrect the identity of the individual road inside the office and to direct travel to the proper desk within the building by vigorous solicitation outside. Whether or not the union ticket office is legal under the Anti-Trust Act is a matter of dispute among railroad men. In the Union Pacific-Southern Pacific merger case, the prosecuting officers attached much importance to the consolidation of ticket offices as infractions of the law, and after dissolution all consolidated offices were abandoned. But it is probable that in this case the Government attorneys were examining outward signs of a more significant inward agreement, and that the joint ticket office would not in itself have been considered a restraining combination. Certainly if the individual corporate units are preserved, the fact that they all reside under one roof can be no more illegal than the annual automobile show. This would seem to be a case where the railroads have raised a legal doubt for the purpose of stopping them from doing what they did not in any case wish to do. Other unification policies in passenger service included the introduction of a universal mileage book, standard ticket forms and baggage rules, and the abridgment of time-tables. Attempts to standardize dining-car service struck at the very heart of individualism, and the results were not altogether successful.

Advertising and all work for the stimulation of traffic was stopped under federal operation except that which concerned itself with agricultural development. A sharp decline in traffic after the war ended forced the Administration into a campaign of advertising to stimulate travel. With the return of the roads to their owners, the managements felt keenly the necessity of active campaigns to restore their traffic diverted under war necessities. In view of the serious financial condition of the railroads, advertising and traffic development plans have been worked out with more care as to their immediate effect, and waste has been carefully avoided. Closer contact is being developed between the railroad and the shipper. The prompt closing of "off-line" freight offices by the federal administration seemed natural in view of the fact that they were primarily soliciting agencies in a competitive market. But it was discovered later that they had been of material service to shippers in a variety of ways that had to do with information concerning rates and shipments. No satisfactory substitute for this personal relationship was developed during federal control.

To promote uniformity in operation, there was created an Operating Statistics Section which was to do for operation what the Interstate Commerce Commission had done for accounting. It was to decide upon operating statistical standards and make them effective and to analyze and disseminate operating results. Its purpose was to make use of all the operating statistical data prepared for the Interstate Commerce Commission, and to require such additional information as was essential to a complete exhibit of physical performance and of unit costs of operation. Its plan for the standardization of statistical practice was made effective on August 1, 1918, and its work was developed with such efficiency that its standards and reports have found a permanent place in railroad administration. Eight standardized monthly reports were required from Class I roads (those having operating revenues in excess of $1,000,000 per annum) covering such data as freight and passenger train performance, locomotive and car performance, locomotive and train costs, and the distribution of locomotive hours. It is of especial note that statistics of car and locomotive performance place much more stress than was ever laid before upon the time element in equipment performance, a most significant factor in a final determination of operating efficiency. While much of the material had been gathered by roads for many years, there had been no uniformity in method or in the meaning of the figures. It is now possible to compare operating results on the various roads without qualification for differences in methods of accumulating data and computing units and averages. As a result of the wide distribution of the summarized reports, railroad officers know much more than they did before about their relative performance and many know more about their own operations. In fact, officers on many of the larger roads are now requiring similar data and comparisons for the different operating divisions of their systems. The effect of this statistical work, while not measurable with any accuracy, is distinctly in the direction of an awakened and more intelligent interest in the efficiency of operation.[1]

In the Division of Accounting considerable saving was effected in consequence of the unification of operations. Car hire was eliminated and all accounting therefor went with it. Much simplification was introduced into the car-repair and joint-facility accounts. Much of the controversy over interline apportionments and freight claims was eliminated. Yet it is obvious that the savings were meagre in comparison with what would be made under a permanent system of unified management. It was an interim period. It was not desirable to break the series of accounting and statistical reports prepared by the Commission. The contract with the Government necessitated the maintenance of accounting identity. Two sets of books had to be kept, and much new labor was involved in following up the many details of the contract. This was all incidental to the temporary lease, and hampered the Division in making the showing in economies that it might under other conditions have been capable of doing.

In the field of maintenance many practices were standardized and the principles of unification introduced. Locomotive repair-shops were pooled regardless of ownership, thus reducing distance to which locomotives were sent for repairs and the time they were out of service. Standard practice was introduced in many phases of maintenance and inspection, and the policy of inspection was extended to take the place of commercial insurance, which was abolished. Joint purchase of supplies was undertaken wherever possible. The most sweeping inno-

[1] For more detailed discussion of the statistical practice, see article by William J. Cunningham, who is responsible for the development of the plan, in Annals American Academy, November 1919, entitled "The Accomplishments of the United States Railroad Administration in Unifying and Standardizing the Statistics of Operation."

vation and the one which met with the strongest opposition was the introduction of standardization into the manufacture of locomotives and cars. The Director-General, in his seven months' report of September, 1918, stated that there were said to be prior to the war 2,023 different styles of freight-cars, and almost as many of locomotives. At the time of his report, twelve standard types of freight-cars had been decided upon, and six types of locomotives in two weights. With interchangeable parts, it was expected that these relatively few types could be more rapidly repaired, particularly when off their own lines, and that the stock of repair parts could be reduced. Moreover, it had already been demonstrated that the speed in production of new equipment was materially increased. Aside from the natural opposition of the locomotive and car builders to this policy, there were many expert railroad-maintenance engineers who felt that the policy of standardization had been carried too far, and that many roads were consequently unable to secure the equipment adapted to their peculiar needs. This was particularly the case with locomotives, which to be efficient must be adapted to the many local conditions of physical plant and operating methods, such as alignment and grades, nature of fuel, strength of bridges, weight of track, and capacity of roundhouses, turntables, and sidings. Efficiency in operation had been sacrificed to efficiency in production. Probably the reasonable policy lay somewhere between the two extremes. While experimentation should be sufficiently encouraged to assure a steady development in efficiency of equipment types, and the railroads should be free to order those types that are best suited to their needs, the public should not be asked to bear the burden of all the variations from standard that the ingenuity of builders can devise, and induce the railroads to purchase.

There was less opposition to the standardization of the freight-car. In fact, many of the larger roads had been pursuing this policy for years, and the influence of such national organizations as the Master Car Builders' Association had been in the same direction. It is only necessary to recall the assistance of this organization in the establishment by the Interstate Commerce Commission of safety standards, beginning with the automatic coupler and air-brake nearly thirty years ago, to realize that standardization is no new problem in the design of railroad equipment. Freight-cars travel freely about the country, whereas locomotives seldom leave the home line. Cars must receive at least emergency repairs wherever they happen to be. There is a large saving in time and expense if cars and repair parts can be standardized, at least in the case of equipment that travels most widely and is not limited to the carrying of special traffic in particular sections.

The controversy in which the most acute differences of opinion arose between the railroad corporations and the federal administration related to the equipment ordered by the Director-General in accordance with the types determined upon and allocated to the different railroad systems. The Administration ordered 1,930 locomotives and 100,000 freight-cars. No passenger-cars of any sort were purchased. This was in 1918, no orders being placed in 1919 because of the uncertainty as to the date of termination of federal control. Most of the locomotives were accepted, but vigorous protest was raised against the allocation of cars. Many roads insisted that the equipment was not adapted to their needs and they all objected to taking and paying for equipment at war prices which would later have to be written down to a lower price level. This controversy is one of the main issues in the final adjustment of the compensation between the roads and the Government.

Two other steps involving far-reaching consequences in the direction of unification were taken, those relating to the express companies and to the waterways. With the express companies each railroad had a separate contract, and these contracts varied widely in their stipulations concerning the handling of different kinds of traffic. There was necessity for a uniform contract applicable over the entire railroad net. Accordingly, a corporation known as the American Railway Express Company was created to take over the existing companies during the period of federal control. With this new corporation the Railroad Administration made a contract[1] in June 1918, which contained an agreement for division of income that in a way foreshadowed the provision of the Transportation Act of 1920 for the distribution of railroad net revenue. Of its gross transportation revenue, the express company was to turn over to the Director-General 50.25 per cent, which was the average for the previous ten years of the payments by the express companies to the railroads. Out of the balance, enhanced by the earnings upon roads not under federal control and by income derived from other sources than transportation, the express company was to defray its expenses, rentals, and taxes. From any balance remaining, it reserved 5 per cent for a capital stock dividend. The next 2 per cent on the par value of the stock was to be divided equally between the company and the Government, the company's portion being used for dividends or general corporate purposes, and any remainder was to be used to accumulate a guarantee fund of 10 per cent on the capital stock to insure stability of dividends. Any income in excess of that needed for the guarantee fund was to be divided upon a somewhat complicated basis between the company and the Government, in which the latter got the larger share. Moreover, when at the end of the contract the guarantee

[1] U. S. Railroad Administration Bulletin No. 4 (revised), page 85.

was distributed, the Director-General became the beneficiary to the extent of three-fifths thereof. By presidential proclamation the American Railway Express Company was taken possession of on November 16, 1918, with the proviso that the Director-General might at his discretion continue the operation of the company under the contract of the previous June. Express matter was thereafter sent by the most direct route and express-cars were utilized without regard to ownership.

By the Federal Control Act the President was authorized to expend from the revolving fund what he deemed necessary or desirable for the utilization and operation of canals, and the purchase or construction and operation of equipment on inland and coastwise waterways. A Marine Department was created under the Railroad Administration. Because of the requisitioning by the Government of a large amount of coastwise tonnage for war purposes, the remaining private lines were disposed to accept only the most profitable tonnage, and an additional burden was in consequence thrown on the railroads. Accordingly, the Railroad Administration not only took over all railroad-owned steamships but also, under the President's war powers, fifty-one ships belonging to four private companies. These private vessels were returned to their owners after the armistice. In April 1918, the New York Barge Canal Section was created, and the leasing and construction of equipment was undertaken.[1] In July the Cape Cod Canal was taken over to provide an inside waterway free from submarine danger. Dredging and other maintenance work was at once undertaken, and traffic began moving in volume in the fall. In the same month the Mississippi and War-

[1] The New York Barge Canal is a public highway owned by the State of New York. It never came into the possession of the Director-General, but the Railroad Administration operated boats upon it in the same way as did other operators.

rior Waterways Section was created. The fleet of the Kansas City-Missouri River Navigation Company was purchased, and barges were leased from the Corps of United States Engineers. Construction of towboats and barges was authorized. So far as the Mississippi was concerned, there was little development of water traffic beyond that which originated along its banks. Grain southbound and sugar northbound were the only commodities of any importance. The amount of freight actually handled was negligible. The causes assigned for the large deficit in the operating statement were defective power for the handling of barges and inadequate terminal capacity and facilities. For the coal business between the Warrior River, Alabama, and New Orleans, equipment was purchased and contracts let for new construction. The Delaware and Raritan Canal across New Jersey was operated by the Administration as an incident to its control of the Pennsylvania Railroad, which is the lessee of the canal. The Chesapeake and Ohio Canal was guaranteed against loss.

To encourage water traffic, joint through freight rates, both class and commodity, were published, applicable to water lines on the Mississippi and Warrior Rivers and to the New Jersey canal section, which enjoyed a differential of 20 per cent against all-rail handling. But more was needed than favorable rates to develop this form of co-operation. Transfer facilities were lacking altogether or were hopelessly obsolete. The Government's experience with attempts to revive traffic on the New York Barge Canal reveals the fundamental obstacles to an immediately satisfactory solution. There were no unloading facilities on the banks of the canal, and manufacturing industries, because of the prohibitive terminal expense, refused to receive their coal by water. There were no adequate terminals at the lower end of the water route, and canal-boats were obliged to await with their loads the pleasure of the ocean steamships, thus seriously delaying traffic movement. The differential between water and rail rates was not satisfactory to shippers, and the management, because of costs of operation, could not afford to drop the water rate lower. During 1919 Government craft carried a total eastbound and westbound tonnage of only 166,000 tons, for which it received a gross revenue of $510,000. The larger proportion of this tonnage was grain eastbound. The operations for the year developed a deficit of $161,000. Costs of water transportation were affected by the same war influences that prevailed elsewhere and efforts to increase efficiency by the addition of improved equipment met with the same difficulty that the railroads were facing, a more imperative need elsewhere for the materials of construction. Nothing of any significance was accomplished during federal control in the effort to make the water facilities the handmaiden of the railroads. Nothing more than a beginning was made in any direction. No water traffic of any importance was created. One and all the experiments closed their accounts with a deficit.

This cursory survey of the operating policies of the federal administration brings out the fact that there were in the mind of the management two distinct objects, at times conflicting in their effects. The first was to operate the roads as a unit for the purpose of making the largest possible contribution to the winning of the war. This was the dominant motive during the year 1918 up to the signing of the armistice. The second purpose was to increase efficiency and reduce the cost of railroad operation by the introduction of co-operative methods, wherever possible, by setting aside the individual selfish interests of the particular road in favor of the larger interests of the country as a whole. Through argument and entreaty and by even more stringent means, more efficient methods were sought in the operation of trains, the delivering and loading and unloading of cars, and the elimination of wasteful practices born out of the competitive struggle. The campaign for more efficient operation went along with the war programme. In many cases development of efficiency was an aid to speedier and more effective handling of war-supplies and troops. But in many instances the war necessity compelled the sacrifice of the principles of sound operation to the higher demands of the immediate exigency.

As has already been indicated, it is well-nigh impossible to measure with any accuracy the savings of unified operation. Clear-cut economies there undoubtedly were, through the elimination of competitive practices such as advertising and outside agencies, through reduction in passenger service, abolition of fire insurance, elimination of many forms of joint accounting, and to some degree through unification of terminal operation and the consolidated ticket office. But general comparisons of conditions that refuse to remain static must be accepted with caution. Conditions of operation change rapidly. The elimination of one obstacle to economical movement often creates another and a wholly unexpected one. A comparison of the situation as it actually worked out with what is assumed would have been the situation if unified operation had not prevailed can have little value. In this period of rising prices and wages and declining labor efficiency, the really important thing was not to save money but to get the job done, and that as quickly as possible. Emphasis upon economies was largely for political purposes,[1] and to meet the criticisms of those who had opposed from the beginning the assumption of the roads by the Government.

[1] In a letter to the regional directors, October 24, 1918, Director-General McAdoo urged that trips be taken by officials for the purpose of coming into contact with local industries and associations and explaining the general policy of the Railroad Administration, and said: "Also explain the advantages that have accrued and will accrue

However, it was natural to assume that once the war was over, the federal administration would be in a position to devote its entire attention to the development of an efficient national transportation agency in which all competitive wastes would be avoided. But the public demand for the abolition of restrictive regulations and for the restoration of pre-war privileges was too great to be resisted, and the co-operative enterprises and the various arrangements for reducing operating costs disappeared one by one. Railroad executives who had given of their services unreservedly during the war to the federal administration withdrew to renew their relations with their former corporations, or to assume new positions in the railroad service, and their duties with the Government were taken over by men of less outstanding ability who were obviously carrying on until the end should come.

Following the armistice, passenger service was promptly increased. Coal-zoning, the sailing-day plan, short-routing, solid-train despatching quickly vanished as federal policies, and joint terminal arrangements began to go to pieces. The year 1919 was a period of most unhappy uncertainty in which, as we shall see, the federal administration was urging a new lease of life, and in which without this assurance it felt itself unable and unwilling to undertake any long-time constructive policy. It was a period of slow disintegration so far as the general programme of co-operation in force in 1918 was concerned. However, the lessons learned through the process of trial and error in matters of national co-operation should not be lost. A discussion of this problem will form a part of the concluding chapter.

in the future by the improvements in transportation conditions worked out by the Railroad Administration and which are bound to be continued permanently because of their efficiency, economy, and expedition in the handling of traffic."

CHAPTER XI

RATE REGULATION

SUFFICIENT has been said to indicate that the Government, if it was to make from the operation of the railroads a financial showing at all satisfactory, would be compelled to take vigorous steps to increase its revenues. The Federal Control Act of March 1918 granted to the Railroad Administration a rate-making power that was almost unrestricted. The President, whenever in his opinion the public interest required, could initiate rates, fares, classifications, and regulations by filing them with the Interstate Commerce Commission, and these rates and regulations were not to be suspended by the Commission pending final determination. They were to take effect upon such notice as the President should direct.

Finding itself facing the possibility of a huge deficit, primarily as a consequence of wage increases and the increase in cost of materials and supplies, the Administration announced on May 25, 1918, a 25 per cent advance in freight rates, effective June 25, and an advance in passenger fares to a minimum of three cents per mile, effective June 10, with a half-cent additional per mile for the privilege of purchasing Pullman service.[1] Additional regulations concerning Pullman travel still further increased the cost for those seeking the more luxurious accommodations. The new rates were made specifically to apply to both state and interstate traffic. In many cases, due to changes in minima and in the methods of application, the increases in freight rates were much in excess of 25 per cent.

[1] This extra charge was cancelled after the armistice.

The method by which the increases were accomplished must have won the envy of all railroad officials who had struggled through protracted hearings with federal and state commissioners, and had been obliged in the end to accept increases, if any at all, far below what they deemed necessary to meet their needs. The Director-General explained that action was necessarily delayed until the Federal Control Act could be passed; that the correction and adjustment of individual items in a structure so vast would have been impossible in any brief space of time, and that, after conference with the Commission, and after investigation of existing conditions and a careful estimate of probable results, it was decided to take quick action that would spread the increase as equitably as possible over the entire country. While the Administration doubtless gave the matter mature consideration, the public was not taken into its confidence, and had to content itself with newspaper rumors. There is little question that the summary manner in which the increases were put through was deliberate, and designed to forestall any interference that might spring from public discussion. In fact, such a procedure was anticipated in the Federal Control Act itself, which reduced the power of the Commission from that of suspension of rates to that of making findings, after hearing complaints concerning rates actually in effect.

These increases were intended so to enhance net operating revenue that the "standard return" payable to the carriers under their contracts could be secured without drawing upon other Government funds. But obviously such a plan could be based on estimates only, as it was impossible to foretell what the effect upon traffic would be from the increases in rates. So far as passenger traffic was concerned, the deliberate intention of the high charges was to reduce travel and to free roads and equipment for more important functions, a purpose that largely failed of effect. As for freight traffic, there was some prospect that the higher rates would be more or less directly reflected in higher net earnings, for transportation demand, in view of war emergency conditions, was largely inelastic, essential commodities having to move regardless of cost. But the results of the year 1918 in no way fulfilled these optimistic predictions. For the twelve months the net railroad revenue fell short of the amount required to meet the "standard return" by over $200,-000,000. The only district that earned its standard return was the Southern district, comprising the states east of the Mississippi and south of the Ohio and Potomac. The result in the South was due in large measure to the fact that investment in betterments did not begin to show results until federal operation was under way; in other words, that the years upon which the contract was based were years of light earnings. The bargain of the Southern roads with the Government was consequently an unfortunate one for them.

The reasons assigned by the Director-General for the outcome in 1918, in which the operating ratio had risen to 81.3 per cent, are all connected directly or indirectly with war conditions, the necessity of moving war freight expeditiously regardless of expense, the loss of men to the draft and to railroad service abroad and the substitution of inexperienced labor, and the rapid increase in cost of labor and materials. Moreover, while wage increases were largely effective from January 1, the railroads received the benefit of rate increases for only the last six months of the year. As late as January, 1919, Director-General McAdoo expressed the conviction that with the return to more nearly normal conditions the deficit would not only be wiped out but reductions in rates might gradually be made, and that earnings would show an improvement for each month over the previous year. But in spite of these optimistic predictions, the financial condition of the railroads grew worse instead of better. The operating ratio fluctuated from month to month during 1919 from a high point of over 92 per cent in February to a low of 76 per cent in August and back again above 90 per cent in December, and reached a record height for the entire period of federal control (nearly 98 per cent) in February 1920, the last month of Government operation. Roads whose net operating income fell short of the standard return by over $200,000,000 in 1918 failed to reach the standard return in 1919 by nearly $400,000,000, and the aggregate deficiency for the twenty-six months of federal operation was over $900,000,000.

Out of 203 roads reported by the Bureau of Railway Economics, the number that earned more than their standard return was 76 in 1918 and only 44 in 1919. Retrospection is of course far safer and more illuminating than prophecy, particularly in a period when conditions were constantly shifting and the country was face to face almost daily with problems for the solution of which there was little if any precedent. But even granting all this, the amazing optimism of Director-General McAdoo, which pervaded his testimony before congressional committees and his various public utterances, had little justification. Director-General Hines explained in his final report the reasons for the unfavorable financial showing of the previous fourteen months. He said that could the rate increases which became effective in June, 1918, have been put in force on January 1, there would have been no fall in net operating income below the standard return during 1918, nor up to October 1, 1919. The bad financial showing of 1919 was due to the sudden slump in business following the armistice and resulting in part from the steel and coal strikes in the fall of the year.

There has been much discussion of the question whether a wiser policy of rate making would not have required gradual increases in rates to meet in part at least the growing expenses resulting from increased costs of materials and of labor.[1] It is frequently asserted that it was a matter of indifference whether the people paid the guarantee in the form of taxes or of freight rates; it was a war cost to be borne in any case. But the answer is

[1] This question of the relation of railroad rates to prices during the war, or the burden of the railroad rate, has so many points of contact with our discussion that it will be of value to present here the facts. The following tabulation has been prepared by the Bureau of Railway Economics from data taken from the Statistics of Railways of the Interstate Commerce Commission, and from the wholesale prices of 327 commodities determined by the Bureau of Labor Statistics of the U. S. Department of Labor. These commodities are averaged together in proportion to their relative importance. The year 1913 is taken as the base.

RELATIVE INCREASE IN FREIGHT RATES COMPARED WITH INCREASED COMMODITY PRICES, 1919–1921. (1913=100)

YEAR OR MONTH	AVERAGE RECEIPTS PER TON-MILE CENTS		INDEX NUMBERS OF WHOLE-SALE PRICES, ALL COMMODITIES	INDEX NUMBERS OF RETAIL PRICES, 43 ARTICLES OF FOOD	INDEX NUMBERS OF RETAIL COAL PRICES	
	ACTUAL	RELATIVE			PA. ANTHRA. (CHESTNUT)	PA. BITUM.
1913....	.719	100	100	100	100	100
1914....	.723	101	100	102	100	105
1915....	.722	100	101	101	101	103
1916....	.707	98	124	114	109	112
1917....	.715	100	176	146	121	134
1918....	.849	118	196	168	134	144
1919....	.973	135	212	186	154	152
1920....	1.052	146	243	203	183	198
Sept. 1920....	1.151	160	242	203	200	223
Oct. 1920....	1.226	171	225	198	204	230
Nov. 1920....	1.263	176	207	193	206	230
Dec. 1920....	1.209	168	189	178	206	226
Jan. 1921....	1.210	168	177	172	204	218
Feb. 1921....	1.254	174	167	158	201	210
Mar. 1921....	1.335	186	162	156	198	205
Apr. 1921....	1.334	186	154	152	188	195
May 1921....	1.251	174	151	145	188	191
June 1921....	1.278	178	148	144	188	191

It will be noted that even as late as January 1921, when deflation had set in and many were crying out against the burden of the high freight rate and demanding its reduction, wholesale prices were still 9 points and retail prices 4 points above freight rates. During the entire period under consideration rates lagged behind prices in their upward advance.

not so simple. Aside from the obviously more business-like method of making an industry pay its way, and making the public realize definitely that they are getting only what they are paying for, there is the other and far more intricate question of the incidence of the burden in the two cases. It cannot be correctly assumed that the two situations would be identical. Yet if we look upon federal control as wholly a war policy, then there was justification perhaps in distributing the war cost as widely as possible, and the tax method rather than the freight-rate method would be efficacious for the purpose.

However, Director-General Hines defended the policy of the Administration on the grounds of expediency. The complexity of the rate structure, the enormous number of adjustments in rate relationships that had been necessitated by the horizontal increase in June, 1918, were deterrents to another advance. Freight-rate readjustment is so disturbing to business that no change ought to take place except when the reasons are imperative, and there was great uncertainty at this time as to the need for the increase. The belief that rate increases would be used as occasions for unnecessary increases in price, and thus aggravate an already desperate situation was another deterrent. An increase at this time would also have made more difficult the handling of the wage problem. Toward the end of federal control there was an obvious unwillingness to act. The policy then was to pass the problem on to private management. In the face of the general feeling prevailing throughout the year, no rate increase could have been put promptly into force by the Director-General. In deference to the public attitude it would have been necessary to ask the Commission to pass upon the increase, and this would have meant delay. Moreover, it was ingeniously argued that any rate increase required to cover the expenses of federal control would not have been sufficient in any case to meet the larger expense of private operation, and as the roads when again in private hands would have to secure further increases, the public interest would be better served by having the entire advance come at one time.

Any attempt to reach a final conclusion on this question involves much speculation as to what would have been the effect upon business of another moderate increase in rates by the Administration, as compared with the somewhat radical increase necessitated in August, 1920, when the roads were again in private hands. We cannot now determine whether business would have adjusted itself more easily to the gradual method, neither do we have the means of knowing to what extent the increases would have been multiplied in prices. From the standpoint of the individual railroad, it is obvious that a more courageous policy on the part of the Administration during the period of federal control would have been preferable, because it would have facilitated the process of transfer of the roads back into private hands. But Director-General Hines, in his exhaustive review of his policy, reached the conclusion that in any case rates could not have been advanced fast enough to meet the rapidly changing conditions, and that, everything considered, the policy adopted by the Administration was "vastly more in the public interest than any other policy that could have been adopted with reference to the rate matter."

Under the rate-making power, the federal administration had the unique opportunity of putting on trial a uniform classification, a goal which regulating authorities have been endeavoring to reach for thirty years. For many years the railroads have had a uniform classification committee at work endeavoring to reconcile the conflicting interests of different industries and sections and the railroads serving them, and from time to time the work of these committees has come officially under the eye of the Commission. In 1912 Western Classification

No. 51 was suspended[1] by the Commission and thoroughly examined. Certain fundamental principles were laid down for the guidance of railroad committees in their future work. In 1919, in the Lumber Classification Case,[2] the Commission announced fundamental guiding principles of a sound classification. But in all cases where the matter has arisen it has confined itself, so far as the broader issue was concerned, to general suggestions and limitations. In spite of the unquestioned power possessed by it since 1910 to prescribe a uniform classification, the Commission has preferred, because of the complexities, the enormous detail, and the necessary compromises involved, to confine its activity to stimulating the carriers and to leave the execution of the project to them.

The Railroad Administration in 1918 appointed a committee to take up and complete the work which had been begun by the carriers' committee ten years before. The completed consolidated classification was not put into force by the Director-General as he had power to do, but was submitted to the Interstate Commerce Commission for its approval. After extended hearings, the Commission recommended the adoption of the classification so far as it concerned general rules, commodity descriptions, packing specifications, and estimated and car-load minimum weights, but generally disapproved the commodity ratings because they effected such a large number of increases in rates, particularly in Eastern and Southern territory. So far as separate state classifications were investigated, the Commission concluded that the local situations must needs be worked out fully after careful investigation, and that no benefit was to be gained by substituting at that time the consolidated schedule for the various state classifications.[3] In accord with the

---

[1] 25 I. C. C., 442. The opinion includes a complete history of the movement for uniform classification.

[2] 52 I. C. C., 598. [3] 54 I. C. C., 1 (Sept., 1919).

Commission's suggestions, the Railroad Administration filed Consolidated Freight Classification No. 1 with the Interstate and state commissions, effective December 30, 1919. The Consolidated Classification Committee created during the Railroad Administration has now been made a permanent organization by the carriers and is proceeding in the direction of uniform ratings.

CHAPTER XII

In his proclamation taking possession of the roads, the President directed that the systems of transportation taken over should remain subject for the time being to all statutes and orders of the Interstate Commerce Commission and the state commissions, but that any orders thereafter made by the Director-General should have paramount authority. Such sweeping authority as was assumed by the President under his war powers, and as was further specifically delegated to him by the Federal Control Act in March, 1918, could not but run foul of existing regulating bodies. The very first order of the Director-General, dated December 29, 1917, authorized the carriers to disregard established routes whenever necessary in the interest of economy and efficiency, and thereby superseded Section 15 of the Interstate Commerce Act, which protected carriers against being short-hauled and which granted to shippers the right to route their freight. By throwing all railroads into one operating system and authorizing the utilization of all terminals, equipment, and facilities, regardless of ownership, this same general order removed the protection granted by Section 3, which gave to carriers exclusive right to use their own tracks and terminals.

But in the matter of rates, as already noted, the limitations upon the Commission's authority were particularly severe. Section 10 of the Federal Control Act gave the President power to initiate rates and put them into effect as an incident to the exercise of his war functions. When once the rates were in effect, complaints might be filed

167

with the Commission, which was then to hold its hearings and to render decisions as to the reasonableness and justice of the rates.[1] Thus far the procedure was a return to that which prevailed between 1906 and 1910 and before the power to suspend rates was conferred upon the Commission. But the analogy was not a close one. For the Commission was instructed by law to give due consideration to the fact that the transportation systems were not in competition, but were being operated as a unit. Moreover, whenever the President found and certified that in order to defray the expenses of federal operation and cover the compensation to the carriers it was necessary to increase revenues, the Commission was required in passing upon such increased rates to take into account the finding and certificate of the President, together with such recommendations as he might make. This rate-making power of the President set aside Section 6 of the Interstate Commerce Act, which required thirty days' notice of a change in rates, for the amount of advance notice of any change was now at the discretion of the President.

This new procedure inevitably grew in importance. The sudden horizontal increase in rates in June, 1918, created a multitude of maladjustments and threw out of gear a closely interlocked rate structure. It was necessary to establish agencies that could handle these local problems in behalf of the central administration. Accordingly, freight traffic committees were organized, consisting of

[1] From Circular No. 1-A, issued by Division of Traffic, U. S. Railroad Administration, July 1, 1918, to traffic committees, railroad and water lines under federal control: "As no authority other than as required by this circular is necessary to change rates, fares, charges, classifications, regulations, or practices applying wholly on carriers under federal control, no application should be made to the Interstate Commerce Commission or to any state commission for authority to advance or modify rates, . . . nor for authority to publish changes therein on short notice, and any such applications made heretofore should be withdrawn."

three general committees at New York, Chicago, and
Atlanta, and a large number of district committees.
These committees, numbering either three or five members each, contained representatives of railroad and shipping interests. At the beginning, the former were always
in the majority, but later representation was equalized.
It was the duty of these committees to conduct hearings and make recommendations for adjustments. Final
action was taken by the Division of Traffic in the Director-General's administration after consultation with the
Division of Public Service. Disagreements were adjusted
by the Director-General. Advice was frequently asked
of the Interstate Commerce Commission and of state
commissions before rates were finally put into effect.

This system of rate adjustment emphasized the sub-
ordinate position that the Interstate Commerce Commission was perforce compelled to take. Moreover, once
the war was over, the system was attacked by shippers'
organizations as autocratic, and Congress was urged to
restore the full powers of the Commission with respect
to suspension and investigation of rates. It was argued
that no disinterested body with authority to act was in
existence, and that the Director-General could decide controverted questions without any semblance of a hearing.
This feeling ripened into a bill which passed both houses
of Congress in November, 1918, giving to the Commission power to suspend rates initiated by the President,
and coupling with it a provision prohibiting the President
from increasing intra-state rates without the prior approval of the state commissions. In his veto message
the President expressed himself as agreeable to the restoration of the power of rate suspension by the Commission, but he could not accept a law that deprived the
federal government of power to make changes freely in
intra-state rates, at the time when the Government was
solely responsible for the operation of the railroads. He

insisted that the practice followed by the Railroad Administration of consulting the Interstate Commerce Commission on matters of fundamental policy insured adequate representation of the public interest, and avoided divided action and delay. The attitude of the Administration toward the method of rate adjustment that it was pursuing is found in the comment of Director Prouty of the Division of Public Service.

"In all my experience with rate making and rate regulation in this country, which goes back almost a quarter of a century, there has been no time when the interest of the shipper in the matter of rate changes was as well protected as it is under the system now in effect, and there never has been a time when on the average, rate changes were made as intelligently and as speedily. I have long insisted that it was of vital importance to the shipper to participate in those preliminary discussions which resulted in the recommendation of a change; and I am confident that, whoever operates the railroads of this country, this idea which is now for the first time recognized will be in some form perpetuated." [1]

Director Prouty's suggestion of carrying over into peace times the plan for conferences between shippers and railroads at the seat of trouble is worthy of serious consideration. Much time and expense would be saved in expediting cases before the commissions and many cases would never have to go there at all. The lack of such official agencies of co-operation is a serious criticism of our regulation policy. It is encouraging to observe that the joint-conference plan in an informal manner is still in use. The restoration of the powers of the Interstate Commerce Commission has removed the main ob-

[1] Hearings, Senate Com. on Interstate Commerce. February, 1919, page 857.

jections to these committees entertained by the shippers' organizations. The elaborate organization of the war period has not been restored, but the spirit of co-operation which is being exhibited between railroad and shipper organizations gives promise that some plan that shall provide a medium for the airing of disputes and a method of orderly procedure for their handling will eventually become a permanent part of our traffic machinery.

In this same connection it is of interest to examine the Division of Public Service of the Railroad Administration, a department that grew almost inevitably out of the new relationship of the railroads and the public. Service and charges were wholly under the control of the Government administration, which felt called upon to examine constantly its own efficiency, and to justify its policy to its patrons. This division expanded its functions steadily, and was of especial importance during the second year of federal administration. It was responsible for the traffic committees already described, upon which the shippers were represented. It created special terminal committees to increase efficiency at these points. It had advisory power, and later joint jurisdiction with the Division of Traffic over rates, and handled all complaints concerning rates filed by the public. It supervised the relationship between the Railroad Administration and the state commissions, and through its Bureau of Complaints it disposed of a multitude of grievances that poured in by letter from discontented shippers and travellers.[1] Many matters of freight and passenger service never before regulated were taken cognizance of. The enthusiastic Director of the division called it a full-

---

[1] Adjustments made by the Bureau of Suggestions and Complaints ranged all the way from the installation of additional passenger-trains down to the inclusion in the menu on the dining-cars of shredded-wheat biscuit, at the request of a passenger who stated that he missed this cereal from the menu on that train for the first time in six years.

fledged public-service commission, which was something of an exaggeration, in view of the fact that the agency that performed the service and made the rates was the same that entertained the complaints and conducted the investigations. However, its experience was doubtless of material influence in extending the Commission's regulating power over service in the legislation of 1920.

While the war legislation did not in so many words shear the Commission of its power to determine the reasonableness of rates once a complaint had been presented, yet when the question was one of adequate revenue rather than one involving the rate on a specific shipment, it at once became a question of public policy in which the Commission was left with little discretion. The findings and the certificate of the Director-General, the personal representative of the President of the United States, were given by the statute a weight that left the Commission little choice except to approve the schedule as a whole.

Such issues as have given the Commission the opportunity to assert its independence of the federal Railroad Administration may be illustrated by the case of Willamette Valley Lumberman's Association v. South Pacific Co.[1] This was a case of undue preference. Complaint was entered before the Director-General instituted his increases in June, 1918, and the preference was enhanced by this increase. It was the argument of the Director-General that the words "reasonable and just" in the Control Act had a meaning different from that applied to them in the Act to Regulate Commerce, and that the rates initiated by the Director-General were in themselves and in relation to each other presumed to be right, and could not be changed without an affirmative showing that they were wrong. The first contention the Commission denied. To the second, it replied that there was

[1] 51 I. C. C., 250 (1918).

no authority in the Control Act for perpetuating during federal control a rate adjustment that was unlawful under the Act to Regulate Commerce; that the increases initiated by the Director-General were merely superimposed on the existing basis of rate adjustment, which all the evidence showed was unreasonable and unjust. "It is inconceivable," said the Commission, "that the Congress did a vain thing in conferring upon this Commission power to determine whether or not the rates initiated by the Director-General are just and reasonable." An appropriate order was entered against the defendants, including the Director-General.

The authority of the Commission was again challenged in connection with various applications for relief from the 4th Section (the long and short haul clause), and it was urged that the power to grant relief was in suspense during the period of federal control. It was the position of the Commission,[1] maintained throughout this period, that the Act to Regulate Commerce was in full force, except so far as it was inconsistent with the Federal Control Act, that there was nothing in the Control Act or in the President's proclamation to indicate that Section 4 was a hindrance to the prosecution of the war and should be set aside, and that accordingly it would be enforced. Generally speaking, the Director-General declined to regard carriers' applications for relief from Section 4, and during the federal-control period most of the applications filed were by roads not under Government operation. Yet in numerous instances rates were established by the Director-General that constituted violations of the clause and which remained in effect during federal control. Correction of these maladjustments has proceeded slowly during 1921.

So far as rates not under federal control were concerned, they were subject in all their interstate relations

[1] 51 I. C. C., 356 (November, 1918).

to the Act to Regulate Commerce, and the Commission still had its former jurisdiction over joint traffic between federal and non-federal roads. But this jurisdiction covered a relatively insignificant portion of the traffic of the country.

In the field occupied by the state commissions, the federal Railroad Administration exhibited even less regard for the sensibilities of regulating authority. General Order No. 28, increasing freight and passenger rates, was made specifically applicable to intra-state as well as interstate traffic. In matters of service the Railroad Administration proceeded with almost no recognition of even the existence of state commissions. Relations became strained as a consequence of the creation of district traffic committees, already described. It became the practice of many railroad officials to disregard the jurisdiction of state commissions and to take up rate matters with these traffic committees instead. This was only natural, because the ultimate determination of the rate rested with the Railroad Administration in Washington rather than with any state authority. Local feeling became articulate in resolutions adopted at the meeting of the National Association of Railway and Utilities Commissioners in October, 1918, in which the members demanded full authority on the part of the states, and declared that in any event it was the duty of each state commission to exercise and maintain its authority to the extent that it might deem the public interest demanded. It declared further that "the Association is emphatically of the opinion that any plan for the future operation of the railroads should fully safeguard the powers of local tribunals, responsible to the people of the several states, with respect to rates, service and facilities intra-state in character." The issue was most sharply drawn in connection with express rates which were filed by the Director-General in 1918. Suits were instituted against their application intra-state in Nebraska, Iowa, South Dakota, and Minnesota. These issues were all disposed of by the Supreme Court decision in the North Dakota case mentioned later.

During the war, the Federal Railroad Administration never squarely met the issue and never officially interpreted its powers. In practice, it initiated state rates and filed them with the state commissions "for information only." In matters of service, it asserted its complete authority. Early in 1919, the war being ended, and plans being under way for a return to a peace basis, the Railroad Administration, after conference with representatives of state commissions, announced a formal policy in matters that might come into conflict with state jurisdiction. Transportation systems under federal control were to continue subject to the lawful police regulations of the several states in matters relating to spur tracks, railroad crossings, safety appliances and train service, and it was to be the policy of the Director-General to cause the orders of the state commissions to be carried out. Attention was called, however, to the financial condition of the roads, and it was assumed that expenditures would be ordered by the state commissions only after full consideration of the needs and difficulties of the United States in operating the railroads. As for rate matters, the Directors of Traffic and Public Service were ordered, before authorizing important advances in rates, state or interstate, to submit them for advice and suggestion to the commissions in the states affected. Carriers were ordered, for the purpose of maintaining the continuity of state records, to file with state commissions, for information only, all rate schedules and annual and other reports required by state statutes. As to the division of authority over rates, the conference disagreed, and the Director-General announced his purpose to expedite a decision at law by the appropriate tribunal. The opportunity arose in a case in North Dakota in which the Supreme Court of that state directed the issue of a peremptory writ of mandamus, ordering the railroads to desist from collecting on intra-state business any other charges than those on file with the State Board of Railroad Commissioners. Upon appeal the Supreme Court of the United States upheld the authority of the Director-General as a war power and sustained the rate-making functions embodied in the Federal Control Act.[1] Notwithstanding this decision, the Director-General continued to seek the advice of state commissions in matters affecting rates. Their assistance was as a rule cheerfully offered, and was influential in shaping the final conclusions.

[1] 250 U. S., 135 (June 2, 1919).

CHAPTER XIII

THE GOVERNMENT AND LABOR

As has been already pointed out, the critical character of the labor situation was one of the factors that led to the nationalization of the railroads during the war. Trouble had long been brewing, the gravity of which railroad managements had been unable to abate. Long before our entrance into the war, railroads traversing manufacturing sections were losing their men to munition plants and other industries, some roads turning their mechanical forces over two and three times in the year. Wages were steadily rising and the quality of service was, because of war-pressure, steadily falling. With the inauguration of the draft, the situation became still more acute, invading not only the mechanical forces but all departments of the railroads. From that time on the experience of railroads throughout the country was the same, a constant struggle to hold their organizations together, and continuous concessions in wages. Former methods of negotiation were abandoned. Threatened strikes overnight necessitated adjustments on a few hours' notice to avoid breakdown of the organization. Very considerable increases in wages took place in the classes of telegraphers, station clerks, platform labor, and the like, and among the mechanical forces wages soared to unprecedented heights. One of the classes that received the largest percentage of increase was that of unskilled labor.

The labor problem, so far as it affects train operation, concerns itself with the activities of the four brotherhoods, which include in their membership nearly all the employees in the classes of locomotive enginemen and firemen, conductors, brakemen, flagmen, and other train-men, approximating 400,000 men. It will be recalled that a nation-wide strike of all these employees set for Labor Day, 1916, was only averted by the passage by Congress of the Adamson Eight Hour Law, and that under threat of a strike the railroads granted the basic eight-hour day provided for by the congressional enact-ment without waiting for the decision of the Supreme Court concerning its constitutionality.

Here the matter rested until November, 1917, when the increasing cost of living and the wage increases being granted in other industries produced an uneasiness among the rank and file of some of the trainmen's organizations which it was apparently impossible for the leaders to suppress. When it became clear that definite demands for increases were being formulated and that, in spite of the efforts of the official federal mediator, a clash was impending, the President called the leaders of the four brotherhoods into conference on November 22. The public information concerning the results of this con-ference is contained in two statements, one of which was given out by the brotherhoods, and was as follows:

"The men who comprise the railway brotherhoods are thorough Americans, therefore they believe in American standards of living, and in consequence of this realize that standards of pay that were established in 1912 and 1913 are inadequate to meet present-day prices for com-modities, and for that reason are demanding an increase in present rates that will meet half at least of the increase in cost of those things which they are compelled to pur-chase.

"They want to co-operate in every way that is at all possible in the successful prosecution of the war, and they fully realize that the most serious thing that could occur during the conduct of war would be any interruption of railway transportation, and they, in common with the great body of the people, are determined to do everything within the bounds of reason to avoid such interruption.

"Being fully conversant with their attitude and desire in this matter, we are in a position to give the assurance that, if the situation should arise which would threaten the interruption of transportation the men whom we represent would be more than willing to discuss and consider any solution of the difficulty which presented itself, doing so in the spirit of patriotic co-operation, and would undoubtedly co-operate with the government to the utmost extent in arriving at a just, equitable, as well as patriotic conclusion."

The other statement was the President's, to the effect that "he had got from the interview exactly the impression conveyed by the statement of the heads of the brotherhoods, namely, that the men whom they represented were not inclined to contend for anything which they did not deem necessary to their own maintenance and the maintenance of their families, and that they would be willing in case any critical situation of controversy should arise to consider any proposed solution in a spirit of accommodation and of patriotic purpose."

On November 19 the Railroads' War Board sent a letter to the President in which it declared, in answer to his inquiry as to the railroad attitude concerning the manner of settlement of wage disputes during the war, that they adhered to the principle of arbitration as a general rule of action, but, to prevent interruption of operation in the midst of war, they would place their interests in the hands of the President for such disposition as the public welfare might require.

Two of the brotherhoods presented on December 1 to practically every railroad in the country demands for

increases approximating 40 per cent, and the others had
the matter under consideration when the Government
took over the roads. Co-operation under the Railroads'
War Board had accomplished much from the operating
standpoint, but it was of little use in the handling of the
labor question. It represented management compactly
organized which, in the face of the serious financial situation, was inclined to grant increases in wages only after
being clubbed into submission.

One of the divisions set up by the federal administration was the Division of Labor, the head of which was
the chief of the Brotherhood of Railroad Firemen and
Enginemen. One of the first general orders of the Director-General created a Railroad Wage Commission, under
instructions to make a broad general investigation that
should include the relation of railroad wages to those in
other industries, and the relation of different classes of
labor to each other, the wage conditions in different parts
of the country, the immediate emergency of the war, and
the high cost of living. The recommendations of this
Commission for immediate relief were based upon an investigation of the increase in living costs since December,
1915, and recommended increases for all employees receiving less than $250 per month, graded from an increase
of 43 per cent for all receiving $50 per month and not
less than $46 (under $46 a flat increase of $20), down to
an increase of $1 for those receiving above $248 and not
more than $249 per month. These increases were applied
to the rates in effect December 31, 1915, and were to be
diminished by the amount of any increase received since
that time. Reductions in hours were not to be regarded
as increases in pay. Existing hours of service and existing rules and conditions of payment were not to be dis-
turbed during the war period. It was pointed out that
80 per cent of the employees were receiving not over $100
per month, and that the number receiving from $150 to

$250 per month included less than 3 per cent (excluding officers).

Director-General McAdoo, in putting this award into effect, made some additional increases by way of the establishment of minima for the shop crafts and common labor, but the most significant departure from the recommendations of the Wage Commission was the formal recognition of the principle of the "basic eight-hour day" in all railroad employment, a principle which had been sanctioned by law for the train organizations through the passage of the Adamson Act. However, overtime was to be paid pro rata unless existing agreements provided otherwise.

Following the suggestion of the Wage Commission, a Board of Railroad Wages and Working Conditions, advisory to the Director-General, was set up to hear and investigate matters relating to inequalities in pay and regulations and the larger questions of labor policy. There were also created in succession four bipartisan boards of adjustment, consisting equally of representatives of the railroads and the employees, to which under a signed "memorandum of understanding" the railroad managements and the unions of organized employees agreed to submit their controversies growing out of the interpretation of wage schedules, that could not be adjusted locally on the individual systems. For the adjustment of disputes with unorganized employees, an official was appointed under the Division of Labor of the Railroad Administration.

So far as wages were concerned, the increases granted by the original Wage Commission proved inadequate, particularly for those classes that had received increases since December, 1915. The outcome was an apparently endless series of increases for various classes, including the shop crafts, clerks, telegraphers, employees of express and sleeping-car companies, and finally the four brotherhoods in April, 1919. The Board of Railroad Wages and Working Conditions announced that these increases were generally less than those granted for similar work outside, but were awarded with the idea of creating a wage structure that would survive the war period. This war cycle of wage increases, officially declared to be complete in the spring of 1919, had accumulated an addition to operating expenses estimated at $965,000,000 per year. The table[1] on the following page, prepared by the Railroad Administration, analyzes these increases for the two years, and shows when each increase became effective. According to Director-General Hines, the increases when measured on the basis of hourly rates were only slightly over 100 per cent, which were not as great as in many other industries.

But the employees were by no means satisfied. Comparing their increases with those of men engaged in nonrailroad employment and feeling the pressure of a constantly rising cost of living, all classes made further demands. Unauthorized strikes broke out, and the trouble came to a head in August when the question was officially taken up by the President of the United States. He took the ground that no general demands for permanent increases should be granted until the question could be determined whether the prevailing cost of living was to continue indefinitely. It was the time when the Attorney-General was making his spectacular and futile descent upon the alleged profiteer, and the employees at the suggestion of the President laid aside their demands to await the fall in the cost of living which they were given to think was speedily to result from the Administration's policy. Of course nothing came of it, and early in 1920 the employees urged a prompt granting of the increases on the ground that a sufficient time had elapsed

[1] From hearing before subcommittee of House Committee on Appropriations, April 12, 1920, page 210.

ESTIMATED ANNUAL INCREASES IN COMPENSATION
BASED UPON AWARD OF RAILROAD WAGE COM-
MISSION AND SUPPLEMENTS THERETO

	EMPLOYEES AFFECTED	EFFECTIVE DATE	ESTIMATED ANNUAL INCREASE IN PAY-ROLL, CHARGEABLE TO OPERATING EXPENSES
General Order 27 (substantially recommendation of Lane Commission)	All employees receiving less than $250 per month	1918 Jan. 1	$360,000,000
Supplement No. 4	Shop employees	"	209,000,000
Supplements 7 and 8	Maintenance of way employees and clerks	Sept. 1	190,000,000
Supplement 13	Agents and operators	Oct. 1	25,000,000
Supplements 14, 17, and 18	Policemen, dining and sleeping car employees	1919 Jan. 1	8,000,000
Supplements 15 and 16	Enginemen and trainmen	"	60,000,000
Increase in pay under equalization adjustment effective May 1, 1919	Shop employees	May 1	50,000,000
Time and one-half for overtime allowed	Enginemen and trainmen in road freight service	Dec. 1	38,000,000
Time and one-half for overtime and other adjustments in pay	Maintenance of way employees Clerks	Dec. 16 1919 Jan. 1 1920	25,000,000
Total...			$965,000,000

to demonstrate that the high level of prices was to continue. But the President now urged that they should await the return of the roads to their owners, which had already been arranged for, and should make use of whatever machinery for labor adjustment Congress might provide in the legislation then pending. Following the passage of the Transportation Act of 1920, it took still further outbreaks on the part of labor and urgent solicitation on the part of the labor leaders to obtain action by the President for the appointment of the Railroad Labor Board, upon the shoulders of which now fell the accumulated burden of a year of labor controversy. It has been necessary to describe in detail the slow and reluctant steps in the history of labor's efforts to get satisfaction, in order that one may appreciate the significance of the outlaw strikes of 1920 and the difficulties that labor leaders experienced in keeping their membership in hand. Dissatisfaction with the dilatoriness of the Government was wide-spread and anarchic elements were quick to take advantage of the situation. While the federal administration had doubtless some defense for its attitude in the impending return of the roads to their owners, yet a careful survey of the last year of federal operation reflects little glory upon its handling of the labor situation in its broad national aspects. It is a period which should be thoughtfully investigated by one who is attempting to decide whether Government operation of railroads is the proper policy for the United States.

From the standpoint of those who are seeking a satisfactory form of organization for the peace-time settlement of industrial conflicts, the bipartisan adjustment boards of the war period are of more than transitory interest. These boards were proposed by Director Carter of the Division of Labor as a means of restoring the morale and efficiency of the employees and as a substitute for the arbitration board which had proved so unsatisfactory in the pre-war period. It was argued by the Director that partisanship would disappear and judicial-mindedness would take its place when there was no longer a neutral arbitrator present to divide the forces into hostile camps. That these four boards accomplished the work assigned them with extraordinary success, there is no doubt. The labor leaders stood by the Government. A large majority of the decisions of these boards were unanimous, and there was agreement in practically every one of the thousands of cases before them. Railroad Adjustment Board No. 1, which took jurisdiction over controversies involving the four brotherhoods, functioned more smoothly than the other three, because negotiations in this field were based on a longer experience with collective bargaining. In every case that came before it its decision was unanimous.

The origin of this particular board is interesting. It will be recalled that in March, 1917, a committee of the Council of National Defense intervened, at the request of the President, to prevent a strike of the four brotherhoods over their demand for the immediate introduction of the eight-hour day. Their award was accepted by carriers and employees, but it had to be applied to 150 railroads with their hundreds of individual contracts and with their complex and varied agreements. It was obvious that controversies would arise and that some agency would be necessary to interpret the agreements. Accordingly, the railroads and the brotherhoods set up a bipartisan commission of eight members as interpreter of agreements. This "Commission of Eight" was in existence until superseded by Railroad Adjustment Board No. 1, four of the old members taking places on the new board.

The success of the Commission of Eight and likewise of its successor, both from the standpoint of the performance of its specific job and from that of its ultimate effect upon the public welfare, is due to two facts. First, it was a board of experts of long experience in dealing with the intricate questions of railroad wage schedules. There was no guessing, no splitting of differences. Decisions were the reasoned judgment of experience. In the second place, its authority was strictly limited. It had no power to fix new wage scales or conditions of employment. Its duty was to interpret and apply wage schedules already generally in force. There is no opportunity under such limitations for collusion between railroads and employees at the expense of the public. A bipartisan board with power to make an initial wage award, and hence in position to pass over to the public whatever increases it sees fit to make, would be quite another matter.

Increase in the wage bill was not the only result of the labor machinery set up during the war, nor was it the most significant result. The increases were inevitable and, as has already been said, were moderate compared with those made outside. Of much more significance were the standard rules and working conditions that emanated from this centralized authority. At the very beginning of federal operation the Director-General announced that no discrimination would be made in employment because of membership or non-membership in labor organizations. This had very definite results. It provoked a declaration by the unions in favor of the open shop, and an assurance of benefits to non-union employees under existing agreements equal to those accorded to members. It stimulated the introduction of unionism upon roads where it had not before prevailed and where in many cases it had been definitely prohibited by the managements.

As already indicated, the Director-General formally established the basic eight-hour day for all railroad labor. This was followed up by supplementary orders based upon recommendations of the Board of Railroad Wages and Working Conditions, which contributed materially to convert a theoretical into an actual eight-hour day. Where previous to federal control classes of labor had by negotiation secured to a considerable extent the eight-hour day with time and a half for overtime, the policy was extended to all employees in that class throughout the country. Where labor had not won this advanced position previous to federal control, pro rata payment was authorized for the ninth and tenth hours and time and a half thereafter. In connection with the establishment of this basic policy the Director-General, in order to meet the emergency demands for repair of equipment, appealed to the shop forces as a patriotic duty to accept an arrangement for a seventy-hour week. This was effected and continued in force until the armistice, when it was promptly reduced to the eight-hour-day basis with time and a half for overtime.[1]

Under the same central organization, standard working rules were established providing for uniform administration of discipline and the maintenance of seniority principles. The question of the continuation or abolition of piece-work in the shops was put to a vote of the employees themselves, and following the will of a "substantial majority" piece-work was done away with on one road after another. There was to be no discrimination in pay for women's labor and that of colored employees.

Inevitably the standardizing process led up to the movement for national agreements that would assure uniform conditions throughout the country. In contrast

[1] The Railroad Administration conceded to men in freight service, for the abandonment of certain allowances and arbitraries, time and one-half for overtime, effective December 1, 1919. This was the feature that had been waived at the time of the passage of the Adamson Eight Hour Law.

with the situation among the trainmen, the shop crafts, when the roads were taken over, were working under different rates and different conditions on the various roads, and were even shifting from one road to another to take advantage of superior conditions. After much negotiation a national agreement was finally approved and made effective October 20, 1919, which defined the working conditions with more particularity than was done in the general orders issued by the Administration. This agreement was followed by one with the maintenance-of-way employees, effective in December. Another was signed with the clerks, effective January 1, 1920, another with the firemen and oilers, January 16, and finally one with the signalmen, effective February 1, 1920. It should be observed that all of these agreements were negotiated after the President had announced his intention to return the roads to their owners, and that three of them were signed after the President had issued his proclamation of relinquishment.

It was these national agreements, standardizing practice throughout the country irrespective of local conditions, that furnished the matter of most serious controversy before the Railroad Labor Board after the return of the roads to their owners, and the issue involved will be discussed in the later connection. It is sufficient at this point to note the gains that railroad labor made in its strategic position during the period of the war. It deserves great credit for its loyal and efficient service, and the country is particularly under obligation to its leaders for their patience and restraint during the trying year and a half following the armistice, when the Government put them off with one pretext after another. But for all this they exacted their pay. Their goal was a definite one, and they advanced toward it with unwavering step. Their purpose could not be better stated than in the words of Director-General McAdoo in his annual report for 1918. "But for the possible early return of the railroads to private control it could safely be said that the logical conclusion of the work of the present Board of Railroad Wages and Working Conditions would be standardized rates, standardized days, and other standardized conditions of employment for all employees on railroads under federal control."

It is not without significance that the leaders of the railroad unions and a large body of the membership indorsed the movement for permanent nationalization following the war experience. This sudden shifting of position on the part of the leaders, most of whom had previously been opposed to the policy, can be interpreted as a shrewd estimate of what federal management meant to them. They had had their first taste in the Adamson Act. Upon this as a foundation they built up their powerful national organization of the war time, under the sympathetic observation of the first Director-General and with the active assistance of his Director of Labor. It is no exaggeration to say that the gains made by railroad labor during the twenty-six months of federal operation in the power of collective bargaining, in the development of union organization, in the standardization and nationalization of practices and policies, were greater than in the entire previous period of their existence. That they desire to perpetuate these gains under private operation is no more than human.

To the question of the loyalty and efficiency with which labor worked during federal operation, there is no exact answer possible. There was a constant turnover due to the greater attractiveness of other industry and to the call for military service. Labor was diluted and inefficiency resulted. The patriotic stimulus during 1918 doubtless kept the labor effort up to the maximum, but it was not as productive as pre-war labor. Under the uncertain conditions of the following year, when employees were in doubt as to who their future employer was to be, when agitation for Government ownership was active among them, when, moreover, the development of national standards and the increasing centralization of wage adjustment were breaking down the old personal relationship between manager and men, there was a noticeable decline in morale and a lessening of efficiency. However, it was the conclusion of Director-General Hines, reached after long and careful observation of the labor situation, that the war spirit resulted in less effective work everywhere, and that on the whole the decline in efficiency was greater in other lines of industry than on the railroads.

The frequently reiterated charge that the federal administration carried on its pay-rolls several hundred thousand unnecessary employees had no basis in fact, and arose from the general introduction of the eight-hour day, which increased necessarily the number of persons performing the work. Director-General Hines in his final report presented a table showing that while the number of employees increased, the number of hours worked remained almost the same, and in 1919 slightly declined. Neither did the hours worked keep pace with increase in traffic. Portions of this table are here reproduced.

	CALENDAR YEAR			
	1916	1917	1918	1919 (Partly estimated)
Number of employees..	1,647,097	1,723,734	1,820,660	1,891,607
Hours worked........	5,189,790,716	5,406,878,384	5,641,820,405	5,126,142,664
Average hours per employee per month...	263	261	258	226
Per cent of year 1916:				
Hours worked......	100	104.2	108.7	98.8
Revenue ton-miles..	100	108.3	111.2	100.2
Passenger-miles.....	100	113.8	122.9	133.6

CHAPTER XIV

No complete income account or balance-sheet has been issued by the Railroad Administration that shows in simple fashion the transactions between the railroads and the Government. In fact, there have been so many offsetting accounts and adjustments that probably no such simplified statement is possible. It is not the intention here to follow this financial relationship in detail, but merely to set forth the significant transactions and the more important results. In any survey of the finances of the period it should be recalled that the Government's interest did not end with the return of the roads to their owners, but continued for an additional six months in the form of a guarantee, which was an extension of the contract of the control period. From the standpoint of finance there is little distinction between the two periods, and they will be treated together in this discussion.

The terms of the contract between Government and railroads need not be repeated in detail, but the pertinent provisions should here be recalled. In addition to the guarantee of an annual net operating income equivalent to the average of the three test years, the Director-General was required to charge to operating expense a sufficient amount for maintenance and depreciation to make sure that the roads would be returned to their owners in as good condition as when received. Any excess expenditures deemed necessary in the interest of safety to overcome previous undermaintenance were to be charged to

---

[1] In the preparation of this chapter the author has been greatly assisted by studies (unpublished) made by the Bureau of Railway Economics.

the roads. Additions and betterments that were undertaken for war purposes were to be paid for by the Government, all others were to be charged to the carriers. But no deduction from the amount owed by the Government to the roads could be made by the Government to cover maintenance or betterments that would impair the ability of the carriers to meet interest, sinking-fund, and tax requirements. The Director-General could allocate motive power to the roads to the extent he deemed necessary. The $500,000,000 revolving fund might be used by the President not only to cover deficits in operation but to provide for additions and betterments, to cover maturing obligatibns, to reorganize bankrupt roads, and to purchase the securities of the roads. In other words, the Government's funds were to be used for two main purposes: first, to cover any deficit necessary to fulfil the contract with the carriers, and, second, to provide capital necessary for additional facilities and for refunding.

In the first place, it will be necessary to determine the total of funds available to the federal administration, which it employed in its capacity as lessee of the railroads. By the Federal Control Act of March 1918, $500,000,000 was appropriated as a revolving fund to be used for the various purposes already described. This fund proved insufficient to meet the operating deficit of 1918, to provide for necessary additions and betterments, and to take care of critical financial situations on certain properties. Accordingly, a request was made in January 1919, for an additional appropriation of $750,-000,000. It is not without its bearing upon the fundamental problem whether a Government can safely be intrusted in time of peace with the management of its transportation facilities that this appropriation failed of passage in the Senate because of a political filibuster, creating thereby a most serious situation in the Railroad Administration, and compelling resort to every possible expedient to secure funds. Payment of bills was post-poned, loans were called, the assistance of the War Finance Corporation was invoked, the War Department paid $100,000,000 of claims without waiting for the necessary vouchers. By the time Congress met in extraordinary session, the request of the Railroad Administration had increased to $1,200,000,000, but Congress appropriated only the $750,000,000 originally asked for. This was available on July 1.

The request for $1,200,000,000 had been based upon the belief that deficits in operation were at an end. But with the fall of the year came the steel and coal strikes and the sharp decline in earnings. This, combined with the fact that the congressional appropriation fell short of the estimated requirements by $450,000,000, again placed the Railroad Administration in a position of financial difficulty. But no further appropriations were available until the passage of the Transportation Act of 1920. In that measure Congress appropriated $200,000,000 for the purpose of winding up the Government's relations to the railroads, and, in response to the request of Director-General Hines in April following, appropriated an additional $300,000,000. Therefore there was available to the Railroad Administration from January 1, 1918, to September 1, 1920, by direct grant a total of $1,750,-000,000.

Furthermore, the Transportation Act of 1920 provided that any valid claims against the Administration arising out of transactions during the period of federal control should be paid out of the loan fund which the Act established. These claims have been estimated at $40,000,-000, and this amount should be added to the assets of the Administration, making a total available by congressional grant of $1,790,000,000.

Technically speaking, the Administration's treasury was also enhanced by its expropriation of cash balances from the railroad treasuries—"working balances," as they were called. These balances, taken over at the beginning of federal control, aggregated over $300,000,000. But it should be noted that at the same time the Administration assumed outstanding current liabilities to an amount estimated to be in excess of the cash obtained. Hence, these additional funds had little or no significance for the transactions of the control period.

Reference has already been made to the assistance of the War Finance Corporation during the trying months of 1919. Certificates of indebtedness were issued by the Government to roads in lieu of cash to the amount of $193,000,000, which the roads used as collateral for loans, either from the banks or the War Finance Corporation, to the extent of about 80 per cent of their face value, the Government agreeing to reimburse the roads for the difference between the 5 per cent interest that the certificates bore and a maximum of 6 per cent that the railroads might have to pay. These certificates to the amount of $92,000,000 were likewise issued to equipment companies to whom payments were due. They were all retired out of the $750,000,000 appropriation available July 1.

The operating side of the Government's account may best be presented in tabular form.[1]

Deficit from operation of Class I roads, Jan., 1918–Feb., 1920	$677,513,152
Deficit, other railroads, Pullman Co., refrigerator-car, and steamship lines	43,011,129
Deficit, American Railway Express	38,111,742
Deficit, inland waterways	2,449,739
Amount needed to replace stocks of materials and supplies taken over	85,204,618
Net interest and other debt adjustments	40,233,396
Expenses R. R. Administration to March 1, 1920	13,954,980
	$900,478,756

[1] From statement of Director-General Hines before subcommittee of House Committee on Appropriations, April 1920, page 84.

In addition, the administrative expenses of the Railroad Administration from March 1, 1920, to December 31, 1920, were estimated at $3,445,222, which brought the total net loss through 1920 up to $903,923,978.

In a letter to the House Committee on Appropriations dated May 5, 1921, Director-General Davis, in charge of the liquidation of the affairs of the Railroad Administration, raised the estimate of the operating loss to the Government considerably beyond that of Mr. Hines in the previous year—the result of more complete information in relation to the contract obligations of the Government. The controversy as to whether the short lines were under federal control and were entitled to compensation for the first six months of 1918 before they were formally relinquished having been decided by referees in favor of the railroads, an allowance for this had to be added. Unfinished contracts on inland waterways were by the Transportation Act of 1920 made an obligation of the Railroad Administration. Then there were claims for loss and damage arising out of the Minnesota forest-fire in 1918, personal-injury claims, fire losses on carriers' property, omitted or underestimated allowances for undermaintenance of road and equipment, and additions and betterments made solely for war purposes. All of these items, it was reckoned, would add $300,-000,000 to the original estimate, thereby establishing an operating loss of over $1,200,000,000.

But this estimate was based upon the assumption that the Administration could settle with the roads under its interpretation of the upkeep section of the standard contract. It was the contention of the Government that the contract recognized the impossibility of determining maintenance at the beginning and end of federal control by any physical comparison, and that a full compliance would be secured by adjusting differences by the accounting method and measuring the liability of the Adminis-

tration for labor and materials by the amount expended
for the same purposes during the three-year test period,
after equating for changes in price. The carriers, on
the other hand, argued that they were entitled to a
physical comparison, so that, quoting the standard contract, "the result shall be, as nearly as practicable, the
same relative amount, character, and durability of physical reparation." This contention found its support in
the demonstrated "inefficiency of labor" resulting from
employment of inexperienced workmen, the abolition of
piecework, and a generally lowered morale. A day's work
did not bring the same result during the war as before,
and the loss to the road was not compensated by a payment of the difference in wages. But the fate of this contention is probably indicated in the ruling of the Interstate Commerce Commission in August 1921,[1] which it
made in connection with the fulfilment of the statutory
mandate requiring it to determine the amount that the
carriers could charge to maintenance during the six
months' guarantee period. Had the contract contemplated, says the Commission, a determination of the
relative efficiency of labor at different periods, it would
have said so in unmistakable language. Any method
involving comparison of actual physical results would
lead to prolonged controversy and reliance upon opinion.
The clear and easily applied test was that which was
based upon the accounts and in which due allowance
was made for changes in wages and in hours of service
per day.

It was Director-General Hines's view that maintenance
on the whole had been in accord with contract, that the
roads were returned in as good condition as they were
received. He held that many roads were overmaintained,
and that this overmaintenance would more than offset
the undermaintenance that prevailed elsewhere. But

[1] I. C. C. Finance Docket No. 1176.

Director-General Davis explained that the claims for undermaintenance would run from $700,000,000 to $800,000,000 when all the roads had completed their surveys, and that as the Administration's claims for overmaintenance were not sufficient in amount to offset these demands, some allowance would have to be made for this item. However, he reported that he had settled claims up to July 15, 1921, aggregating $226,000,000 for $68,000,000, which seems to indicate that the railroads had exaggerated their claims for trading purposes, and were disposed to shrink them in face of an offer of cash.

There is no way of reaching an accurate conclusion as to the condition of maintenance of way and equipment at the end of federal control. No physical inventory of materials and supplies was made when the systems were taken over, neither was there any physical survey of the roads themselves. In 1919 there was a disposition on the part of the Director-General, because of the operating deficit, to reduce maintenance expenditures to the narrowest limits. It was evidently easier and safer to entertain claims for undermaintenance from the roads than to prove and sustain the fact of overexpenditure when the final settlement day should come. There is general agreement among unprejudiced experts that in those items capable of measurement, such as ties, rails, and ballast, deficiency undoubtedly existed. Way and structures, generally speaking, were in poorer condition at the end of the period than at the beginning. While locomotives were well maintained, cars were not. Physical depreciation there undoubtedly was, but the carriers were unable to establish the claim and to make it consistent with a reasonable interpretation of contract requirements.

The Administration policy concerning capital expenditures and the method of payment therefor by the carriers has aroused much public interest and comment and prolonged controversy. It is therefore of importance to consider it in detail. Based upon an investigation of capital needs made immediately upon the initiation of federal control, there was authorized by the Division of Capital Expenditures during 1918 the amount of $1,279,-000,000, of which $573,000,000 was for additions and betterments, $659,000,000 for equipment, and $47,000,-000 for extensions, branches, and other lines. Aside from appropriations made directly for war purposes, approval was confined to such expenditures as were necessary for safety in operation, or to provide a needed increased capacity, and any expenditure not required for these purposes was in most cases deferred.

The policy was laid down by the Administration of authorizing improvements to effect permanent economies only when the economy was so great that the cost could probably be saved during the period of federal control. Hence the large items of expenditures were additional main tracks, yard tracks and sidings, shop buildings, engine-houses and appurtenances, and locomotives and cars. Standardized locomotives to the number of 1,930 were ordered and 100,000 freight-cars of the less specialized types. No passenger-cars of any sort were purchased by the Railroad Administration.

In 1919, the war having ceased, the Administration took the position that inasmuch as it was clear that Congress and the people wished a prompt return of the railroads to private operation, no expenditures should be made from Government funds unless absolutely necessary. Equipment orders in 1919 were confined to 600 locomotives, and in general the expenditures covered contracts entered into previous to the armistice. Moreover, the failure of the $750,000,000 appropriation in March 1919, necessitated rigid economy and forced a postponement of even such expenditures as had been contemplated. By the time the money was available in July, demands of all sorts had so increased, and the assurance of a speedy return to private operation was so much greater, that no projects of any kind were undertaken.

The following table, constructed from a statement of Director-General Davis to the Senate Committee on Interstate Commerce, shows succinctly how the relations of Government and carriers concerning capital expenditures stood in the spring of 1921.

CAPITAL EXPENDITURES—PERIOD OF FEDERAL CONTROL

Expenditures for new equipment (100,000 cars and 2,000 locomotives):		
Paid for in cash by the carriers...	$71,000,000	
Equipment trust certificates issued..........................	310,000,000	
		$381,000,000
Additions and betterments chargeable to the carriers:		
Long-term notes already taken by the Government.................	61,000,000	
Unfunded........................	702,000,000	
		763,000,000
Total capital expenditures, period of federal control.................	....	$1,144,000,000

The average expenditure of less than $600,000,000 per year for the war period is evidence of the faithfulness with which the Administration adhered to the policy of authorizing only such projects as were imperatively needed.

Equipment purchased was allocated from time to time to the various roads according to the Administration's estimate of the needs of the carriers. This policy aroused vigorous protest because of the high cost of equipment, the excess over normal being a burden that the roads insisted should be borne by the Government as a war cost. Moreover, they claimed either that they did not need equipment at all or that they could not use the type that was assigned to them. This controversy was the most bitter and persistent that arose in the relations of railroads to the Government during the entire period of federal operation. And only when it became clear that they could not buy equipment to any greater advantage, and that the equipment must be had, did the carriers finally accept it. They were induced to yield by an arrangement under which the Government undertook temporarily to carry the cost for them. Equipment trusts for 100 per cent of the purchase price were accepted from the various roads. Under an act approved in November 1919, the Government had the option of holding these notes until maturity, of selling them on the market, or of placing them behind an issue of obligations by a nonprofit national equipment corporation to be organized for the purpose. Some roads paid for the equipment in cash, but many issued equipment notes. These were held by the Government and amounted, as shown in the table, to $310,000,000. They are payable in annual instalments, and limited in maturity by statute to fifteen years.

It was the opinion of Director-General Davis that the unfunded expenditures for additions and betterments would not need to be completely funded, as some companies would take care of portions of the indebtedness by cash payment, and others would not be able to furnish security satisfactory to the Government. He thought the necessary funding would be under $500,000,000.

In addition to these investments there were miscellaneous financial transactions effected during the war period which must be included. Long-term notes amounting to $44,000,000 consisted principally of collateral loans to the New Haven road. Holdings of stocks and bonds of railroad companies to the extent of $35,000,000 included bonds of the Boston and Maine purchased to promote the reorganization of that road and to finance certain additions and betterments. In this category was also included American Railway Express Company stock to the amount of $3,600,000 and Southern Railway bonds for $2,350,000. Receivers' certificates were also purchased, among them being those of the Denver and Salt Lake and the International and Great Northern.

There was $14,500,000 invested in inland waterways represented by boats, barges, dredges, and machinery. None of this is immediately recoverable, as the Railroad Administration was instructed to turn over all this property to the War Department.

The definitive obligations of the carriers held by the Railroad Administration on August 1, 1921, including equipment trust obligations, amounted approximately to $440,000,000. Estimating the additions and betterments still to be funded at $500,000,000, the Government would have an approximate total temporary investment in the railroads of the country of $940,000,000. This is on the assumption that the securities held were not to be disposed of through direct public sale or through the medium of the War Finance Corporation or other agency. Such a stake in the railroads retained for a decade might exert a profound influence upon our transportation policy.

This financial estimate has had to do with the federal-control period which ended on February 28, 1920. But under the terms of the Transportation Act the Government offered a shelter to the carriers for another six months in the form of a continuation of the standard contract. For the roads that accepted this guarantee the aggregate Government obligation was an operating income of about $418,000,000.[1] As the roads showed for this period an actual operating deficit of over $250,000,-000, the cost to the Government for the period was $668,-

[1] These figures are for Class I roads only, no others being available.

000,000. These figures exclude the operations of thirty-nine Class I roads that declined to accept the guarantee and operated on their own account.

By the Transportation Act, detailed provision was made for settlement of accounts between the Government and the carriers. Section 207 authorized the Government to set off its obligations to the roads against the amounts due to it "so far as deemed wise by the President," but this process of set-off was limited by the terms of the standard contract which protected the roads against being deprived of the funds necessary for taxes, interest, and sinking funds. Moreover, this limitation to the use of the set-off method was further extended to protect the roads in a continuance of the dividend payments made during federal control, and to assure them a working capital equivalent to one-twenty-fourth of their 1919 operating expenses. The remaining indebtedness not offset in this manner could be funded by the carriers for a period of ten years at 6 per cent. Carriers might issue equipment trust securities to cover equipment purchased through the Government, and all issues put out by railroads under this section were exempt from the necessity of authorization by any authority, state or federal.

Settlement by the Government was to be made promptly at the conclusion of the guarantee period upon certification by the Commission, and it was further arranged that upon Commission certification advances might be made during the guarantee period of such sums as were necessary to meet operating expenses and fixed charges, the Secretary of the Treasury being directed to make the payments upon the execution by the carrier of a contract which would protect the Treasury against overpayment. This provision was interpreted by the Treasury to mean that no partial payments could be made except during the guarantee period, and that after its expiration only one payment could then be made, which should cover a final settlement with the carrier. Due to delays by the railroads in preparing their claims and by the Commission in examining and certifying them, most of the roads were by this ruling deprived of any payments at all until they should have reached a final settlement with the Government. This meant that approximately $600,000,000 was indefinitely tied up at the time when the roads were acutely in need of funds. It was necessary to secure relief from Congress, which was granted in the form of an amendment to the Transportation Act on February 26, 1921 (Section 212), authorizing the Commission to certify partial payments to the carriers without waiting for final settlement and directing the Treasury to pay them.

Because of the difficulty experienced by the railroads in the summer of 1921 in securing funds, and the imperative need of such funds for restoring equipment and liquidating current obligations for materials and supplies, and because of the presumed stimulus that the supply of funds would furnish to business in general, urgent representations were made to Congress and the President against the set-off method of adjusting the indebtedness of the carriers to the Government. Instead of allowing the policy to continue of funding the net indebtedness of the railroads to the Government, Congress was asked to authorize the machinery by which the gross indebtedness of the carriers to the Government might be funded, and the carriers in their turn receive in cash what was owed to them by the Government on operating account. A bill was introduced which conferred upon the War Finance Corporation power to purchase securities accepted by the Director-General of Railroads in the funding of railroad indebtedness, and therewith to provide the funds with which to settle the accounts of the railroads against the Government for compensation, depreciation, and maintenance. In short, it amounted to loaning to the railroads by the Government the difference between the gross and the net amount of the debt owed to the Government by the carriers for additions and betterments. In connection therewith the railroads informally agreed to waive their claims for undermaintenance based on the inefficiency of labor in order to hasten settlement, without surrendering any of their rights in court in case there was a failure to settle. The justification for this proposed legislation from the railroad standpoint lay in the fact that these expenditures were imposed upon the roads under the war powers of the President, many of them without their consent. To offset expenditures for additions and betterments by payments due the roads for compensation virtually classed these expenditures as immediately payable out of current income. But no executive in normal times would have thought of incurring obligations of this size to be reimbursed from current income. He would have contracted long-time obligations. The Government was taking advantage of its preferred position as lessee to enforce to the limits of its power a contract which was imposed over the carriers' protest, and which in its effect was violative of sound principles of corporation finance.

In reply, it might be noted that the additions and betterments that were most seriously objected to by the roads during the war period were those of equipment, which were funded up to 100 per cent by the Government. Other expenditures, as already explained, were kept down to the minimum, and none at all were contracted for after 1918. Judge Lovett, in charge of capital expenditures, himself an able railroad official, slashed ruthlessly the estimated capital needs which the railroads had submitted in response to his request. Safety of operation and required operating capacity were almost the only recognized grounds for expenditure. Again it should be noted that while the Government in its offset policy was demanding the payment of additions and betterments out of current income, it was not requiring this payment at the expense of taxes, interest, sinking funds, or dividends. It was a payment out of surplus income.

What it all amounted to was an additional loan to the railroads, the proceeds of which should be turned over to them in cash. There was no legal or equitable obligation on the part of the Government to do this. It was a matter of public policy, and the defense for it, if there was any, lay outside the contract relationship of Government and carriers. The real defense for the plan was stated in the message of President Harding accompanying the proposed bill as follows:

"Railway solvency and efficiency are essential to our healthful industrial, commercial, and agricultural life. Everything hinges on transportation.

"After necessary and drastic curtailments, after harrowing straits in meeting their financial difficulties, the railways need only this financial aid which the fulfilment of our obligations will bestow to inaugurate their far-reaching revival. Its effects will be felt in varied industries, and will banish to a large degree the depression which, though inevitable in war's aftermath, we are all so anxious to see ended."

To release frozen credits, to start moving the wheels of industry, these were the real arguments for the bill. It was an emergency situation to be handled by emergency methods.[1]

For the purpose still further of "enabling carriers . . . properly to serve the public during the transition period,"

[1] The proponents of the bill could not secure immediate action, and the gradual improvement in the investment market resulting in the sale by the Government of railroad securities held by it, led to the shelving of the measure.

there was appropriated $300,000,000 as a revolving fund out of which the Government might make loans to the carriers. These loans were to be contracted within two years after the termination of federal control, and the application to the Commission was to be accompanied by evidence that the funds were necessary to enable the carrier properly to meet the public need for transportation, and that the carrier was able to repay the loan. Loans at 6 per cent not to exceed five years in duration could be certified by the Commission to the Treasury, and the advice and assistance of the Federal Reserve Board might be invoked.

After consultation with interested organizations, the Commission tentatively allotted the loan fund to certain specific purposes, the purchase of freight-cars and locomotives, additions and betterments to promote freight-train movement, the meeting of maturing indebtedness, the needs of short-line railroads, and the settlement of claims against the United States arising out of federal control. Up to August 20, 1921, loans amounting to $226,000,000 had been made from this fund.

While no exact figure can be given indicating the financial outcome of federal control, it is evident from this brief review that the out-of-pocket expense to the Government, the war cost, in the operation of the railroads, including the guarantee period, will amount to not less than $1,850,000,000, and this without the recognition of claims for undermaintenance. In addition, the Government's investment in railroad securities may reach $950,-000,000, which is in the form of obligations maturing at different times during the next decade and a half.

Summary of Federal Operation

Inasmuch as each phase of federal operation has been examined and adjudged, it becomes unnecessary to esti-

mate at length the period as a whole. It divides itself
naturally into two parts, the war period of eleven months,
ending with the armistice, and the interim period from the
end of 1918 until the roads were turned back on March
1, 1920. So far as the first period is concerned, there is
almost a universal feeling that the undertaking was essential, and that while mistakes may have been made
in operating policies, these mistakes are more readily
discernible now than they could have been at the time.
The causes detailed elsewhere that led to taking possession were a sufficient justification. Every one worked
with loyalty and enthusiasm, from the highest executive
to the humblest employee. On the whole, the results were
gratifying and the year must be regarded as a success.
Problems that loomed up huge and insoluble in December, 1917, particularly the labor problem and the problem of finance, were both handled in such a way as not
only to prevent a stalling of the transportation machine,
but to accelerate its efficient working as a part of the
war organization. The financial deficit of $200,000,000
was wholly due to the fact that wage increases were in
effect from January 1, while rate increases took effect
not much before July 1, and this deficit was a justifiable
charge against war account.

The second year is more difficult to estimate. At the
beginning there was a difference in point of view between
the Railroad Administration and the railroads as to when
federal control should cease. It became clear before many
months, however, that the public was not favorable to a
further continuance of federal operation, and that the
roads would go back as soon as Congress could arrange
the procedure. In fact, in his message to Congress cabled
from Paris in May, 1919, the President had announced
that the railroads would be handed over to their owners
at the end of the calendar year. Therefore, the Railroad
Administration in 1919 was engaged in the thankless

task of holding the properties together until the day of official dissolution. No long-time plans could be initiated. It was a day-to-day administration settling only such problems as were absolutely necessary to keep the plant in operation. This situation was aggravated by the failure of Congress to pass the necessary appropriations, and by the steel and coal strikes in the fall of 1919. It was satisfactory neither to the public, the railroads, nor the Railroad Administration. It was a case of waiting upon the will and wisdom of Congress.

Whether federal operation on the whole was more costly than private operation would have been is an idle question, because private operation would have been an impossibility. No thorough and satisfactory co-operation on a voluntary basis could have been effected under existing law, and it is not clear that railroads would have co-operated successfully, even if they could. Whether or not federal operation was wasteful and unnecessarily costly rests largely upon one's conclusions as to the Administration's labor policy. In matters of operation, there were many savings effected through co-operation, some of which have been retained under private management. On the financial side, the Government's aid was indispensable and may perhaps have saved the roads from bankruptcy. Capital could have been secured in the market by the individual roads only at prohibitive prices, if at all. The Government provided at reasonable rates the funds needed for capital investment and bridged the gap between rising costs and revenues. With the popular feeling against price increases affecting their ability to raise their rates, with the irresistible demands for wage increases, and the constantly rising prices of materials and supplies, most of the railroads would have escaped bankruptcy, if at all, only by the most narrow margin. It is doubtful whether any but the most substantial of the carriers, those with large accumulated surpluses, and with outside sources of income not subject to federal confiscation, could have weathered the storm at all.

For the labor policy the Government was responsible. It established the eight-hour day with time and a half for overtime, it drew up the national agreements, it accelerated the development of unionism. It broke down local discipline and gave the individual employee a national outlook and a sense of national brotherhood. It is too soon to judge what the ultimate outcome will be, and whether it will work to the benefit of all concerned. Certainly, for the time being, this policy increased seriously the difficulties of the railroads in restoring their individual systems to efficient working condition. And it accounts to a large degree for the deficit financiering of the Railroad Administration,—this combined with the indisposition to increase rates to meet increased expenses, a policy already sufficiently discussed. But with all the indictments against the Administration in mind, one could not in the transition year following the war have looked with complacency upon a régime of private operation, in which railroads would have been compelled to grant constant increases in wages, would have been obliged to seek additions to capital in the open market at constantly increased prices, and would have appeared before the Commission as suppliants for corresponding increases in rates to meet these increased costs. The effect upon prices with its tendency to multiply the increase in the price charged would have been deplorable. And it must also be remembered that increases in rates do not bring immediate response in revenues, and in some instances bring no response at all. The more we study the situation, the more probable it appears that the railroads, if thrown upon their own resources immediately after the armistice, would have failed to make a record materially better than that of the federal administration.

The results of federal control are summarized as follows by Director-General Hines in his final report:

"It made practicable a war transportation service that could not have been otherwise obtained; its unification practices have increased the utilization of the inadequate supply of equipment so that an exceptionally large transportation service has been performed in the busy periods of 1919 with a minimum of congestion; it met the emergency of the unprecedented coal strike in a way which private control could not have done and absorbed a heavy financial loss on that account which would have proved highly disturbing to private control; it provided more additions and betterments and equipment than private control could have provided during the difficult financial period of 1918 and 1919; it dealt fairly with labor, and gave it the benefit of improved and stabilized working conditions which were clearly right; it not only did not cost more than private control would have cost during the same period, but cost considerably less on account of the economies growing out of unifications, and the total burden put upon the public (through rates and taxes) on account of railroad costs was substantially less than would have been necessary if the railroads had remained in private control and rates had been raised enough to preserve their credit; it protected the investment in railroad properties, whereas without federal control those investments would have been endangered; and it turns the railroads back to private control functioning effectively, with a record of exceptional performance in an exceptionally difficult winter, despite the disruption caused by the coal strike, and in condition to function still more effectively with the normal improvement to be expected in the weather and in other conditions."

THE RETURN TO PRIVATE OPERATION

CHAPTER XV

On December 24, 1919, the President of the United States issued his proclamation announcing the return of the roads to their owners on March 1, 1920. Thus was the immediate future of the railroads definitely settled, and Congress warned to speed up in shaping legislation under which the roads were to operate when the Government should withdraw its protection. It was evident that the problem of the immediate future could not be solved by a mere withdrawal of the Government from the scene of operations. One glance at the railroad income account would have disposed of any such supposition. Some provision must be made by which earnings should cover expenses if financial disaster was to be warded off, and, more than this, the confidence of the financial community must be restored if credit was to be available for all the pressing capital requirements that had perforce been laid one side during the war and its aftermath. On the operating side, there was much to be done to transform a nationally conceived organization into efficient individual operating units. Labor organization and morale had to be reconstructed. Equipment scattered to the far ends of the country was to be returned to its owners. If the statements of officials are to be accepted, there was an enormous amount of maintenance work to be done, both on road and equipment, before facilities could be restored to pre-war standards. These difficulties of the transition stage were responsible for the granting of a "guarantee period" to be discussed presently. But the legislative opportunity was used to the uttermost for the introduction of many innovations

long advocated. The mental upheaval following the
war made it easy, apparently, to put through projects
that would have seemed formidable undertakings in normal times. Moreover, the popular reaction against Government operation developed into an almost unanimous
approval, from public and corporations alike, of much
more extensive and effective Government regulation.
So that the legislation passed on the eve of the return
of the railroads to their owners provided not alone the
means necessary to make this transition safe but included an elaborate amendment of the Interstate Commerce Act.

This legislation was the result of extended and profound investigation by those leaders in Congress who
were directly concerned with railroad affairs. President
Wilson, in connection with his preparedness message to
Congress in December, 1915, had recommended the creation of a commission to inquire into the condition of the
railroads. A Joint Committee of House and Senate was
appointed the following July under instructions which
revealed the problems that the public was seeking to
solve. It was ordered to investigate Government ownership, incorporation of carriers, proposed changes in the
Interstate Commerce Act and in the organization of the
Commission, and the controversy, rendered acute by
Supreme Court decision, concerning the delimitation of
authority of federal and state commissions. This committee, the life of which was twice extended and whose
activities, continuing at intervals through 1916 and 1917,
were ended only by the initiation of federal operation,
accumulated a mass of information,[1] and through its
hearings placed the leading experts on record concerning the problems at issue. The signing of the armistice in November, 1918, brought again sharply to the

[1] Hearings before Joint Committee on Interstate and Foreign Commerce, 64th Cong., 1st Sess., Nov. 20, 1916, to Dec. 19, 1917.

front the future of the railroads. In his annual message in December the President frankly admitted that he had no solution, and that the only conclusion he had reached was that it would be a disservice to the country and to the railroad owners to return to the old conditions unmodified. Some new element of policy was necessary to remove restraint and insure development alike of all forms of transportation,—railroads, waterways, and highways. While negative in tone, the message was in essence a plea for the development of co-operation and a rejection of the idea of permanent nationalization. Upon the heels of this message came the annual report to Congress of the Interstate Commerce Commission. This body was likewise dominated by the desire for greater co-operation of all agencies of transportation and a closer working interrelationship of existing railroad lines. It declared that whatever policy of management might be adopted, there should be provision for prompt unification of all lines in time of emergency, and in normal times a reasonable merger of lines and facilities sufficient to promote the public interest. It urged a limitation of railroad construction to what was needed by the public, and the development of water transportation and its co-ordination with rail. On the general issue of public as against private ownership and operation, the Commission expressed no opinion, but confined itself to stating the legislative demands that would arise under either plan and the points at which the public interest must be adequately safeguarded.

Shortly thereafter Director-General McAdoo submitted a formal statement to the Senate Finance Committee, urging an extension of Government control from the statutory period of twenty-one months after the signing of the peace treaty to January, 1924, or a period of five years. A consideration of this suggestion by committees of Congress opened up the entire problem of the railroads' future and gave opportunity for the presentation of the many plans out of which the Transportation Act of 1920 was shaped.

It would be impracticable, even though it were informing, to analyze all the varied proposals, advocated with a skill and an earnestness and backed by a popular interest such as has never before been experienced in this country in connection with railroad legislation. There were the official proposals from the Government, including those of the Directors-General and the Interstate Commerce Commission. There was the plan of the railroad executive managements presented by the Association of Railway Executives. The shipping and business interests were most adequately represented in the proposals of the National Transportation Conference organized by the United States Chamber of Commerce. Other organizations of "citizens" constituted themselves into leagues for the purpose of giving weight to ideas which their founders desired to have incorporated into law. The counsel of the railroad brotherhoods proposed the "Plumb Plan." Individuals in considerable numbers offered suggestions which ran all the way from modifications of those previously suggested to complete schemes of their own, and all of these plans were elaborated in hearings before the appropriate committees of Congress. The legislators who were to be responsible for the final bill were literally overwhelmed with specific advice, criticisms, and suggestions upon every possible phase of this complicated question.

It will be helpful to present briefly a few of the more significant phases of this extraordinary discussion. First in order came the proposal of Director-General McAdoo, ably supported later by his successor, Director-General Hines. It was a plea for a continuation of existing control for another five years. It would take the railroad question out of politics for a reasonable period and before it should become involved in the approaching campaign. It would give composure to railroad officers and employees who were now in a state of restless uncertainty. It would permit the planning and execution of a comprehensive programme of railroad betterments that would immensely increase the efficiency of the machine. It would give the railroads the benefit of the credit of the United States, so that financing could be successfully accomplished. Moreover, and this was the real reason for the proposal, it would give an opportunity to test under normal conditions the value of unified control, and thus put the country into a position to find intelligently a permanent solution for the railroad problem. For those who believe in a far greater degree of co-operation between railroads than now prevails, this proposal had much to commend it. A five-year period would have offered a much needed opportunity to force upon the individual railroads many projects for co-operative operation, the accomplishment of which under present conditions will long be prevented by the jealousy or indifference or selfishness or conservatism of individual executives. But Mr. McAdoo's proposal failed to take account of popular feeling. An impatience to get back to a peace basis, an unwillingness to submit longer to a control that even under war conditions was in many respects arbitrary and autocratic, robbed this project of all popular support. The public would have none of it. In spite of its attractive possibilities in developing the principle of co-operation, the plan contained features so objectionable as to condemn it wholly, unless one were an advocate of permanent nationalization. A continuance of the existing contracts with the railroads meant a continuance of the Government guarantee, a fixed amount to each road, without any regard to the efficiency of its operation. The guarantee had already proved demoralizing under war conditions. It would have been destructive of all individual efficiency by the end of a five-year period. Then there was the rapidly declining morale of the labor organization on the individual road, the destruction of individuality by such measures, for example, as the scattering of cars regardless of ownership or adaptability to special situations, the constant emphasis upon the superior claims of national interest as against the local needs of the carrier. All this would have resulted in a scrambling of the systems from which the individual railroad would probably have never emerged. Moreover, the financial obligations of the roads to the Government, already large at the end of federal control, would at the end of another half-decade have become a burden that they could not have individually assumed, and the obvious alternative would have been nationalization. Whether so intended or not, the proposal was too definite a bid for Government ownership to meet with any popular indorsement.

The proposals of the Interstate Commerce Commission were merely an extension of the suggestions contained in its annual report for 1918 already referred to, except in one respect. It had reached the conviction that with the adoption of appropriate safeguards for regulation "it would not be wise or best at this time to assume Government ownership or operation of the railways of the country." Accordingly, its specific recommendations were in accord with this view and were largely in the nature of amendments to existing legislation growing out of its experience with the problem. They included the abandonment of limitations upon pooling and consolidation, the power to prescribe a minimum rate, the emancipation of railroad operation from financial dictation, the regulation of the issue of securities, the elimination of the twilight zone of jurisdiction between federal and state authority, more efficient use of equipment and more liberal use of terminals, and the solution of the problem of specialized facilities and the private car.

The Association of Railway Executives presented the plan which was supported by virtually all railroad managements, the leading features of which were federal incorporation of all interstate carriers, voluntary consolidation of existing lines, joint use of equipment and terminals when the public interest required, regulation of security issues by the Interstate Commerce Commission, and exclusive regulation of all rates, state and interstate, by the same body. In connection therewith, the association proposed a statutory rule of rate making, which was to declare that the level of rates should be such as would provide a revenue sufficient to cover expenses and a fair return on the value of property, and to maintain the credit of the roads at a level that would attract new and necessary capital. The plan also contemplated the creation of a Federal Transportation Board which should take from the Interstate Commerce Commission all of its present duties except those of rate regulation, accounting, and valuation. It was also to have the duty of certifying to the Commission the amount of revenue needed by the roads to meet the requirements of the statutory rule.

Comprehensive plans were submitted by the National Association of Owners of Railroad Securities and by the United States Chamber of Commerce. From these two came the rate section substantially in the form in which it was finally adopted. The Security Owners' Association played an influential, a unique, and an altogether unprecedented rôle. It consisted very largely of bondholders in the form of insurance and trust companies and savings institutions, which felt that their interests were not being fully considered by the active managements of the roads. It represented a new departure in railroad politics, the first organized attempt of railroad creditors on a national scale to participate in the solution of the railroad problem. Moreover, it meant a somewhat new

conception of the place of the bondholder in railroad
management.   The issue was later sharply drawn when
in the most critical period of the labor controversy in
the spring of 1921 a committee of this association invited the brotherhood leaders to confer with it with
reference to the problem.   This brought a protest in
the form of a letter from President Smith of the New
York Central Railroad to President Warfield of the
National Association of Owners of Railroad Securities,
in which Mr. Smith took the position that the board
of directors of the New York Central and the officers
appointed by it represented the New York Central and
its stockholders in all matters of management.   He denied the right or propriety of intervention by bondholders
in the labor situation.   Reply was made by Mr. Haley
Fiske, president of the Metropolitan Life Insurance Company, who was one of the conferees.   Mr. Fiske called
attention to the fact that his company had a financial
interest in the New York Central through bonds and
otherwise to the extent of $32,000,000, and that this in-
terest was a vital one.   As one of the "owners of the property," the Metropolitan Life Insurance Company was
interested in promoting co-operation between the railroad administrations and their operatives and in saving
its interests from the disaster which was felt might follow
from the situation then prevailing.   This incident has
been related for the purpose of setting forth a significant
issue which is sure to arise again.   Is the old legalistic
conception of the corporation still dominant in railroad
affairs?   Is the bondholder a creditor pure and simple,
whose only proper concern is in the safety of his principal and the regular payment of his interest?   Two factors in the situation would seem to suggest a negative
answer.   In the first place, capital for permanent investment is secured quite as extensively from the sale
of bonds as from the sale of stock, and in recent years

the former method has been far more generally resorted to. It is not the intention of railroads to any considerable degree to pay off these bonds at maturity other than through a refunding process. The bondholder is a permanent investor in the business. Furthermore, his security, although nominally found in many instances in the property of the corporation, is actually in its earning power. It is impracticable in most instances under foreclosure proceedings to dismember the property of a railroad corporation for the satisfaction of the creditors. What the bondholders desire is prompt reorganization, with a restoration of earnings sufficient to pay their interest. If then the bondholder is a permanent investor and looks to the earnings of the corporation for his security, he has a vital personal interest in management and is entitled to express it on all proper occasions. To be sure, if he uses his influence to promote the exclusive interests of the bondholders without regard to the "residuary legatees," the stockholders, he is acting quite as unjustifiably as is railroad management when it warns creditors to keep hands off, but no such attitude can be attributed to this association. The work of the railroad bondholders during the discussion of new railroad legislation was constructive, and much of the credit for the outcome must be accorded to them.

Throughout all the various plans, with the exception of the "Plumb Plan," to be separately described, there ran a fundamental similarity in constructive suggestions. Without further discussion of individual proposals, it will suffice to summarize the suggestions that, with variations in matters of detail, were found in most of the comprehensive schemes.

1. An almost universal opinion in favor of private ownership and operation with increased powers given to the regulating authorities.

2. Consolidation of carriers into a relatively small

number of systems varying from thirty-five to a single corporation. In some plans consolidation was compulsory, in others voluntary, but they all sought to preserve competition in service, and they all provided that consolidations were to be created with the permission of the Commission and to be under its control.

3. Consolidation to be accomplished through federal incorporation, and in some proposals through the creation of holding companies.

4. Supervision of the issue of securities by the Interstate Commerce Commission.

5. The addition to the duties of the Commission of the responsibility of assuring to the roads adequate revenue.

6. Suggestions for assuring a definite return to the roads ranging from a guarantee on securities or property, to a mandate prescribing the necessary rates to insure a definite income.

7. A shortening of the period allowed the Commission for the suspension of rates.

8. Provisions for adjustment of labor disputes ranging all the way from mere conciliation boards to compulsory arbitration.

9. Proposals for federal agencies to carry the new powers into effect, including regional boards, and an enlarged and strengthened Interstate Commerce Commission.

In view of the fact that the so-called "Plumb Plan" contained proposals quite at variance with all other suggestions made, and was indorsed and is still supported, at least nominally, by the organized employees, the scheme will be set forth here in outline. It provided for the purchase by the Government of the railroad properties. The operating lessee of the roads was to be a national corporation without capital, the direction of which was to be in the hands of fifteen men, five representing the public and appointed by the President, five chosen by the classified employees, and five by the operating officials. Surplus after payment of expenses and fixed charges was to be divided equally between the Government and the employees, the operating officials receiving twice the dividend granted to the classified workers. When the Government's share in any given year was more than 5 per cent of the gross operating revenue, the Interstate Commerce Commission was obliged to reduce the rates sufficiently to absorb this surplus. A sinking fund was to be set aside from gross operating revenue to retire the Government securities with which the roads were to be purchased. Extensions were to be financed by the Government, although, so far as possible, the burden was to be shifted to the communities benefited. The Commission retained its rate-fixing powers. Labor adjustment was in the hands of bipartisan boards composed equally of officials and employees, with appeal to the directors of the corporation.

It is not necessary to go into any elaborate discussion of the merits of this plan. It did not meet with the public support that was evidently expected. It produced almost no influence upon Congress. It was backed by organized labor, and officially the plan still has labor's indorsement in the campaign being conducted by the Plumb Plan League. The serious plight of the railroads makes fertile soil for the sowing of Government-ownership propaganda. Thus far the public has not shown any signs of enthusiastic indorsement, and in fact there are evidences that the leaders of railroad labor are at times, in their negotiations with their employers, finding their obligations to the Plumb Plan somewhat irksome. It may yet prove a millstone about their necks.

The plan has the superficially attractive feature that it eliminates all private gain from railroad operation, monopolizes the roads in the public interest through the employment of Government funds, and gives the public a share in the prosperity of the industry through a reduction in rates corresponding to the increase in net revenue. But its success would depend upon the development of a sense of public responsibility and a degree of efficiency among railroad employees that experience hardly justifies one in assuming. Without such efficiency, without cordial co-operation between official and classified employees, without the utilization of the highest degree of executive talent and managerial capacity, the predicted results would not appear and the scheme would fail. It should be noted that this is not a plan for state socialism. Mr. Plumb disbelieves in Government operation in a democracy, and declares that it is sure to fail. It is rather a form of Guild Socialism, in which the Government puts its property into the hands of trustees to be operated for the joint benefit of the public and of those engaged in its operation. It is foolish to dismiss a scheme of this character by simply denouncing it as Sovietism, and hence anathema. No special form of organization has any inherent right to existence in a democracy. It is a question of expediency. The public wants service under the most favorable circumstances. Will the Plumb Plan, all things considered, work to the greatest public good? So far as any one can judge, the public at present thinks not, and a careful analysis of the provisions and their probable working confirms the public judgment.

On October 23, 1919, the Cummins Bill was reported to the Senate, where it passed on December 20. The Esch Bill meanwhile had been reported to the House on November 10 and passed on November 17. A comparison of the two bills revealed divergencies so marked in character that it was evident that the new Act would be a conference measure, and so it proved. The compromise measure, action upon which was speeded up by the President's proclamation announcing the return of the roads on March 1, emerged from conference on February

18. It passed the House on February 21 and the Senate on the 23d, in both by substantial majorities. President Wilson affixed his signature on February 28, and on the next day at midnight the roads reverted to their owners under the instructions of the presidential proclamation of the previous December. To the examination of the more significant features of this statute attention will now be directed.

The Guarantee Period

But attention must first be called to the "guarantee period," which has already been under consideration in connection with the finances of the war period. The termination of federal control at 12.01 A. M. March 1, 1920, carried with it the provision that the President should then relinquish possession of all railroads, and that the powers relating to control over operation and charges should cease. Similarly all powers relating to the purchase, construction, or operation of waterways, and the purchase of securities or the use of the revolving fund, were to expire, except as they were exercised to complete existing contracts. All waterway facilities owned by the Government were to be transferred to the Secretary of War, who was to assume all contracts and to continue operation. Settlement of all questions involved in the contract with the railroads was to proceed as rapidly as possible, and funds and the machinery of settlement, as already discussed, were provided to expedite the process.

It was enacted that no rate or fare, or any classification or regulation that affected the rates or the value of the service, which was in effect when federal control ceased, could be reduced prior to September 1, 1920, without express approval of the Interstate Commerce Commission. This extended for another half-year the war powers of the federal commission over intra-state rates and practices. But Congress went further than merely to protect carriers in the preservation of the rate base. It set up a "guarantee period" of six months from March 1, 1920, during which the carriers were to receive one-half the annual compensation guaranteed them by their war contracts with the Government. This was granted to take care of the roads until they should be able to stand alone. Their equipment was scattered, the morale of their organizations impaired, if not destroyed, the physical condition of property and equipment was below the demands of service. They needed increased rates to cover the deficits which the Government had been caring for out of the public treasury. Recovery would take time, and to have thrown them immediately upon their own resources would have resulted in wide-spread disaster. In general, contract conditions under which the roads had been operating were continued for the guarantee period. In order to secure the benefits of the guarantee it was necessary that each carrier should file with the Commission by March 15 a statement accepting the provisions of the Act. This meant essentially that the carrier should turn over to the Government all income in excess of the guarantee. Thirty-nine Class I roads declined to accept this contract, preferring to operate independently and "take a sporting chance" of profit or loss.

CHAPTER XVI

THE PROBLEM OF RATES

THAT section of the Act which Senator Cummins declared to be the one about which "the bill revolves" prescribed a detailed method of rate making. It opened with a declaration of policy addressed to the Interstate Commerce Commission. It declared that in the exercise of its rate-making authority, the Commission should prescribe such rates as would give a fair return on the aggregate value of the property used in the service of transportation. In determining the net operating income that would constitute this fair return it was to take account of honesty, efficiency, and economy of management, and whether reasonable expenditures had been incurred for maintenance. It was from time to time to determine what percentage upon property value would constitute a fair return, such percentage to be uniform for the various rate groups into which the country was to be divided. In reaching its conclusion as to the proper percentage to apply, it had to give due consideration to the transportation needs of the country and the probable demand for increased facilities. For the first two years, until March 1, 1922, the rate of return was prescribed by Congress and was to be 5½ per cent on the value, to which the Commission might, in its discretion, add ½ of 1 per cent to make provision for capital expenditures in the form of improvements or betterments. The value of the property of the carriers was to be determined by the Commission, which was authorized to make use of the results reached by its Bureau of Valuation so far as they were available. The Commission shall, said the statute, "give due consideration to all the elements of value recognized by the law of the land for rate-making purposes, and shall give to the property investment account of the carriers only that consideration which under such law it is entitled to in establishing values for rate-making purposes." It is to be hoped that the Commission knows what this means.

Then follows the feature that is new to American legislation. Congress announced that as it was impossible to establish uniform rates upon competitive traffic that would adequately sustain all the carriers engaged in such traffic, and which were indispensable to the communities they serve, without at the same time granting some of the carriers an income unreasonably in excess of a fair return upon the value of their property, any carrier receiving such excessive return held the excess as a trustee and must dispose of it as Congress should direct. The method of disposal was this. If a carrier enjoyed net railway operating income in excess of 6 per cent of its property value, one-half of such excess was to be paid into a reserve fund maintained by the carrier until this reserve reached 5 per cent of the value of its property, and thereafter it might use its share of the excess earnings for any lawful purpose. The reserve fund might be drawn upon for dividends, interest, or rentals in any year in which the operating income did not amount to 6 per cent. The other half of the excess operating income above 6 per cent was to be paid to the Commission, and was to go into a railroad contingent fund which was to be administered as a revolving fund under its direction. Therefrom loans might be made to carriers to meet capital expenditures or to refund securities, or the Commission might purchase equipment and facilities for lease to carriers. Loans were to be made at 6 per cent. They were to be protected by adequate security, and the carrier was to demonstrate its need for the money and the public interest to be served by the expenditure, and to furnish reasonable assurance of ability to repay at maturity. Lease contracts for equipment were to provide a rental charge sufficient to cover depreciation and a return of 6 per cent upon the investment. Any carrier building a new line of railroad might be relieved by the Commission for a maximum of ten years from dividing excess earnings derived from the new construction. That the existence of an excess revenue divisible with the Government was not to be deemed evidence of excessive rates was indicated by the provision that no shipper would be permitted to recover for excessive rates on the ground that a particular rate might contribute to the excess income paid by the carrier to the Commission.

So much for the bare bones of the statute. A careful analysis of its provisions reveals many novel features. At the outset, let us dispose of some of the common misconceptions with reference to it. In the first place, the law guarantees nothing to any individual carrier, and its guarantee to carriers as a whole or by groups is a distinctly doubtful one. There was much support in the congressional hearings for a provision that would guarantee to railroads a minimum return, either upon investment or upon securities. This would have meant that independent of rates charged or traffic handled, independent of the showing of the income account, the corporation would have been assured of a definite return to be made up, if there were a deficit, from contributions by the Government. No proposal could have been better calculated to destroy all incentive to efficiency and economy in operation. It would have applied to railroading the cost-plus contract that the Government found so disastrous during the war. There is little doubt that the unfavorable results shown in railroad operation under federal control after the armistice, and particularly during the guarantee period, March to September, 1920, were in part attributable to the existence of a Government guarantee. Expenses could not be and were not guarded by the Government, and the same vigilance was not to be expected on the part of operating officers that would have been displayed had they been responsible for results to their boards of directors alone.[1] A guarantee such as the war contract provided, with no danger of loss and with no possibility of extra profit, destroyed all individual interest in results. As has been noted elsewhere, this is the most persuasive argument against the five-year extension plan advocated by the Directors-General. It could have ended only in Government ownership, and that is the necessary outcome of any guarantee plan. The Government's financial interest steadily increases and the pressure for conversion of this financial claim into a genuine title to property becomes irresistible.

What the law provided was that the railroads should be divided by the Commission into regional groups and that the Commission should so adjust rates that the carriers of each rate group might earn 5½ per cent upon the aggregate value of the property of the group. This would result in a higher rate of return for some roads and a lower rate for others, depending upon relative efficiency in management, favorableness of location from the traffic or the operating standpoint, and general condition of the property as the result of past policies and experience. This rate of return that the Commission was instructed to provide, be it noted, was not a return upon securities, but a return upon property. Whether this would yield anything to the stockholder after fixed charges had been

---

[1] The Commission was required to fix the amount to be included in operating expenses as a maintenance charge during the "guarantee period." But obviously it was physically impossible for the Commission to watch the expenditures on the individual road in any effective manner. The results of such regulations as it laid down could not appear until the roads came to make their settlements for the "guarantee period" with the Government.

satisfied depended upon the conservatism of the capitalization and the relation of bonds to stock. A road with small bonded debt and low stock capitalization relative to the value of its property would be able to pay generous dividends under this plan, but a road heavily over-capitalized, with a preponderance of funded debt, was not likely to have much surplus income for distribution to stockholders. However, this did not materially alter the situation from that which obtained before the Act was passed.

Again, it should be noted that the carrier was not robbed of all incentive to increase its net earnings. If it was one of the class of the less prosperous roads that might be expected to earn less than 6 per cent, there was the opportunity to bring the business up to a 6 per cent basis. There was no less of an incentive up to a certain point than prevailed under the old method of rate making. One computation showed that during the "test period," 1915–1917, 109 out of 162 Class I railroad systems operating 89 per cent of the mileage of the country failed to earn 6 per cent on their property investment. Hence the requirement of a division of excess earnings with the Government was likely for some time to come to affect only a small minority of the roads.

In the case of the more prosperous roads the limit to earnings was an elastic one. If any carrier earned in excess of the 5½ per cent or 6 per cent return, it retained but 50 per cent of this excess. The balance it had to turn into a national fund for the benefit of transportation as a whole. It was not, be it noted, turned over to the less prosperous roads. There was no pooling of earnings. The Government took possession and administered the fund, and no road secured any portion of it except by paying for it. The portion that the carrier retained was not at first subject to its free disposition. It had to accumulate a reserve for dividends, interest, and rentals until the fund reached 5 per cent of its property value. Then any further accretions were at its unhampered disposal. This requirement recognized that it was impossible wholly to stabilize earnings, that traffic and operating conditions would produce fluctuations from year to year which the Commission could not anticipate, and could not prevent if it did. It was a device to stabilize the return to the bond and stock holder at a figure that public authority regarded as a fair return.

Whether the elasticity of the limit to earnings was adequate to insure private initiative and efficient management could only be demonstrated by actual experiment. The limitation was vigorously opposed by the carriers. It should be noted in this connection that after March 1, 1922, the Commission adjusted the rate of return, and it is obvious that in making such adjustment the question whether the existing rate had proved high enough to establish credit would be a pertinent consideration.

Why this method of recapturing earnings was introduced into the law is stated in the statute itself and has already been quoted. It was an attempt to solve what had been dubbed for many years "an insoluble problem." It has gradually developed from a debatable proposition into an axiom that rates on competing railroads must be the same. How, then, were rates to be so fixed as to provide a reasonable return to the weak or badly situated road and keep it out of bankruptcy, and at the same time prevent the better situated or managed line from enjoying an unreasonably high return? The railroad executives had argued before committees of Congress for a simple statutory rule, which should require that the level of rates prescribed by the Commission should not only be reasonable but should be sufficient to protect existing investment and attract the capital necessary to maintain and extend the properties in compliance with public requirements. Their attitude toward the problem of competitive railroads of unequal strength showed an indisposition to meet the issue squarely and see it through. They suggested rates that would sustain the "average" road. The road that could not measure up to this standard was to suffer the fate it deserved. As for roads that earned a return much higher than the average, that was left open for future consideration.

That this has always been one of the difficult problems of regulation is apparent to any one familiar with the decisions of the Commission in cases involving rates to be prescribed for competitive carriers. As far back as the Spokane Case in 1909 the Commission said:[1]

"The whole territory served by these defendant lines must be considered and the existence of all these railroads to that territory is absolutely essential. . . . We must, therefore, in fixing these rates, have regard not altogether to any one particular railroad, but to the whole situation and must consider the effect of whatever order we make upon all these defendants."

In the investigation of rates in official classification territory in 1911, in which the Commission denied the increases requested, Commissioner Prouty sought to apply the rule just quoted to the situation facing him. He concluded to take the three lines, the New York Central, the Pennsylvania, and the Baltimore and Ohio, as typical and then added:

"Under rates reasonable for these three systems there may be lines whose earnings will be extravagant, but that is their good fortune. There may be lines which cannot make sufficient earnings, but that is their misfortune. We ought not to impose upon this territory, for the purpose of allowing these defendants additional

[1] 15 I. C. C., 393.

revenues, higher rates than are adequate to these three systems considered as a whole." [1]

In the many cases involving rates on competitive lines that were in different financial circumstances, shippers opposing the increases invariably stressed the high earnings that would result to the more fortunate roads. There is little doubt that the reluctance on the part of the Commission to grant increases was in part due not to a failure to realize the necessities of many roads, but to an unwillingness to accord to the better located competitors earnings in excess of what they had a right to collect from the public. For the fundamental cause of the difference in earnings between the prosperous and the poor road was not always difference in efficiency of management but often difference in the traffic productivity of the territory served, a difference which was in part, at least, the result of accidental location. Yet the road with light traffic was essential to its community and should within reason be sustained. No method of meeting this troublesome problem had existed heretofore except the unsatisfactory one of striking an average. The Commission's burden was now immensely lightened by the new provision which determined first what the rate of return should be for the particular territory, and then provided for the disposition of excess earnings. No longer need the public fear exploitation through excessive rates, neither should it be concerned that a railroad system which is reasonably necessary will not be awarded rates high enough, at least to give it a fighting chance for life. The public and the large majority of the roads should benefit from this provision which relieves the Commission of the hampering circumstances that formerly beset it.

Railroads brought their heaviest guns to bear to dem-

[1] 20 I. C. C., 274.

onstrate that the whole recapture plan was unconstitutional, and eminent counsel was employed on both sides to argue the question before committees of Congress. It was the contention of railroad counsel that earnings from reasonable rates were the property of the carriers that performed the service, and that any device such as the creation of a trust, was a deprivation of property without compensation and, therefore, unconstitutional. It was pointed out that even though specific rates had not been passed upon by commissions, nevertheless the regulating authority had been in existence for many years and rates that were undisturbed could not be presumed to be unreasonable. It was contended that the attempt to recapture earnings was wholly unprecedented, that statutes and courts had confined themselves to restraint of the rates from which the earnings were derived, and had never attempted to take away what had lawfully come into the possession of the carrier. Moreover, it was contended that the scheme placed an unfair burden on the patrons of the prosperous road to furnish transportation for other communities, and that the plan could not be defended as a valid exercise of the taxing power, because the property was not taken for proper governmental purpose or for public use upon payment of just compensation. It was merely a device for solving a difficult situation, a plausible defense for which had been sought in law.

The position of the proponents who carried their point and persuaded Congress to try the plan, was that no railroad corporation could be considered by itself, that the exigency in which roads of varying financial strength were operating side by side required that if increases in rates were to be made at all, the obstacle which had so long blocked the way to adequate relief for the weaker road,—that the relief would confer an excessive return upon the prosperous competitor,—must be removed. The only thing that the plan confiscated was the opportunity on the part of certain carriers to earn excessive returns. In answer to the claim that such procedure was unknown in law, it was pointed out that many states in their early history granted charters which provided that earnings beyond a certain per cent on the stock were to be turned back to the state. Of course this contention was purely academic, for none of these state provisions was ever judicially tested. Moreover, the maximum rate of return was often fixed so high that it was never reached, and, if it had been, there would have been nothing there to divide, for the roads were free to pad their operating expenses, and in most states stock-watering flourished without interference. Whether the plan will stand the legal test and whether, if it does, it will accomplish its purpose are questions for the future. For, like many of the early roads whose dividends were limited, the carriers have not attained to that happy state when they yet have anything to divide. However, it is difficult to characterize the clause as confiscatory in the face of the application of the same principle on a large scale in our taxation policy. It is the principle of the excess-profits tax—a tax of 50 per cent upon differential profits above a certain fixed amount.

Assuming the constitutionality of the clause, the question arises as to its practical working. The fact that it is in a sense a guarantee necessitates a close watch on the part of the Government of the way in which gross earnings are expended. A mandate is given to the Commission to see that railroad operation is honest, economical, and efficient. The extent to which the Commission is capable of doing this will determine to a degree the operating income to be divided. In the multitude of railroads and their wide geographical distribution lies the difficulty of adequate supervision of operating accounts by the Commission. Yet under the accounting regulations of the Commission there is a definite limit beyond which the carrier cannot go in charging expenditures to operation. The railway operating income, which is the item subject to division with the Government, contains all transportation earnings except what are necessary to cover operating expenses, taxes, and the settlement of certain joint-facility accounts between roads. Capital expenditures must be made from net operating income and cannot be charged to operating expense. So far, then, as regulations are concerned, the Government's share of operating income is protected, but the situation will require eternal vigilance on the part of the Commission's examining force.

What will be the effect of this provision upon the supply of new capital is another question. What the capital market is to be and what place railroad securities will occupy cannot now be more than guessed at. It was insisted by the railroad executives that the clause was drawn in the interest of the bondholders and that it would seriously interfere with the policy of capitalizing through issues of stock, for it would tend to reduce the probable return of the stockholder who assumes all the risk to a rate approaching that guaranteed to the bondholder. If that should turn out to be the result, it would furnish strong ground for modification, as the tendency has been far too strong in recent years toward the use of funded obligations to obtain new capital.

There are many technical problems of administration involved in the working out of the law. There is the question as to what constitutes the value of railroad property "held for and used in the service of transportation." This was of course the fundamental question in the application for increased rates in the summer of 1920. Little help is to be derived from the statute, which authorizes the Commission to utilize the results of its valuation survey so far as these are available, and to give to the book accounts of the carriers such consideration as they are legally entitled to. It was hardly possible that the Commission could rely to any large degree upon the work of the Bureau of Valuation beyond the use of the general principles and experience derived from the preliminary surveys, and the advice of experts directly engaged in that work. For at the time of the hearings on rate increases, the Commission had fixed no final valuation for any carrier, and had served upon carriers only nine tentative valuations covering 4,688 miles of road. Most of the roads were small. Some of them were in the hands of receivers. The reports on these roads omitted many factors that the carriers contended should be inserted before final valuations were declared. Yet it was the carriers' contention that the results of the work then completed abundantly established the position that the cost of reproduction of the properties would be found, when the valuation was finished, to be substantially in excess of the amounts shown in the property investment accounts. They accordingly urged the acceptance by the Commission of the book accounts of the railroads as a basis for the computation of the fair return prescribed by Congress, although recognizing the weakness in many respects of these accounts as an accurate measure of value. In its rate decision rendered on July 29, 1920, the Commission did not clearly indicate how it arrived at its estimate of property values. It stated that so far as the valuation work had produced results showing general tendencies and principles, it gave consideration thereto. It appeared to have followed the suggestions made by Justice Harlan in Smyth v. Ames as to the proper considerations to be taken into account in determining value, such as the probable earning capacity of the properties under particular rates prescribed by law, the sums required to meet operating expenses, the amount and market value of bonds and stock. More-

over, it considered the investment accounts as they had
been under supervision since 1907, and it gave attention
to the carriers as going concerns with their requirements
of working capital. From a consideration of all the facts
of record, the Commission found the value of the railroad properties and fixed this value at approximately
$1,100,000,000 less than the book accounts of the car-
riers. The detailed figures are given in the following
table:

	BOOK COST OF ROAD AND EQUIPMENT, DEC. 31, 1919	PROPERTY VALUE FIXED BY THE COMMISSION, JULY 29, 1920
Eastern group...........	$9,038,194,615	$8,800,000,000
Southern group..........	2,183,923,124	2,000,000,000
Western group...........	8,818,454,872	8,100,000,000

This reduced the property investment accounts of the
Eastern carriers by about 2½ per cent and the Southern and Western carriers by over 8 per cent.

Attempts were made in Congress, while the bill was
pending, to prevent the use of book accounts of the railroads as evidence of value of property, on the ground
that these accounts were commonly manipulated and contained many worthless items, the results of an earlier
and more irresponsible period of railroad accounting.
But the conservative policy of many of the roads, the
reconstruction of property accounts that has taken place
in many cases, the facts that have been revealed by the
valuation investigations now under way, the general
information in the possession of numerous accounting
officers who have had oversight of accounting practice,
all lead to the conclusion that however unsatisfactory
the property accounts of many roads may be, an enormous real value is there represented which can be con-
fidently used as a sound basis for rate making. Moreover, this account is gradually improving through the

exercise by the Commission of the accounting authority granted to it in 1906. The "cost of road and equipment" of all carriers, excluding switching and terminal companies, as reported by the Commission, increased from $13,000,000,000 on June 30, 1908, to over $19,000,-000,000 on December 31, 1919. This increase of over $6,000,000,000 is equivalent to over $25,000 per mile on the 235,000 miles of railroad represented in the 1919 figure. Surely, with all this value actually present in the property, there is little ground for the wholesale denunciation of railroad accounts with which the public is being constantly bombarded.

It will be of interest to follow further the rate decision of the Commission in 1920[1] as the first application of the new principles in rate making. In conformity with the authority granted by Congress, the Commission divided the country into four rate groups: the Eastern, Southern, Western, and Mountain-Pacific. These groups corresponded substantially with the classification territories, and with the groups into which the railroads had been thrown for statistical purposes by the Commission, except that the Western group was divided, and the territory west of the Colorado common points, being in a better financial condition than the eastern portion and enjoying higher rates, was made a separate group.

The next step was to prescribe such rates as would presumably yield a return of $5\frac{1}{2}$ or of 6 per cent upon the "fair value" of the aggregate property of each of the rate groups. The method of determining value has already been described. The Commission decided to allow the carriers the additional $\frac{1}{2}$ of 1 per cent for "improvements, betterments, or equipment . . . chargeable to capital account," so that its rate computations were made upon an assumption of a 6 per cent return. How the expenditure of the additional $\frac{1}{2}$ per cent is to

[1] Ex parte 74, 58 I. C. C., 220 (July 29, 1920).

be supervised does not yet appear. It will of course become a practical question only in the case of those roads that earn in excess of 5½ per cent. Roads that earn less will presumably be under no obligation to spend any definite per cent of earnings on betterments. Those of the Eastern group received an increase in charges for freight service of 40 per cent, the Southern group an increase of 25 per cent, the Western group 35 per cent, and the Mountain-Pacific group 25 per cent. Increases were also granted in passenger and Pullman fares. That the Commission was disposed to give the carriers full opportunity to earn the maximum permitted by law was evident from the fact that it followed very closely the per cent of increase requested by the carriers, a rate of increase which had been calculated by them in the most generous manner possible. The traffic figures which they employed to compute gross earnings under the new rates were those of the year ending October 31, 1919, which was the lightest traffic year since 1916, and the cost data from which they estimated their probable operating expenses were those of March 1920, which date was practically at the peak of high prices. The decision of the Commission worked out statistically to give the roads an operating income about 20 per cent higher than the average of the three "test years," 1915–1917, which was the standard return guaranteed during federal control. Said the Commission in commenting upon this decision:[1]

"The only basis of comparison available in determining the rates which should be established . . . is to be found in the volume of traffic in the past, and estimates of the expenses, volume of traffic, and other relevant factors likely to exist in the near future. Necessarily, rates so established have an element of uncertainty be-

[1] Annual Report, 1920, page 10.

cause the costs, volume of traffic, and other factors to be encountered by the carriers are not ascertainable with exactness. It is therefore impossible to speak with confidence as to results until a reasonable period has elapsed."

Because of the peculiar nature of the New England rate situation, it will be of interest to follow the decision of the Commission in "Ex parte 74" a little further. The New England roads, although struggling with many problems peculiar to themselves, such as excess of passenger traffic and of less-than-car-load freight traffic, the pronounced terminal character of their operations and the predominance of short hauls, elected to join the Eastern group of carriers and throw themselves on the mercy of the Commission for relief from their peculiar difficulties.[1] The Commission included them in the Eastern group but made no special rate rulings applicable to them, contenting itself with urging that the Eastern carriers give careful consideration to the divisions of joint rates which should recognize the disproportionate needs of the New England carriers. But all attempts to accomplish a result satisfactory to New England through voluntary negotiation with trunk-line carriers failed and the Commission was obliged to consider the problem formally. Its decision in July 1921,[2] found that the existing divisions of joint rates were violations of the Act, in that they were lacking in uniformity, equality, system, and order, but that the testimony being of a general character did not afford a basis for a valid prescription of divisions of through rates. Accordingly, the record was to be left open for readjustments to be proposed by the interested carriers.

[1] The Commission had granted to New England increases in both freight and passenger fares in April, 1918, just previous to the increase in rates ordered by the Director-General. (49 I. C. C., 421.)

[2] 62 I. C. C., 513.

In this decision there were four dissenting opinions, and it is with the position of the dissenters that this discussion is concerned, for it helps to bring out the significance of the new rate policy. The amendment of 1920[1] provides that the Commission, in exercising its power over equitable divisions of joint rates, shall give due consideration to efficiency of operation, the amount of revenue required to pay operating expenses, taxes, and a fair return on property, and the importance of this transportation service to the public. Also it must take into account whether any participating carrier is an originating, an intermediate, or a delivering line, and any other circumstance that would warrant a departure from the mileage basis of rate division. It was the view of the majority of the Commission that the problem of division of joint rates should be handled item by item upon specific and detailed evidence. On the other hand, the minority, in a forceful argument, maintained that the purpose of the Act was to assure a sound and healthy national transportation system, and that the financial needs of the New England carriers were a vital consideration, because important carriers with conservative property investment were near the brink of financial trouble. A prompt remedy was required and the Commission was imposed specifically with the duty of taking care of critical cases of this character. If the general theory of the rate section of the Act is sound, and if it is sustained by the public and the courts, it is a fair prophecy that the minority view in this case will eventually become that of the majority. Certain it is that with a deadlock prevailing between trunk-line and New England carriers and disagreement among the trunk lines themselves, the Commission in shifting the problem back to the roads has merely gained a respite, not an exemption, from its obvious responsibility.

[1] Sec. 15 (6).

In spite of all favoring circumstances, the outcome of the general rate case was disastrous. For a few months it appeared that the financial troubles of the railroads had been solved, but soon traffic fell off sharply, and by the first of the year 1921 many of the roads were not earning their operating expenses. While in some instances, particularly as applied to heavy commodities like agricultural products, the rates may have been too high and have resulted eventually in checking traffic, a study of the industrial situation during the summer and fall of 1920 reveals the signs of approaching general depression. Employment was decreasing, the consumers' purchasing power was declining. Dullness was transmitting itself from retailer to wholesaler and back to manufacturer and producer of raw materials. This movement, which had to run its inevitable course, was already under way before railroad rates went up.

Now that the rate section has been treated in detail, its most significant features may be briefly summarized. Before the passage of the Act of 1920 Congress had not gone beyond the point of laying down the general principle that rates should be reasonable and non-discriminating. The determination of the specific rate and the probable consequences thereof were left to the judgment of the Commission. In this Act Congress assumes direct responsibility for deciding what is a sufficient return upon the property of a carrier. To be sure, it limits its authority to two years, turning the power thereafter over to the Commission, but for the time being it declares what, in its judgment, is a fair return upon the fair value of railroad property. Doubtless it was guided in the determination of the rate by the experience of the Commission in earlier rate cases of large proportions. In the 5 per cent case in 1914, the Commission had held that an average operating income of 5.64 per cent upon the property over a period of fourteen years was smaller than was demanded in the interests of both the general public and the railroads.

In the next place, Congress specifically declared for a return to the carriers based upon the value of their property. To be sure, this was a policy which was becoming general among regulating bodies, and had been gaining steadily in favor ever since the decision in Smyth v. Ames in 1898. Yet its specific establishment here is not without significance. While no guide for the determination of fair value is laid down, the Commission is instructed to make use of the results of its valuation survey as rapidly as they are available. The settlement by the courts of what constitutes fair value in connection with the controversies that will arise in the valuation of individual railroad properties will eventually fashion a rule that will be followed by the Commission in the administration of this rate section. One bogey at least should be well-nigh disposed of, and that is the bogey of overcapitalization. Return on capital securities received no attention in this statute. The stockholder gets whatever there is to divide after the operating income has been drawn upon for the contractual obligations. But the return which the Commission is under obligation to assure to the carriers is a return on property, not on securities.

Finally, the Congress has laid upon the Commission an obligation which, if it existed before, was not clearly indicated in the statute, an obligation to provide the public with adequate transportation, and to see to it that the carriers under honest and efficient management earn enough to assure to the public this service. And this means a credit with the investing community sufficient to obtain the funds necessary to keep pace with public requirements. That this is a change in conception of the function of the Commission will be evident to one who has followed the decisions of the Commission in detail, particularly those having to do with rate problems covering large territories. There has been a growing tendency in the Commission to insist upon a broad interpretation of its powers, and away from the narrow judicial attitude which confined itself to the reasonableness of a specific rate or schedule, without reference to the effect upon the general financial condition of the carriers. This growing tendency was discussed and illustrated at length in connection with the important rate cases of the first half of the decade, and it is this point of view that is embodied in the rate section of the Transportation Act of 1920. Congress has, by express grant, placed upon the shoulders of the Commission the responsibility of providing, through its rate-fixing powers, the transportation service that the public interest demands.

CHAPTER XVII

THE PROBLEM OF RATES

(CONTINUED)

1. *Rate Suspension*

In the Transportation Act of 1920 there was no disposition to eliminate the rate-suspension power of the Commission. Its value as a protection to the consuming public was too thoroughly appreciated. But there was a feeling, with which the Interstate Commerce Commission itself was in sympathy, that the time within which rates could be held in suspense was needlessly long, that the carriers, even in cases of wide extent and large import, were entitled to a decision in a period short of ten months, that if the Commission was overburdened with cases and found itself unable to render prompt verdict, the obvious solution was an enlarged Commission, properly organized to take care of its work; that, in other words, the railroads should not be made to suffer for the inadequacy of the Commission's machinery. Many cases had dragged along interminably, and in many instances the Commission had been obliged to request from the carriers a further extension beyond the ten months' limit, which was usually acceded to. Shipper and carrier alike would be benefited by a shortening of the period of uncertainty and much expense would be saved.

To be sure, the Commission had improved steadily in the efficiency with which it had handled its cases, due in part to an enlarged personnel, in part to a more systematic organization and division of authority among groups of commissioners. By an Act passed on August 9, 1917,[1]

[1] U. S. Stat. L., vol. 40, page 270.

the membership of the Commission was increased from seven to nine,[1] and it was authorized to act through subdivisions, which it could create to any number it desired. To these divisions the Commission could assign any function arising under the Act, and any decision of a division was to be of the same effect as though made by the entire Commission, and was subject to rehearing by the Commission. Questions involving reasonableness of rates or discrimination required a membership of three in the division, and valuation questions a membership of five.[2] In conformity with the statute, the Commission was divided into three divisions, and it was provided that any division might call upon the entire Commission for advice or for the assignment of additional commissioners for the hearing of specific cases. Except for important cases which are reserved for hearing by the entire Commission, cases are now assigned, considered, and disposed of in rotation, one of three divisions sitting in argument, while the other two are disposing of cases and handling the variety of auxiliary functions. Among the three divisions are distributed the various administrative and supervisory functions which the Commission has gradually accumulated during its life, such as oversight of safety-appliance and hours-of-service acts, valuation, suspension of rates, transportation of explosives, long and short haul applications and those for posting and filing of rates, and the disposition of cases heard by examiners. In the reorganization, provision has been made for keeping the entire Commission in close touch and harmonious co-operation with the activities of the subdivisions. Hence,

[1] Increased to eleven by the Act of 1920, since which time the Commission has increased the number of divisions from three to five. The increase of administrative duties with the Act of 1920 has materially added to the labors of the Commission. See Annual Report, 1920, page 3.

[2] Amended in 1920, so that each division is to consist of at least three members. Sec. 17 (2-4).

efficiency has been gained without sacrificing the unity necessary to the preservation of its authority and prestige.

With this reorganization and the resulting efficiency, it was not only safe but wise to shorten the period of rate suspension, and this was done in the Act of 1920. The first period of suspension remains as originally prescribed —120 days—but an extension is now limited to 30 days, making the entire period 5 months instead of 10. Rates are automatically to go into effect at the end of this period if the issue is not decided, but if increased freight rates are involved the Commission may require the carrier to keep an account showing by whom, and in whose behalf, payments have been made, and if the decision is adverse to the carrier to refund with interest such portion of the increased rates as is found not to be justified.

The curtailment of the suspension period has had a stimulating effect upon the Commission's procedure. Under previous conditions, a majority of cases required the full ten months' period, the average time for all cases being about eight months. Cases were set for hearing thirty to sixty days after the tariffs were suspended, and were handled in a routine manner. Now they are advanced for hearing, given precedence over most other Commission business, and every effort is made to reach speedy decision.

Since the new law went into effect the Commission has found it possible to dispose of all suspension cases except a very few, which were unusually voluminous or contained matters of peculiar difficulty, within the allotted time of five months. In case the Commission finds it cannot reach a decision within the statutory period, it requests from the carriers a voluntary suspension for an additional time. In every instance the carriers have complied, although in one or two cases this compliance has been realized only after the Commission had intimated that otherwise it would compel the carriers to keep an account and refund the increases with interest in case they were later found to be unlawful. It appears, then, that the refund provision of the law finds its greatest usefulness at present as a club that the Commission may swing over the head of the carrier.

It is fortunate that this refund procedure was not made mandatory upon the Commission, for this cumbersome method may well prove to be impracticable. It is an attempt to strike a middle ground between making effective the new rates before they have been passed upon, and thus, in case they are eventually disapproved, loading the shipper with unjust burdens for which he cannot be recompensed, and, on the other hand, preventing, for a number of months, the collection by the carriers of rates that may eventually be approved, and thus depriving them of justifiable revenue. This compromise gives an appearance of fairness that it does not actually possess, for, as has been already noted, freight rates in large measure find their way into price. The shipper or consignee who pays the freight bill in the first instance may have his name recorded on the books of the railroad as the person "by whom or in whose behalf" the amount was paid, but long before the Commission has rendered its decision he will have reimbursed himself through his sales. If he later becomes the recipient of a refund, he recovers the freight charges twice over. There may be instances when the process does not work in this fashion, and it may be within the capacity of the Commission to distinguish cases. If so, it is fortunate that the power to require this refunding procedure is discretionary.

The same problem has long been present in reparation cases, that is, in the award of damages against a carrier for unreasonable or discriminating rates, a power granted to the Commission in 1906.[1] The Supreme Court has

[1] Sec. 16 (1).

held that in a discrimination case the damage to the complainant, if any, may be the exact difference between the rates paid by the complainant and by his competitor. But whatever the damage is, he must prove his damage with the same degree of certainty that would be required for a judgment in court.[1] But when the reparation concerns an unreasonable rate, neither the Commission nor the court has required proof of damage, but has contented itself with deciding that the measure of damage is the difference between the rate paid and the reasonable rate. The shipper may have passed the rate on in the sale of his goods, and in most cases has done so. But, says the court,[2] "the general tendency of the law, in regard to damages at least, is not to go beyond the first step. . . . The carrier ought not to be allowed to retain his illegal profit, and the only one who can take it from him is the one that alone was in relation with him, and from whom the carrier took the sum. Behind the technical mode of statement is the consideration well emphasized by the Interstate Commerce Commission of the endlessness and futility of the effort to follow every transaction to its ultimate result. Probably in the end the public pays the damages in most cases of compensated torts."

But the Commission properly points out that this attitude of the court implies that the shipper has suffered from extortion, and hence is entitled to his damages, whereas the fact is that when the carrier charged the rate, which later the Commission decided was unreasonable, that rate was the legal rate, and neither carrier nor shipper knew whether it would later be held to be unreasonable. Determination by the Commission that the rate was unreasonable constituted a finding that the carrier had committed a public wrong from which it should not be permitted to benefit, but it was not necessarily an evidence of private damage for which the shipper was entitled to

[1] 230 U. S., 184 (1913).　　　　[2] 245 U. S., 531 (1918).

recover. With this in mind, the Commission has recommended that the law affirmatively recognize that in cases of unreasonable rates private damage does not necessarily follow a violation of the act, and that the damage sections be so construed that no person shall be entitled to reparation except to the extent that he can show damage.[1] With this the Commission has linked the proposal that its function shall be confined to the finding of an unreasonable rate as of a particular time, and that the award of reparation be placed wholly in the courts, thus relieving the Commission of an enormous task somewhat alien to its proper functions.

From the standpoint of mere bookkeeping, there are objections to the reimbursement plan of the Act in the mass of detailed accounting and the consequent expense involved. One has only to recall the experience of the Consolidated Gas Company in New York City, after the adverse decision of the Supreme Court in 1909—the enormous labor involved in the process of refunding payments and the many inequalities that arose through inability to locate patrons—to realize what a tremendous job the law has given to the carriers.

At the very beginning in 1910 the proposal of the "insurgents" should have been adopted, that rates should not go into effect without the previous approval of the Commission. Now that the Commission is better organized, there is far less reason for refusal to adopt this plan than there was then. If the burden is on the carrier to show that the increased rate is reasonable, there is no reason why this demonstration should not be made to the satisfaction of the Commission before the rate goes

---

[1] Annual Report, 1920, page 78. This is a change in the Commission's attitude. In 1908 (13 I. C. C., 680) the Commission said: "If complainants were obliged to follow every transaction to its ultimate result and to trace out the exact commercial effect of the freight rate paid, it would never be possible to show damages with sufficient accuracy to justify giving them."

into effect. Such was the underlying purpose of the Act of August 1917, which expired by limitation on January 1, 1920.[1]

2. Long and Short Haul

The amendment of Section 4, the long and short haul clause, was a gratifying indorsement of the constructive work of the Commission during the previous decade. For the new legislation did no more than to put into statutory form the rules of procedure upon which the Commission had repeatedly acted in specific cases. The amendment provided that (1) the Commission should not permit a charge to or from a more distant point that was not reasonably compensatory for the service performed; (2) if a circuitous route was permitted to meet the charge of the direct route, intermediate points on the circuitous route, which were at no greater distance from points of origin than the length of the direct route, could not be charged higher rates than the direct route was charging; (3) potential water competition was not a sufficient ground for relief from the operation of the clause. All of these principles had been for several years the basis of Commission decision and the instruments with which the anomalous situation in the Southeast was being gradually adjusted. Reasonably compensatory rates at terminal points had to be assured before the Commission would listen to the carrier's prayer for relief. The extent to which circuity of route should be recognized as a justifiable ground for relief had been determined by the Commission soon after 1910, and the establishment of reasonable intermediate rates had been required as a preliminary to any concession. Moreover, for several years pleas of

---

[1] See p. 13. That this would lighten rather than increase the burdens of the Commission is evident when we consider that reparation awarded by the Commission in 1920 amounted to $878,000, and that the amount for 1921 will be larger.

potential water competition had fallen upon deaf ears.[1]
In an extended investigation of the Mississippi River
situation in December 1919, it was denied that river
competition was any longer of a character to justify the
continuance of the lower rates at river points than at intermediate points, and all relief previously granted with
respect to rates between the main river cities was withdrawn.[2] As was pointed out earlier, no effective water
competition had for a quarter of a century been present
in the Mississippi Valley. At the time of this investigation, in 1919, there was nothing operating on the Mississippi in through traffic except five towboats and a few
barges owned by the United States Railroad Administration. There was nothing at all on the Missouri River,
and in local business between river cities only a weekly
service. While there seemed to be much anticipation of
development of water transportation in the valley, and
while many cities were contemplating water-front improvements, there was no indication that private capital
was interested. Any growth in water facilities was to be
in Government-owned vessels.

The effect of the decision here referred to was wide-
spread. It restored rates throughout the Mississippi
Valley to a basis consistent with the 4th Section, and
thereby affected rates to all parts of the United States.
It is the most significant action thus far taken to bring
the transportation situation in the Southeast into harmony with the fundamental principles of interstate commerce law. Rivers and brooks that never served any
useful transportation purpose beyond that of furnishing
the railroads with plausible arguments against Commission rulings can now be returned to their placid solitude
from which they were dragged in the early years of the
long and short haul controversy.[3]

[1] 53 I. C. C., 295 (April, 1919).   [2] 55 I. C. C., 515.
[3] A proposed readjustment of class and commodity rates in this territory was submitted by the railroads, but was in large part disapproved

3. *Minimum Rates*

It is an interesting instance of the persistence of the competitive theory of railroad rates that not until 1920 was the Commission given power to prescribe minimum rates, although in its earliest reports it had pointed out clearly the consequences of this lack of authority.[1] It was the general assumption that the Commission was established to protect the public against excessive rates, that the self-interest of the railroads could be trusted to take care that rates were not too low, and that in any case, if they proved to be too low, it was the railroad that suffered and not the public. This theory was allied with the familiar one that the more railroads a community had, the greater the competition and the more advantageous the rates to the public, a theory which many a community has found, to its sorrow, does not work out satisfactorily in practice. But more than this, leaving the lower end of the rate scale to be manipulated at will by the railroad means a failure altogether to recognize the public nature of the industry, and the fundamental legal principle that this agency must offer to every locality and every commodity rates that are just and reasonable and not unfairly discriminating. To permit a railroad to prescribe any rate it chooses provided it does not exceed a certain maximum puts an unrestricted power of unfair discrimination into its hands. It may for any reason it sees fit give so low a rate to a particular commodity that this commodity does not contribute its fair share of revenue to the railroad treasury, thus imposing an unreasonable burden upon all traffic not so favored. The

by the Commission (64 I. C. C., 107, 306, October 10 and November 15, 1921). The Commission's disapproval was based upon the fact that carriers had removed discriminations against interior points by advancing materially the rates to the water points.

[1] Annual Report, 1893, page 38.

only restraint upon the carrier is that the rate must be publicly filed in accord with legal requirements. There are multitudes of instances of this abuse in railroad tariffs. No power resided in the Commission to interfere.

Again, there was nothing to prevent any restless carrier, which thought thereby to serve its own selfish ends, from upsetting an established rate structure by unwise and unreasonable reductions of competitive rates. Competing carriers could not do otherwise than follow suit, however reluctantly. Competition at terminal points or at common markets among commodities originating in various producing sections led often to the granting of unreasonably low rates at the expense of non-competitive points. So far as these cases could be brought under the long and short haul section, that is, so far as the discrimination against the short-haul point and in favor of the long-haul competitive point involved a like kind of property over the same line, the situation since the amendment of 1910 had been within the control of the Commission, and the Commission, as evidenced in the transcontinental cases, had not only determined whether the competitive rate could be lower than the intermediate rate, but had actually established the differential between them, and this without any statutory authority to prescribe a minimum. But there are many instances which do not violate the long and short haul principle, and yet discriminate in favor of the competitive point to such a degree as to throw an undue burden upon all interior points that are paying non-competitive rates. When a railroad undertakes to put a producing section that it serves into a market in which other producing sections served by other railroads are competing, and in order to do this grants a rate that is unreasonably low for the service performed, the achievement is to a degree financed by all the places along that railroad that do not enjoy the competitive advantage. The dropping of the rate by one railroad in the interest of the producers that it serves simply results in a lowering of the rate by the competing carrier at the behest of its patrons. There was no stopping-point in law. The Commission was helpless. And it not only meant injustice to other shippers and places and commodities, but it meant an instability of rates that was not in the public interest. The old-fashioned rate war was pretty thoroughly discouraged by regulations governing the filing and alteration of rates, but there was still opportunity for a considerable disturbance of the rate structure in times of light traffic, which could only be removed by the power to prescribe a minimum.

In the Act of 1920 this power to prescribe a minimum rate has been added to the power already possessed to prescribe a maximum.[1] It is evident that this clears up once for all the question of the authority of the Commission to prescribe a differential between long and short haul rates, a power which the Supreme Court held the Commission already to possess, but which now has the sanction of a statute. Again, it evidently puts into the hands of the Commission the power to prescribe an absolute rate, a power which Congress in the past has been loath to grant, and which many have believed to be unconstitutional. However, in view of the precision with which Congress has defined the limits of administrative discretion in the various sections of the Act to Regulate Commerce, there is little danger that this added authority will be abused. It is one further step in the establishment of efficient regulation by administrative agency.

[1] Secs. 6, 13, 15.

CHAPTER XVIII

THE conflict of state and nation over the limits of their respective jurisdictions is as old as the Constitution, and need not be reviewed here. Even in its more recent application to railroad problems, it is no new question. In the Wisconsin application of the Granger cases[1] decided in 1876, when interstate transportation was just beginning to assume large proportions, the Supreme Court of the United States said: "Until Congress undertakes to legislate for those who are without the state, Wisconsin may provide for those within, even though it may indirectly affect those without." But this was not allowed to stand long without modification, or at least elucidation, for in the Wabash Case[2] ten years later the court, in a divided opinion, specifically limited the authority of the state to commerce within its borders. "It cannot be too strongly insisted upon," said the opinion, "that the right of continuous transportation from one end of the country to the other is essential in modern times to that freedom of commerce from the restraints which the state might choose to impose upon it, that the commerce clause was intended to secure."

Somewhat slowly and haltingly, but always in the same direction, public opinion and court decision moved. There was a gradual tightening of the federal grip upon the entire transportation system. One of its most interesting recent manifestations has appeared in con-

[1] Peik v. C. & N. W. Ry., 94 U. S., 164.
[2] Wabash v. Illinois, 118 U. S., 557 (1886).

258

nection with safety-appliance legislation. The facts in these cases are typical of railroad relationships everywhere. Cars operating in interstate and intra-state traffic are indiscriminately mixed in the same train and the same employees handle both. To rob Congress of the power to control the safety equipment on cars operating in intra-state traffic defeats the very purpose of the federal law.[1] However, this applied to safety provisions only, and might be regarded as a manifestation of federal police power in the interest of the entire people. It remained for the Minnesota and Shreveport Cases to establish federal supremacy in the field of rate making. To be sure, in the former of these cases[2] the power of the State of Minnesota was left undisturbed, even though the evidence disclosed multitudes of instances in which the orders of the Minnesota legislature and Commission had compelled adjustment of interstate rates to meet the competition of the newly established state charges. But this interference was held by the court to belong to that class of powers which the state was at liberty to exercise in the absence of the assertion of federal authority. The issue had been tried out in the courts without recourse to the tribunal set up by Congress for the determination of questions of discrimination and preference—the Interstate Commerce Commission—and hence the law of the state was in full force. Justice Hughes anticipated the legislation of 1920 when he said: "If the situation has become such, by reason of the interblending of the interstate and the intra-state operations of interstate carriers, that adequate regulation of their interstate rates cannot be maintained without imposing requirements with respect to their intra-state rates which substantially affect the former, it is for Congress to determine within the limits of its constitutional authority over interstate commerce

[1] 222 U. S., 20 (1911).   [2] 230 U. S., 352 (1913).

and its instruments the measure of the regulation it should supply."

The Shreveport Cases[1] brought the issue definitely to a head. In conformity with a policy deliberately pursued by the Texas Commission to allocate Texas markets to Texas jobbers and manufacturers, the commercial interests of Shreveport, Louisiana, just outside the State of Texas, had been seriously discriminated against. For example, the rate that would carry first-class traffic intra-state 160 miles eastward from Dallas on the line of the Texas and Pacific, would carry the same class of traffic interstate only 55 miles westward from Shreveport on the same line. A rate of 50 cents per hundred pounds would carry traffic northward from Houston on the line of the Houston East and West Texas a distance of 118 miles. This destination was only 112 miles south of Shreveport and yet the rate from Shreveport was 69 cents. These two instances are typical of a general policy of rate adjustment. The Supreme Court, sustaining the Interstate Commerce Commission, found an unlawful discrimination to exist under Section 3 of the Interstate Commerce Act, which forbids any undue or unreasonable preference or advantage. It likewise sustained the Commission in finding that the interstate rates were reasonable and that the discrimination must be removed. The discrimination was evident and was direct. It arose out of the rates prescribed by a single carrier for shipments under similar circumstances over its line. The Commission having ordered this discrimination removed, and having found that the interstate rate was not unreasonably high, there was no option on the part of the carrier except to disregard the order of the state commission and remove the discrimination by raising the intra-state rate. It was this action that

[1] Houston East and West Texas Ry. v. U. S. and Texas and Pacific Ry. v. U. S., 234 U. S., 342 (1914); 23 I. C. C., 31 (1912).

was contemplated by the Supreme Court decision. To quote from the opinion of Justice Hughes:

"Wherever the interstate and intra-state transactions of carriers are so related that the government of the one involves the control of the other, it is Congress, and not the state, that is entitled to prescribe the final and dominant rule. . . . It is for Congress to supply the needed correction. . . . So far as these interstate rates conformed to what was found to be reasonable by the Commission, the carriers are entitled to maintain them, and they are free to comply with the order by so adjusting the other rates to which the order relates as to remove the forbidden discrimination. *But this result they are required to accomplish.*"

In 1918 the Commission reviewed its opinion[1] at the intervention of shippers who contended that its order went beyond the necessities of the case. They conceded that the Commission could fix rates between Shreveport and Texas points, but they said the federal authority cannot displace Texas rates and classifications "except within the territory that is substantially tributary to Shreveport." However, the Commission declined to modify its ruling, on the ground that the area in Texas from and to which Shreveport might reasonably expect to ship freight embraced the entire state.

It is unnecessary to follow the later opinions sustaining this doctrine.[2] They all culminated in the legislation

[1] 48 I. C. C., 312.

[2] In its report for 1916 (page 89) the Commission stated that following the opinion in the Shreveport Case, it had already decided over fifty similar cases. In Business Men's League of St. Louis v. A. T. and S. F. Ry. it practically wiped out the Illinois two-cent passenger law. 41 I. C. C., 13 (1916); 49 I. C. C., 713 (1918). 245 U. S., 493 (1918). The doctrine has also had application to express rates in a South Dakota case. 244 U. S., 617 (1917).

of 1920, in which Congress put its seal of approval on the interpretation of the court by making it the law of the land. It is provided, by an amendment of Section 13, that whenever the Interstate Commerce Commission, after full hearing, finds that any rate or regulation imposed by authority of a state causes any undue or unreasonable advantage or preference or prejudice as between persons or localities in intra-state commerce and those in interstate commerce, or causes unjust discrimination against interstate commerce, all of which is declared unlawful, the Interstate Commerce Commission shall prescribe the rate thereafter to be charged that will remove the discrimination or preference, and such rate must be observed by the carrier, "the law of any state or the decision or order of any state authority to the contrary notwithstanding." The Interstate Commerce Commission is authorized, but is not required, to confer with the state authorities with respect to rate relationships, to hold joint hearings with them, and to avail itself of the co-operation, services, records, and facilities of the state authorities,[1] but the only mandate imposed upon the federal body is to notify any interested state of any proceeding contemplated by the Commission.

This would appear to be a power sufficiently sweeping to satisfy the most ardent nationalist. Yet the interpretation of this clause, which the Commission was compelled to set up almost immediately upon the passage of the Act, has extended the scope of federal jurisdiction beyond what many at least must have considered its limits at the time the section was enacted. This latest

[1] A practice of holding joint hearings had grown during the years immediately preceding the war, and both the Interstate Commerce Commission and the National Association of Railway and Utilities Commissioners had urged Congress to grant the statutory authority necessary to make co-operation effective.

development calls for analysis, because if the position of the Commission is sustained by the Supreme Court, it will go far toward depriving the states of any effective rate-making authority. It will be recalled that during the war period the powers of the states were set aside or disregarded as far as was necessary to effect the purposes of federal operation, and that this situation was approved by the Supreme Court.

The Transportation Act of 1920 provided for a continuance of the federal guarantee of income for six months from March 1, and stipulated in connection therewith, and as an obvious corollary, that prior to the end of this guarantee period no rate should be reduced without the approval of the Interstate Commerce Commission. The removal of this injunction upon state action was virtually coincident with the application of the increased rates granted by the Interstate Commerce Commission, which were promulgated in conformity with the congressional mandate instructing the Commission to prescribe rates that would yield the statutory return. In making its estimates as to what the rates should be, the Commission had not differentiated between interstate and intra-state traffic, but had taken the country as a whole, divided it into territorial groups, and prescribed rates for each group that would give an aggregate return of 6 per cent upon the aggregate value of the railroad investment. It should be noted, however, that three state railroad commissioners selected by the National Association of Railway and Utilities Commissioners as its representatives sat throughout the hearings and conferences, concurred in the conclusions reached, and issued a statement to state commissions throughout the country to that effect. Following the authorization of increases by the federal commission, the railroad companies made formal application to state authorities for permission to file schedules applicable to state traffic, corresponding with the increased rates authorized for interstate traffic. Many of the states granted the petitions without reservation, but many granted them only in part, and some denied them altogether. In most instances the increases in freight rates were approved. Most of the denials were in connection with passenger fares that had been prescribed by state legislatures, over which the state regulating authorities held that they possessed no jurisdiction.

The first cases decided by the Commission, those of New York and Illinois in November, 1920,[1] laid down the principles followed in all succeeding cases. The Commission rejected the argument that its jurisdiction over intra-state commerce was confined to instances where discrimination existed affecting particular persons and localities, and insisted that the question at issue was whether interstate commerce had been injuriously affected. Congress directed that the Commission allow rates that would yield 5½ or 6 per cent upon the aggregate property value in each rate group, and the power of Congress could not be denied on the ground that aggregate revenue was a commingling of interstate and intra-state revenue. New York by its refusal to increase passenger and milk rates had deprived the railroads of nearly $12,000,000 annually, and to that extent had defeated the declared purpose of Congress. To be sure, the decision pointed out many cases of preference in passenger fares and milk rates between railroads operating exclusively within the state and competitors operating interstate, and showed how state authorities were enabled to regulate interstate charges by controlling competitive intra-state charges. This is an old story rendered familiar by the Minnesota and Shreveport Cases. But the significant fact is that these discriminations were considered as only a portion of the indictment. State

[1] 59 I. C. C., 290, 350.

regulation injuriously affected interstate commerce, not primarily because specific discriminations prevailed here and there, but because carriers had been deprived of a certain amount of revenue which the Commission, under a mandate of Congress, had determined to be necessary in order that the carriers should earn a fair return. This advanced position taken by the Commission is unequivocally stated in the Illinois Case. "It was stated on argument that about thirty-one states had permitted the same increases in fares as we fixed in *Increased Rates*, 1920. Are the transportation facilities of these states and of the nation to be put in jeopardy by reason of the failure of the other states to conform to the plan adopted by the Congress for the welfare of the nation as a whole? The states gave to Congress the power to protect and promote the instrumentalities of interstate commerce, and as the states' right they look to Congress to exercise that power." Again, in the Nebraska Case,[1] it called attention to the fact that "differences in judgment as among the several state commissions, if each could and would create a rate group of its own, would obviously nullify the fundamental purposes of the Transportation Act." This answers the query that naturally arises in one's mind as to how the Commission's position is to be harmonized with Section 1 of the Act which confers control over intra-state commerce exclusively upon the states. Interference is not in the matter of specific rates, but rather in that of financial policy. It is no longer a question of discrimination. It is one of revenue. Here lies the overwhelming significance of these decisions.[2]

The most serious instances of the burdening of interstate operation by state action are likely to result where

[1] 60 I. C. C., 305 (1921).

[2] Senator Cummins, chairman of the Senate Committee on Interstate Commerce, is quoted by the press as saying (Nov. 23, 1921) that Congress never intended to grant authority to the Interstate Commerce Commission to change an intra-state rate on the ground that such rate

the general level of state rates is out of line with comparable interstate rates. In Smyth v. Ames the Supreme Court held that the reasonableness of a schedule of intrastate rates prescribed by the State of Nebraska must be determined by itself, that the argument that the railroad is an entirety, that its income goes into and its expenses come out of a common fund, has no application when the state is without authority over rates on the entire line. In the situation before us, conditions are reversed. The federal government has assumed authority over transportation as a whole. The railroad is an entirety. No state may assume to divide the authority so long as the matter is of national concern.

It is not without interest to observe that in most cases no evidence was submitted by carriers to state bodies and no hearings were conducted. Railroads brushed aside this technicality and petitioned the federal body directly to enforce the rates it had prescribed. This method of procedure the Commission took cognizance of and commented upon in the Arkansas Case.[1] In response to the insistence by the Arkansas Corporation Commission that the dictates of orderly procedure and the demands of substantial justice required that resort should first be had to state tribunals, the Commission recognized the desirability of co-operation between state and interstate bodies, and admitted that the procedure of the carriers rendered this difficult. "However," it added, "we are here confronted with practical questions for the solution of which Congress has provided a practical course of procedure by means of which substantial justice is assured. Respondents have elected to pursue that course

was not producing a proper share of the total revenues of the railroad. On the contrary, he insisted, Congress specifically declined to give that right, and authorized the Commission to change an intra-state rate only on the ground that such rate discriminated against a person, a locality, or an interstate rate.

[1] 59 I. C. C., 471 (December 1920).

and we are not vested with appellate power under which they might be remanded to tribunals of the state."

Almost directly as a consequence of this position, the decisions of the Commission, when read one after another, appear ruthlessly to sweep away state rate structures and substitute its own, without any attempt at specific and detailed adjustment. To be sure, it invites interested parties, including state authorities, to apply for modification of its findings in specific cases of lack of adjustment. But it is a question whether the law did not contemplate a larger degree of co-operation with state authorities and the working out jointly of a rate structure in which each state should in a way agree to assume its proper share of the transportation burden.

A case now pending in the Supreme Court to test the powers of the Interstate Commerce Commission is on appeal from the State of Wisconsin,[1] but forty-two states have joined in a brief as *amici curiæ*.

[1] 59 I. C. C., 391 (1920).

CHAPTER XIX

RAILROAD CONSOLIDATION AND FEDERAL INCORPORATION

WHATEVER the shortcomings of federal operation, and however unfavorably it may have appeared to affect public opinion on the fundamental problem of nationalization, its influence has been profound upon the legislation that followed the war. In many ways the attempts at unified operation were ineffective, and yet they instilled into the public thinking the idea of co-operation and co-ordination which found its way in part into legislation, and which is likely to lead in the future to still more important results. There was much discussion in Congress concerning the various projects for railroad consolidation, both compulsory and voluntary, and when the bill went to conference a compromise had been reached under which the railroads were to have seven years in which to do their own consolidating, at the end of which time the Government was to step in and compel performance. This clause disappeared in the recesses of the conference room and the bill emerged with compulsion altogether eliminated. What defeated the compulsory feature was doubtless an inability to measure the consequences, the probability of controversy and litigation arising from the intricacies of intercorporate relationships, and an unwillingness to impose the irritating burden of adjustment upon carriers that needed to concentrate attention upon operating problems.

Consolidation takes two forms in the Act of 1920, which might be designated as partial and complete. The former relates to applications for control of one carrier by another through lease or stockholding, or any other device except "consolidation into a single system." In such cases the Commission is authorized after hearing and after determining that the proposed plan is in the public interest to approve the acquisition under such terms and to the extent that it considers reasonable.[1]

Complete consolidation is equivalent to merger or amalgamation. It authorizes two or more carriers "to consolidate their properties into one corporation for the ownership, management, and operation of the properties theretofore in separate ownership, management, and operation." Such consolidation must be effected in harmony with a plan to be drawn up by the Commission. This plan must divide the railroads into "a limited number of systems" in which competition is to be preserved as fully as possible and existing routes and channels of trade and commerce are to be maintained wherever practicable. Moreover, these systems are to be so constructed that while employing uniform charges they can earn a rate of net return which is substantially the same upon the value of their respective properties. This plan when completed is to be made public, hearings are to be conducted, of which the Governor of each state concerned is to be given notice, and at their conclusion the Commission is formally to adopt its plan of consolidation. Its efficacy consists in the fact that any consolidation that takes place must be in harmony with this official scheme.

Formal application for permission to consolidate must be presented to the Commission and a hearing appointed

[1] Although not specifically so stated, this power to approve leases and stock purchases would seem to be exclusive and to supersede the power of the states. The clause in this same section which exempts carriers from the operation of the anti-trust laws so far as is necessary applies to all powers covered by the section, including the power here referred to. It is a fair inference that such exemption would not have been granted had not the powers thereby released been under the exclusive control of the federal commission.

to which the Governors of the states interested must be invited. If the Commission finds that the public interest will be promoted by the consolidation, it may approve the application under such terms as it chooses to prescribe, and the order becomes effective "the law of any state or the decision or order of any state authority to the contrary notwithstanding." The order of the Commission with respect to consolidations, either partial or complete, automatically relieves the carriers from the operation of the anti-trust laws so far as may be necessary to enable them to carry out the order of the Commission. It is further provided that the Commission shall proceed under the Valuation Act to value the properties which it is proposed to consolidate, and that the bonds and stock at par of the corporate owner of the consolidated properties shall not exceed the value of these properties as ascertained by the Commission.

A bare recital of the Act makes sufficiently clear the very considerable and wholly unprecedented power granted to the Commission, a power of which it has assumed the exercise without delay. A plan for the complete consolidation of the railroads into nineteen systems has been prepared at the request of the Commission by Professor William Z. Ripley. This scheme has been revised by the Commission and presented as a tentative plan[1] upon which hearings are to be held in compliance with the statute. To keep within the limits imposed by the statute, and to turn out a model system such as the law contemplates, is by no means a light task. In the first place competition is to be preserved and existing channels of trade and commerce maintained. This means

[1] Consolidation of railroads. 63 I. C. C., 455 (August 1921). The alterations from the Ripley plan have been made with the object of minimizing the dismemberment of existing systems. The project has appeared too late to permit of exhaustive analysis in this volume. The outline of the Commission plan is printed as an appendix, page 371.

that the railroads are not to be consolidated into territorial groups, but that branches, feeders, and paralleling roads are to be combined in such a way as to create larger systems without destroying or disturbing the general trend of traffic or prevailing competition. Combinations are to be on an economic rather than a geographic basis.

Competition is to be preserved, but it is to be competition in service rather than competition in rates. For it is specifically provided that the systems are to be so constructed that with uniform rates they can earn the same rate of return upon their property values. Whether the Commission will be able to arrange these systems so that their earnings and their costs under efficient management will give them the same rate of net return must await the careful analysis of the Commission's plan. Yet indications point to a reasonably successful outcome. Mr. John E. Oldham, a Boston banker, prepared and submitted to congressional committees a consolidation plan[1] quite in harmony with the provisions of the statute just referred to. This analysis demonstrated what was already well understood, that consolidation in its broader and less exact sense had already proceeded apace. Stimulated by the decisions of the courts in 1897 and 1898 which forbade traffic agreements, by the optimism of the investing public during this trust-forming era and the resulting opportunities for promoter's profits, a great variety of combinations had been effected, and it was not until the decision in the Northern Securities Case in 1904 that this movement received its setback. Basing his analysis upon the year 1916, Mr. Oldham found that of the 177 roads earning $1,000,000 or more annually of operating revenues,—the so-called Class I roads, which do 97 per cent of the business of the country,—87 of them were controlled

[1] Consult *A Comprehensive Plan for Railroad Consolidation*, by John E. Oldham. Reprinted from *The Nation's Business*, February 1920.

through stock ownership by 45 systems. These 45 systems with their subsidiaries produced 96 per cent of the total earnings and operated 93 per cent of the mileage. Furthermore, this analysis revealed the fact that the consolidation movement had taken place along the lines that the statute expressly approves as consistent with public policy. Mr. Oldham constructed groups of roads in harmony with the natural consolidation movement, preserving the existing "channels of trade and commerce." He found as between his competitive systems thus created a great similarity in earnings per mile, in relation of freight to passenger traffic, in the character of the tonnage, in the average rates competitive and non-competitive, and in the operating results. Moreover, there was little difference in the operating ratio or in the costs of operation for the different accounts. The real variation among the roads was found to be in the character of their capitalization and consequently in their credit standing. According to his analysis, the roads that were weak because of unfavorable location handled only 10 per cent of the traffic. These were mostly small roads with low income return that could be absorbed into larger systems. The other weak roads (handling 30 per cent of the traffic) were weak because unsoundly financed, either through overcapitalization or because of the excessive proportion of bonds in the total of capital securities. In other words, if this analysis is sound for a considerable proportion of the serviceable mileage, the problem is not a hopeless one. It is a problem of financial adjustment within systems already loosely formed rather than one of merging alien properties. The details of the plan here referred to are not important for our purpose, but the scheme is worthy of examination as an indication that the task imposed upon the Commission is not an impracticable one, and that if a plan can be worked out that meets the requirements of the law and at the same time adjusts itself to a natural economic tendency and appeals to the self-interest of the carriers concerned, the end sought may be possible of achievement without resort to compulsion.

The decision in the Northern Securities Case in 1904 which put an end to the combination of two paralleling roads stretching two-thirds of the way across the conti-nent, was regarded by many as an ill-advised interfer-ence with a salutary movement toward greater efficiency in transportation service. Still stronger was this feel-ing when the Union Pacific-Southern Pacific merger was dissolved, for the genius of a Harriman had grasped the fundamentals of large-scale transportation service and was working out an organization that was bound in the long run to benefit the public at large. Yet, on the whole, the decisions of the court are not to be de-plored. They exercised a wholesome check on a move-ment that was little understood and appreciated by the public and was not adequately safeguarded. The financiers were, to a large degree, left to their own de-vices, and beyond the insistence by the court in the Union Pacific Case that the dissolution should be actual, little authority was available to protect the public inter-est. It is only necessary to look back over the numerous cases of financial maladministration of railroad proper-ties, extending down even to the time of the war, to realize how helpless the public has been in the face of any scheme for financial manipulation.

Consolidation under the Act of 1920 is a very differ-ent matter, accompanied as it is by legislation that controls the form of agreement, the capitalization, the excess earnings beyond a fixed rate, and that places responsibility for methods and results upon the federal authority. Moreover, it is perfectly evident that during the last decade there has been a growing recognition on the part of railroad executives and financial advisers that the railroad business must be managed not only primarily, but solely, in the public interest, and that private interest must be restricted in its activities and in its profits to a degree of freedom that is merely sufficient to secure the necessary financial support. It cannot be said positively that there will never again be financial juggling in the railroad business. It can be asserted that such transactions have been very seriously discouraged.

The introduction of the consolidation plan into the statute was for a very definite purpose. It had long been in the minds of those who were trying to find a solution for the problem of the "weak and strong road"— the problem handled in another fashion in the rate section. It seemed obvious that if the prosperous road could be made to take over its less fortunate competitor, rates that would bring a fair return upon the combined investment would be lower than would necessarily prevail under a system where rates must be high enough to sustain the "weak road" by itself. Earnings of the more prosperous lines were to be diluted in favor of the less prosperous. It is clear that no complete solution of this problem through the agency of consolidation was to be attained unless the competing systems, after the consolidation plan was in effect, were earning substantially the same rate of return upon their respective investments. Hence the instructions in the statute to smooth out all the inequalities in traffic and operation and bring the systems at the end of the year into a similar condition of prosperity. But railroad traffic and earnings and operating efficiency do not work with this degree of mathematical accuracy, and approximation to this ideal is probably all that can reasonably be looked for.

It has already been noted that what Congress is seeking to preserve is competition in service rather than competition in rates. It is a common remark that competition in rates no longer exists, that in spite of all legislative attempts to preserve and enforce it through our anti-trust laws, it simply refuses to function, and that rates are fixed by agreement or informal understanding in the very teeth of the law. This common observation is subject to the criticism that affects all generalization. It is never altogether true. Competition in the sense of violent rate-cutting is, to a large degree, ended. Rate wars cannot be carried on with any degree of success when rates must be filed thirty days in advance of their effective date. Moreover, now that the Commission's jurisdiction extends to the determination of a minimum rate, which gives it authority to suspend and disapprove of a low rate as well as a high one, the old-fashioned spectacular rate war has probably passed into history. But this by no means implies that all competition in rates is gone. Although the customary method at present of making changes in competitive rates is by conference of railroad officials, yet agreement in rates is not assured in advance and is not always reached. A proposal of a member of the conference for a reduction in a rate on a specific commodity to a specified market may be met with flat refusal to agree by the other interested carriers. In such case, the road proposing the change may withdraw its suggestion or it may decide to file the rate individually. In the latter case, it usually happens that the other roads follow suit. This is nothing more than a gentlemanly and somewhat deliberate form of competition. And this form still prevails widely throughout the country. It is to a large degree in the public interest. When it goes beyond this point, as may be the case when some powerful industrial interest brings pressure to bear to secure rates unreasonably low and thus imposes an improper burden upon other traffic,[1] the Commission must

---

[1] See Dunn, *American Transportation Question*, page 65, for an example of an unreasonably low rate on copper.

be relied upon to correct the injustice under its power to prescribe a minimum.

But what is competition in service? Is it the mere equivalent of competition in rates? Is the distinction merely that in the one case you give the same service at a less price, and in the other you give more service for the same price? It all depends upon what is compassed in the word "service." If by service is meant merely the special privileges which shippers have come to expect, such as milling-in-transit, reconsignment, free storage and cartage, average demurrage agreements, and a host of others, it may be conceded that service can be commuted into price, and that there is no distinction in the two types of competition. In fact, these special privileges the regulating bodies now generally require to be filed with the rate and to become a part thereof.

But there is a larger aspect of service which is not concerned with these details of operation. It might best be described as railroad statesmanship, that struggle for traffic which realizes itself in far-sighted measures of territorial development, in projects for improving the public welfare in cities and sections which the road serves, in active participation in the life of the communities that are associated with the particular railroad system. Such competition is precious, it is vital to the healthy growth and development of community and railroad alike, it cannot safely be allowed to disappear so long as private operation of railroads continues. It is one of the big things we are likely to lose if we turn to public ownership. No Government system yet devised has developed men with the vision and the energy and the skill to achieve results in this direction that the competitive railroad system has produced. When our industrial society has become static and transportation means nothing more than the humdrum carting back and forth of the standardized products from one standardized community to another, then we shall be ready for our bureaucratic governmental régime. But that time, fortunately, is not yet.

The question of the constitutionality of the consolidation procedure laid down by Congress will doubtless come up for determination. It is inconceivable that the states, having enjoyed from the beginning almost the sole power over incorporation and consolidation, should tamely submit to this midnight robbery without a protest and should rest content with the small sop of an invitation to witness the act. But the fact that the problem transcends state lines and that its pressure is irresistible makes it seem clear that the states are fighting a losing battle.

There is much sentiment in the country for making this consolidation scheme compulsory. This has been strenuously opposed by the railroads, particularly by the more prosperous ones that have feared the dilution of their earnings through the compulsory absorption of less productive systems. It is a question, however, whether many of these same roads, if they are perchance blessed with a surplus which they are compelled to divide with the Government, will not find it rather to their interest to absorb their less prosperous competitors and thereby reduce their earnings below the rate of return that calls for "recapture." Whether compulsory consolidation will be definitely demanded by the public will depend upon the degree to which voluntary consolidation is successful. For once the advantages of this system are thoroughly understood, the railroads cannot withstand public pressure. Not only does it serve to rid the country of the troublesome problem of competition between roads of unequal competitive strength, but it has direct benefits for the public in the savings in operation. Duplication would be avoided in many ways. Roundabout, unnecessary, wasteful transportation would be eliminated. Traffic would seek the normal and direct route instead of meandering aimlessly about the country at the behest of traffic officials. It is a fallacy far too wide-spread that because a road carries traffic far out of its natural course at the same rate as though the traffic were hauled directly, there is no loss, but rather an actual gain, in the fact of additional service. Unnecessary and wasteful transportation can never by any process of legerdemain be made socially justifiable. The fallacy arises from a contemplation of the individual carrier rather than a consideration of the service of transportation from the standpoint of the society served. Many of our false conceptions arise from the existence in this country of an absurdly large number of separately operated railroad systems. A far sounder solution of our unsatisfactory situation than the plan of Government ownership which many advocate, is to be found in the development of closer co-operation between individual systems, aided and strengthened by a large degree of consolidation.

No better evidence of the change in public opinion concerning the closer relations of railroads to each other can be found than the amendment to Section 5, the anti-pooling section of the Interstate Commerce Act. This section, which forbade agreements between roads for the division of traffic or earnings, was passed as a protest against the practices of competitive roads for the ten years preceding 1887, and embodied the fundamental opposition of the American people to any scheme that gave opportunity for the creation of monopolies. This attitude has prevailed almost continuously since that time, and has found expression in other legislation, notably that for the regulation of industrial combinations. In spite of repeated recommendations by the Interstate Commerce Commission, and the many attempts made in

Congress from time to time, the anti-pooling clause has stood without an alteration since its adoption thirty-four years ago. Yet after the war, when service rather than low rates was the desideratum, and when competition of individual carriers no longer seemed the solution of all ills, when the advantages of co-operation which prevailed under federal operation began to be realized, and when the power of federal regulation in general had gained the support and confidence of the public, the pooling clause was quietly altered to correspond with the spirit of the consolidation plan. The Commission is now given the power to approve and authorize division of traffic and earnings under such regulations as it deems just and reasonable, if it finds that such an agreement will be in the interest of better service to the public or will result in economy of operation, and will not unduly restrain competition.

Whether there will be any incentive on the part of carriers to take advantage of this privilege cannot be foretold, because this is only one of various amendments which will affect the carriers' relations to one another and to the regulating agency. Much water has flowed over the dam since carriers and commissions first began their advocacy of regulated pooling, and the new legislation may render this clause of little importance. Should the consolidation plan be made use of in any comprehensive fashion, it might render pooling unnecessary. If a prosperous road absorbs a weak and troublesome competitor, it has destroyed the reason for a pooling agreement between them. On the other hand, it may develop, even under consolidation, that the larger competitive units thereby created will need a pooling contract to steady the situation. Severe competition between vast consolidated systems contains far more elements of industrial disturbance than the competition of 1887 could possibly have had. Yet the consolidation plan contemplates uniform rates with uniform percentage of profit, which if it works out successfully will remove the underlying necessity for agreements to pool traffic and earnings.

And again, the power granted the Commission to regulate the minimum rate added to its power over the maximum leaves the carrier with so little independence in rate making that rate cutting, the consequences of which were largely responsible for the demand for pooling, is thoroughly discouraged. If the Commission on its own initiative as well as on complaint can put a stop to rates that are too low from the standpoint of the public interest, revenues need not be drained away in foolish competition.

Doubtless at the request of the express companies, the Transportation Act of 1920 gave the Commission power to approve the consolidation of the four express companies—the American, Adams, Wells-Fargo, and Southern—into the American Railway Express Company, which had been the operating agency during the federal period. Upon application of the companies, the Commission gave its approval for consolidation.[1] Some opposition developed at the hearing based upon the danger of monopoly. But the Commission pointed out that competition would still prevail to a lively degree through the activities of the parcel post, the fast freight business of the roads, and the increasing traffic of the motor-trucks. In any case, rates and service were under Commission regulation. Moreover, there was doubt whether the express companies would resume business except under a unified organization that would avoid competitive wastes. A contract with the railroads was approved which was to be substituted for the bargains previously made between individual railroads and express companies. Railroads were to be divided into three geographical groups: East-

[1] 59 I. C. C., 459 (1920).

ern, Southern, and Western. The operating account covering the express business for each of these groups was to be closed monthly. After the deduction of the operating expense items, the balance of the revenue was to be assigned 2½ per cent to the express company and the remainder to the railroads in the proportion that the gross express transportation revenue on each road bore to the aggregate express revenue for the group. When the portion assigned to the express company annually exceeded 6 per cent upon its property and equipment, the excess was to be assigned half and half to the express company and the railroads until 10 per cent was reached by the express company, when any further excess was to be divided one-fourth to the express company and three-fourths to the railroads.[1]

This contract emphasizes what has long been apparent to observers—that the express company is a somewhat superfluous piece of machinery in our transportation system. The principal function involved is the transportation of the express matter for which the railroad properly receives the bulk of the transportation revenue. The negotiation of a single contract by the railroads of a large geographical group with a single express agency emphasizes the fact that they are paying what is necessary to get done for them what they would otherwise perform for themselves. It is a question whether the time has not come for taking the last and natural step. The Government has shown the way by absorbing into the parcel post a large part of the express package business. It would only be necessary for the railroads to perfect their fast freight service and an auxiliary delivery system to complete the job. The business could probably be done at less expense than now, and this saving in expense would accrue to the public in lower rates and to the railroads in higher earnings. In fact, some roads,

[1] 59 I. C. C., 518 (1920).

the Great Northern and the Northern Pacific, for example, have been operating their own express companies for years, and this year the Southern Railway and the Mobile and Ohio have organized their own agency.[1]

Federal Incorporation

Many of the plans submitted to congressional committees at the time of the passage of the Act of 1920 provided for federal incorporation of transportation companies. Some advocated voluntary incorporation, others compulsory. This proposal is not new and its constant recurrence is evidence of an inherent vitality derived from sound and healthy roots. Its fundamental justification is in the fact that a corporation created by the federal government is subject in all respects to its exclusive control, freed from the diversity and conflict of the many state jurisdictions. In connection with all the steps of incorporation and capitalization, the control by a single agency would be far more effective than the multitudinous and conflicting laws of unequal value and severity that now operate upon our railroad companies. But the project met with no considerable support. Bitter state opposition because of the loss of police and taxing powers was anticipated. There would be litigation and years of controversy. Congress clearly shrank from the consequences. It would destroy local autonomy, which many considered a calamity. No united opinion could be obtained as to the constitutionality of the project. It was probable that an act forbidding a state corporation from enjoying the right to engage in interstate commerce would be found to be unconstitutional,

[1] On September 1, 1920, the American Railway Express Company entered into a contract with the Great Northern Express Co. and the Northern Pacific Express Co. to purchase their equipment, the property of these companies having been operated by the American Railway Express Co. since July 1, 1918.

and yet some such ruthless limitation would be necessary if compulsory federal incorporation were to be really effective. Incorporation that was merely permissive would accomplish but little. The obvious purpose of the railroads in advocating federal incorporation, albeit of the voluntary type, was to free themselves from the jurisdiction of the state commissions. Yet this would not necessarily do away with control by the state commissions any more than the present state-chartered companies are free from control of the federal commission, and in any case this freedom from state jurisdiction is being gradually accomplished through the operation of other forces.

Federal incorporation did not become a part of the statute, but if anything were to be undertaken at present in this direction, the first step might well be the creation of federal holding companies with power to purchase the stocks of railroads. This scheme would provide a step in the development of the consolidation plan. The properties could be united at the beginning through a holding company and eventually merged into a single corporation. The federal government, by laying down stipulations under which charters would be issued, could exercise a direct and wholesome and unifying influence upon a situation that in the past has been chaotic in the extreme.

So far as the whole question of constitutionality is concerned, not only with reference to consolidation and to federal incorporation but to all plans for social advancement, the history of the growth of federal power and the attitude of the courts with reference thereto should not lead to despair or even to hesitation. If the project is essential to the public welfare, constitutional objections will sooner or later be swept aside. The court exists to promote, not to impede, the public welfare.

CHAPTER XX

FEDERAL REGULATION OF CAPITALIZATION

AFTER years of agitation and recommendation by official bodies and abortive attempts to enact legislation, the exclusive power has finally been intrusted to the Commission in the Act of 1920 to regulate the issue of securities of interstate railroads. This proposal was one of the features of President Taft's bill of 1910. At that time it was flatly opposed by the Senate and there was not enough favorable sentiment in the House to overcome the Senate's opposition. Accordingly the Act when finally adopted contained an innocuous provision for the appointment of a federal securities commission, which should report upon the entire subject. The personnel of this Commission, of which President Hadley, of Yale University, was chairman, was largely of a character to insure that no path-breaking steps in Government control would be advocated. Publicity was set forth as the genuine cure for all ills. Federal regulation of security issues was opposed because of its doubtful constitutionality and the inevitable conflict that would be engendered with the charter-granting states. Exactly what influence this report exerted it is impossible to say. Its arguments on the points just mentioned, as well as on many others covered in the report, such, for example, as the relation of capitalization to rates, provided much ammunition for conservative use, and probably assisted in delaying action upon this pressing problem. Attempts were made from time to time in Congress to secure a law accomplishing effective control, but they never up to the time of the war came within range of probable enactment.

It is a common assertion that the public is not interested in capitalization, but only in rates, that there is no relation between the two, and that the question of security issues is one for the investor alone. No dictum in the field of corporation finance has had wider vogue and with less justification. There is, to be sure, little if any relation between the outstanding securities of a railroad and any particular rate offered to a shipper, although it would not even here be absolutely true to say that the traffic manager when he figures out a new rate does not have in his mind to some extent the effect of this rate upon the net earnings of his company. But when an entire schedule of rates is under consideration, and particularly when it is under attack by the public before a regulating body, the relationship between the rate schedule and the outstanding securities becomes clear and direct, and it is made clearer by the arguments of the very officials who have so frequently asserted that no relation exists. They urge that rates must not be reduced or that they must be increased, in order not only that they may meet their contractual payments of interest, but also that their shareholders shall have the return to which they are entitled. It becomes then a very real interest to the public whether these securities in the hands of bond and stock holders are representative of actual value and are entitled to a claim on the earnings.

But again, the officials argue much more potently that they must pay an adequate return upon their capital securities in order that their credit in the money market may not become impaired. They are constant borrowers in one form or another, and their ability to obtain funds at reasonable rates, or to obtain them at all, depends in large degree upon how they are treating their own stock and bond holders. This again is a public and not a private corporate problem. For a constant stream of new capital is essential in this rapidly developing country to the furnishing of the service that the public requires. It is short-sighted to assume that the investor alone is interested in the credit of a public-service corporation. We have here, then, a very definite reason for some sort of regulation of security issues, the interest of the public (1) in the disposition that is made of net earnings derived from rates that the public pays, and (2) in the maintenance of a standard of credit which will insure a service that keeps pace with public requirements.

But the public is even more interested, if that were possible, in honest financial management. Reckless speculation, inside looting, carelessness, and inefficiency affect not alone the creditors and partners in the specific enterprise, but operate directly to injure the public. For it all means that funds paid into the corporation through rates for the purpose of covering legitimate expenses, rewarding capital, and insuring the credit necessary to provide betterments and extensions, are dissipated and devoted to personal use, and that the freebooters who escape with the loot leave the stripped hulk to be restored by the public.

One of the curious and widely accepted fables of railroad history is that railroad wrecking is a function of construction finance and that it largely has disappeared with the fading of this era into the past. But one has only to read the reports of the Interstate Commerce Commission issued since 1914, containing investigations into the financial transactions of certain carriers, to realize that human nature has not changed and that eternal vigilance alone is the price of financial rectitude. A few quotations from the Commission's reports of these investigations will serve to enforce the argument.

From the "Frisco" report:[1]

"The sale of securities to the investing public through the bankers at a time when every appearance indicated

[1] 29 I. C. C., 140 (January 1914).

the insolvency of the issuing company, invites and warrants condemnation of all those who assisted or participated in such sale."

From the New Haven report:[1]

"The New Haven system has more than 300 subsidiary corporations, in a web of entangling alliances with each other, many of which were seemingly planned, created, and manipulated by lawyers expressly retained for the purpose of concealment or deception. . . .

"The result of our research into the financial workings of the former management of the New Haven system has been to disclose one of the most glaring instances of maladministration revealed in all the history of American railroading."

From the Louisville and Nashville report:[2]

"The above facts illustrate the manner in which permanent improvements on the Louisville and Nashville have in the past to a large extent been made out of earnings and subsequently charged to the capital account. As the Commission in its annual reports has previously pointed out, only by the fullest publicity and public supervision of stock and bond issues may such increasing of the capital accounts of carriers at the expense of the public be prevented."

From the report upon that monstrosity, the Rock Island Company, in which two holding companies were created out of hand for no other purpose than to deceive the public and line the pockets of the promoters:[3]

"Misrepresentation of assets in reports to stockholders appears to have been a practice of the directors of the railway company. . . .

[1] 31 I. C. C., 32 (July 1914).   [2] 33 I. C. C., 172 (February 1915).
[3] 36 I. C. C., 56, 61 (July 1915).

"The property of the railway company will be called upon for many years to make up the drain upon its resources resulting from transactions outside the proper sphere in which stockholders had a right to suppose their moneys were invested."

From the report on the Pere Marquette and the Cincinnati, Hamilton and Dayton:[1]

Referring to the purchase of a terminal company, "These 'fiscal agents,' without themselves putting up a penny, borrowed $1,500,000 on the notes of the Pere Marquette, purchased worthless stocks at 41, sold the same immediately to the C., H. and D. at 42, which on the same day sold the same to the Pere Marquette at 47. The amount paid by the latter, $1,645,000, was entered as an 'investment,' was subsequently lost by reason of foreclosure of the terminal company bonds, and in 1908 was charged as a worthless asset to the Pere Marquette's 'cost of road and equipment.' . . ."

"The exploitation in 1903, 1904, and 1905 of the Pere Marquette and the C., H. and D. was not an incident of railroad construction. The properties had long been established. Whatever control or regulation of the issue of railroad securities was exercised by the states in which these roads operate was inadequate to prevent the exploiting or to forestall subsequent hasty and unwise reorganization. To the extent that these flotations ultimately lodged in the hands of innocent investors, whether here or abroad, the public was deeply wronged. Whatever control or regulation was had of the properties and operations of the two roads was not sufficient to keep them in condition to satisfactorily serve the population dependent upon them. The result has been the same with each, financial disaster to the carriers, serious loss

[1] 44 I. C. C., 147, 222 (March 1917).

to the holders of their securities, deterioration of their physical properties, and a marked impairment of ability to perform their functions as public servants.

"*Nothing disclosed in the record before us is to be more regretted than the readiness of great banking institutions in our financial centres to loan enormous sums of money upon exceedingly precarious security in aid of such schemes as have been devised in the wrecking of these railroads.* Not only this, but the high officers of such institutions, while acting ostensibly as directors of the railroads, have in fact been little more than tools and dummies for the promoters. The trustees of other people's money seem to have had little compunction about violations of their trusts for the benefit of the promoters, and at their demand."

These are from the cases that became so notorious as to compel official cognizance. But there have doubtless been multitudes of instances of lesser import which have not come to public attention, but which in lesser fashion call for condemnation. It is easy to say that these are isolated cases and to complain because the public generalizes from a few striking instances. But the public would be negligent of its duty did it not rise in indignation at these barefaced lootings of public property. And how can the public refrain from generalizing, when they have observed the passive manner in which other executives have viewed these practices and belittled their significance. Executives and directors of railroad corporations and associated banking-houses who are genuinely concerned in giving the public the best possible service under honest management have been at fault in not publicly condemning these fraudulent practices and repudiating their authors.[1]

[1] The Commission in the New Haven Case comments on the "absence of financial acumen displayed by eminent financiers in directing the destinies of this railroad."

It is pertinent to quote at this point the concluding paragraph of the Commission in the New Haven investigation:

"The revelations in this record make it essential for the welfare of the nation that the reckless and profligate financiering which has blighted this railroad system be ended, and until this is fully done there will be no assurance that the story of the New Haven will not be told again with the stockholders of some other railroad system as the victims."

We have here, then, another sound reason for some form of public regulation of security issues, the necessity of protecting the public against maladministration. These railroads whose financial management has been alluded to as illustrations could not trace their unfortunate condition to the effects of competition or rates or wages or public regulation. A breach of trust cannot be thus covered up. As the Commission well puts it, it was "betrayal from within, not compulsion from without."

Thus far our argument has related to regulation in general. But there is a sound reason for locating this power exclusively in the federal government, and that is found in the conflict of state jurisdiction and the resulting impotency of state authority. Any one who has had to do with the problem of validation of the securities of interstate carriers has appreciated the annoyance and delay, the confusion and the senselessness of conflicting state statutes. The New Haven, the New York Central, and others have experienced this in recent years. It subserves no useful public purpose. It only satisfies local pride. Moreover, the fact that the corporation operates in interstate commerce makes it possible to defeat the requirements of one state by obtaining its franchise in a more liberal one. There can be no satisfactory control of this problem without uniformity and there can be no uniformity without unity of control and administration. This exclusive assertion of power by the federal government may prove to be unconstitutional, as many lawyers assert. But the enormous public advantage to be derived therefrom makes it worth trying, and this very same public advantage is one of the reasons for optimism as to the outcome.

By the recent legislation it is made unlawful for a carrier to issue securities or assume obligations as lessor, lessee, or guarantor, "even though permitted by the authority creating the carrier," except to the extent authorized by the Interstate Commerce Commission. Upon application by the carrier for permission, it is the duty of the Commission to notify the Governor of any state concerned, and state authorities, including railroad commissions, have the right to make such representations as they deem proper for conserving the interests of their communities. Hearings may be held at the discretion of the Commission and the application may be granted or denied in whole or in part and may be modified by supplemental order. The limitations within which the discretion of the Commission is to be exercised are carefully defined by Congress. The Commission may grant the application for an issue of securities or for the assumption of an obligation only when it finds that the application

1. *a.* is for a lawful object within its corporate purposes,
   b. is compatible with the public interest,
   c. is necessary and appropriate for or consistent with the proper performance of its public service by the carrier,
   d. will not impair its ability to perform that service, and
2. is reasonably necessary and appropriate for the purpose.

This guide, somewhat vague and general in character, leaves, as it properly should, a broad power of interpretation to the Commission. However, it is of significance that stress is laid throughout upon the relation of the new securities to the public service. No safer guide could have been proposed and, if followed closely, will end once for all the abuses of the past. The requirement that the issue must be for a lawful object "within its corporate purposes" seems to recognize state authority so far as it is expressed in the charter of the company. An application for a stock issue to be used for purposes not contemplated in the charter granted by the state, even though the purpose were a lawful one, would apparently have to be denied by the Commission. Beyond this, the jurisdiction of the Commission is exclusive and plenary, and it is expressly provided that no other permission for issuance is needed by the carrier.

The Commission's practice has been to examine the charter, including the general incorporation act under which the charter is granted, in case such charter is brought formally to its attention, for the purpose of ascertaining whether the issue of securities requested is within the corporate power of the carrier or is *ultra vires*. But if the charter is not brought to its attention, it disregards it, on the assumption that the carrier, having competent legal advice, will take care to act in obedience to all applicable state statutes. State statutes, if not in conflict with the federal statute, and if introduced in evidence, are observed by the Commission, but in no case is judicial notice taken of them. If the state statutes are in conflict with the federal statute, they are disregarded.

The corporations themselves do not feel free to disregard the various requirements of state statutes and the charters creating them, which prescribe various regulations preliminary to the issuance of securities, such as formal approval in stockholders' meetings, publication of notices, and the like. Railroad counsel are solicitous that every detail should be observed in order that the issue shall not be invalidated. This attitude is enforced by the bankers, who decline to underwrite securities in which the legal formalities have not been complied with. This preliminary work must be done before the attitude of the Commission has been ascertained, and it may often happen that a denial by the Commission renders all the preliminary steps futile. An illustration of such an outcome is found in the first application of the Burlington road. Disapproval of the capitalization plan made it necessary for the management and its financial advisers, after consuming months in complying with the technical requirements of state laws, to begin their work over again. This lack of co-ordination between state and federal authorities will continue so long as there is any doubt as to the legal power of the federal commission to override state law. No corporation can afford to have its securities tainted by doubt as to their validity. But the question of the constitutionality of the Commission's power has not yet been raised.

Not only is the Commission concerned with the emission of securities but, of far more significant public interest, it has to do with the manner in which the proceeds are employed. The use to which the proceeds are to be put must be given in the application. The Commission defines and limits this use in its grant, and penalties, which include the voiding of the issue and fine and imprisonment for the carrier's agent, are imposed for departure from the Commission's authorization. To assist in the enforcement of the section, it is made mandatory upon the Commission to require reports which show in detail the disposition of the securities and the application of the proceeds.

As a protest against the evils of intercorporate juggling

and the abuses of corporate management, it is provided that after December 31, 1921, it shall be unlawful for a person to be an officer or director of more than one carrier without the permission of the Commission, and without a showing that neither public nor private interests will be affected thereby. Furthermore, no officer or director can benefit directly or indirectly from the sale or hypothecation of securities or share in any of the proceeds; neither can he participate in dividends from funds properly included in capital account. These offenses are made misdemeanors punishable by fine and imprisonment. So far as interlocking directorates are concerned, the Commission is likely to permit continuance of the practice in the relations of parents and subsidiaries where the public interest will be promoted by proper system unification, but to discourage the practice where the obvious purpose is to restrain competition and to form an offensive and defensive alliance. In other words, the guiding policy must be sought in the underlying philosophy of all of our legislation relating to combinations and agreements—the Sherman Anti-Trust Act, the Clayton Act, and the Interstate Commerce Act—that competition must not be unduly restrained nor must there be any tendency to create a monopoly.

It is merely a reiteration of a fundamental tenet of corporation finance that dividends should not be paid out of capital. However, it is a somewhat different thing to make such a practice a criminal offense. Forbidding directors to profit in any way from the sale or hypothecation of securities will automatically exclude from railroad directorates all representatives of banking-houses that are acting as fiscal agents for carriers. This is one of the "reforms" that has frequently been demanded by an outraged public which has become suddenly aware of financial juggling that has wrecked the service upon which they have depended. Bankers have many times been discovered to have been the guiding spirits, but attempts at reparation through the courts have always failed. Methods of procedure guided by well-paid counsel in which no traces are left behind, combined with failing memories, have been sufficient to save these men from prosecution. But the exclusion of banking representatives from railroad boards will have an effect not wholly favorable. Many of these men in their capacity as fiscal agents are wise in counsel. They represent a mass of potential credit that can be drawn upon by the railroad as needed. It is a question whether funds will be as readily forthcoming if the representative of the creditors has no seat upon the board.

It is to be regretted that Congress did not take advantage of this favorable opportunity to extend the jurisdiction of the Commission over holding companies, an authority which should embrace their accounting systems and reports, the issuance of securities and the nature of their relation to their subsidiaries. Doubt as to the constitutionality of such a step probably stayed the hand of Congress, but the end was one much to be desired.

Many validations of securities have been effected by the Commission since the new law went into effect, although no complete report is yet available. Beyond making use of the guides to action laid down in the statute, the Commission has not yet worked out any definite code of procedure. However, two cases should be referred to here as revealing the attitude which the Commission is assuming toward one of the most vigorously disputed questions in corporation finance, the right both legal and equitable of a public-service corporation to capitalize its surplus by the issuance of stock and bond dividends. These two cases involve two of the most prosperous roads in the country. The first case was an application of the Chicago, Burlington, and Quincy

Railroad[1] to issue a stock dividend of $60,000,000 and a bond dividend of $80,000,000 with which to assist the Great Northern and the Northern Pacific, owners of nearly 97 per cent of its stock, in refunding the joint bonds issued in 1901 for the purchase of the Burlington road. It possessed a book surplus of $219,000,000 with an actual surplus much in excess of this figure. Its average dividend had been in excess of 8 per cent. The other case was that of the Delaware, Lackawanna and Western Railroad,[2] which requested permission to capitalize in stock its entire surplus amounting to $90,000,000 in connection with negotiations for the disposal of its mining properties. Its average dividend since 1853 had been nearly 13 per cent, and it had distributed annual cash dividends varying from 20 per cent to 72 per cent. It had practically no bonded debt except that of its leased lines. Factors local to each situation played a part in the decisions of the Commission, but we are concerned here only with the one question of fundamental interest.

So far as the issuance of bond dividends is concerned, while there was division of opinion in the Commission as to the propriety of drawing a distinction between bonds and stock, the majority denied the request on the ground that a corporation was not justified in incurring additional fixed obligations without a showing of resulting benefit. However, such a practice is so unique that this part of the decision will have little effect upon financial procedure. Not so with stock. It has been repeatedly claimed by shippers in rate cases and by many thoughtful students of the problem, that when a carrier secures earnings above reasonable dividends and invests them in the property, the public, which has provided these funds through the payment of the rates, has an interest in the property, and cannot be asked again to

[1] I. C. C. Finance Docket No. 1069 (February 28, 1921).
[2] I. C. C. Finance Docket No. 65 (April 18, 1921).

pay a return upon it. Such property is different from that created by the investments of the stockholders. It should not be capitalized, or, if it is, the carrier, taking account of the manner of its accumulation, should share the benefits with the public. The fact that this surplus is the property of the carrier is not a sufficient reason for demanding a return upon it, because no property right is unlimited, and this property has been devoted to a use in which the public has an interest. The fact that the surplus earnings might have been distributed currently to the stockholders as dividends is no defense, because there is no assurance that the high dividend rate thereby created would have been tolerated by the public.

So runs the argument, and its reasoning would be incontrovertible were it not that the railroads have been regulated as to their charges for at least fifteen years. The majority of the Commission, in granting in part the requests for the right to capitalize surplus in the form of stock dividends, declared that there was no proof that the income sought to be capitalized had resulted from excessive rates. Traffic had been carried at rates controlled by state or interstate regulating bodies which were substantially the same as those applied to competing lines. Nor did the Commission find that the return on the property value was excessive. Accordingly, in both instances the decision in favor of the issue of stock dividends was found to be consistent with specific statutory requirements. It is interesting in this connection to find the Lackawanna openly advancing as one of the arguments for a stock dividend that the declaration of as high a dividend as the 20 per cent now prevailing leads the public to conclude that the applicant is receiving an excessive return on its investment. In other words, the federal commission is publicly requested to authorize a 100 per cent watered-stock issue in the hope that it will allay the hostility of an uninformed public!

In reply to the argument that the earnings of a public-service corporation beyond a reasonable return to capital are not the absolute possession of the carrier but are at least the property of a partnership in which the public shares, the majority of the Commission are hardly on secure ground. Their position as stated in the Lackawanna Case is as follows:

"The question of the reasonableness of applicant's past return is not in fact before us at this time. Where the public has found it expedient to adopt a *laissez-faire* policy to encourage utility development, it cannot be said that profits have been illegally collected in the absence of regulation. The title to the surplus has vested without limitation or condition in the corporation and benefits the shareholder. The doctrine of implied trust sometimes applied by courts and commissions to donated property has no application to excessive return, for the payment of rates carried with it no requirement that the funds be left in the business or used for the public benefit. Its strained application to carriers who have made additions and betterments from surplus would only penalize those who came nearest to benefiting the public. The surplus from income was unrestricted legal property of the company, and ceased to be funds of the public, before the decision to divert it to either dividends or additions and betterments was made."

This may be good law, but certainly there can be no universal acceptance of the idea that in the case of a public service in which the investor has been amply rewarded excess earnings are the unrestricted possession of the carrier, to do with them as it sees fit.

One other point of general interest is developed in these two cases; namely, the recognition by the Commission that a substantial surplus is essential to an adequate protection of the public welfare. In neither of the cases did the Commission authorize the full amount asked for, and in both cases it was solicitous that the amount retained in surplus account should be sufficient to provide for emergencies, support borrowing power, afford insurance against obsolescence, provide the necessary investments in non-revenue-producing property, minimize short-term financing, and serve as a general financial balance-wheel. It is in reasoning of this kind that the Commission will perform its great service for railroad finance in the future. Its authority will carry weight with the public and its administrative prestige and legal position will influence the Supreme Court. In spite of the disastrous effects of our long years of neglect, it is still not too late to accomplish constructive results of enduring public value.

CHAPTER XXI

ADMINISTRATIVE POWERS

1. *Service*

As already described, the Commission's first venture into the field of management beyond that of enforcing the various safety provisions, resulted from the passage of the Esch Law in 1917, which gave control over car-service. Experience during the period of federal control with unified direction of car-service was so satisfactory that the Commission urged an increase in its power which should perpetuate the benefits of unification after the roads had been returned to their owners. Moreover, even before the exigencies of war traffic demanded the step, it had become clear that federal regulation of car-service was a necessity if discrimination was to be avoided. For competition in service usually means a somewhat shiftless observance of rules concerning reconsignment, demurrage, and similar privileges. Moreover, competition acts as an incentive to the retention and improper use of cars belonging to other carriers. Voluntary agreements between carriers had failed at times to prevent serious disturbance of a normal car distribution and there was no authority, once the situation was abnormal, that could restore a proper balance. Neither was there any power to compel any carrier to equip itself with cars and thus rid itself of the desire to steal from others. Control was demanded over interchange and return of cars and the compensation for their use. Again, if embargoes were to be erected against the receipt of freight, the power of determination should not rest with the individual carrier. An embargo is a refusal to accept. No agency should be permitted to exercise this privilege without official sanction.

In 1918 the Commission completed an elaborate investigation of the private-car problem.[1] Backed both by the law as amended in 1906, which gave it power over contracts signed by the railroads with private-car companies, and by the Car Service Act of 1917, the Commission, upon the information derived from its investigation, prescribed rates and methods of payment for private cars and regulations for their use. It decided that it was to the interest of carriers and public that the operation of private cars should continue under proper regulation. Apparently the time had not yet come when railroads were to be required to own the equipment of all kinds needed in the performance of their service.

The Act of 1920 clarified and extended the Commission's power.[2] The term "car-service" over which the authority of the Commission prevailed was extended to include the "use, control, and supply" as well as the movement of equipment, and to comprise locomotives and special equipment as well as cars. It was specifically made the duty of each carrier to furnish safe and adequate car-service, but any extension of service must reasonably be required in the public interest and must not involve an expense that would impair the ability of the carrier to perform its duty to the public. Moreover, every carrier was required to make a reasonable and just distribution of cars to the coal mines and, following the ruling of the Commission and the court in the Illinois Central Case, to count in the rating of the

---

[1] 50 I. C. C., 652. This report contains a very satisfactory history of the relation of railroads to the companies furnishing their own cars.

[2] Sec. 1 (10–17).

mine every car used, whether owned by the mine or the carrier.[1]

But the provision of the greatest public interest and importance was that which gave the Commission power, whenever it believed that a shortage of equipment or congestion of traffic or any other emergency requiring immediate action existed, upon complaint or on its own initiative and with or without a hearing, to make such directions with regard to the relations of the property of carriers as should promote the public service. This extended to the joint use of terminals, to preference or priority in transportation, to embargoes, to the issuance of permits. Moreover, if the Commission was of the opinion that a carrier *for any reason* was unable to satisfactorily transport the traffic offered to it, it might prescribe how the traffic should be handled and might distribute it over other lines. Thus was a genuine attempt made to preserve some of the benefits of unified operation during federal control.

The new machinery was promptly brought into action.[2] When the roads went back on March 1, 1920, there was a scarcity of cars which was greatly increased a month later by strikes that tied up equipment and reduced the available supply by one-third. In May the carriers petitioned the Commission to exercise its emergency powers in order that essential products might be moved, such as foodstuffs, coal, and news-print paper. The Commission responded by the issuance of a series of orders designed to make the greatest available use of

[1] Power is given to the Commission to make rules governing special conditions in the handling of live stock. Otherwise the rate must cover all necessary service of loading and unloading at public stockyards. Section 15 (5).

[2] When federal control ended, both the Commission and the carriers restored their separate car-service bureaus, which now keep in constant touch with each other. The railroads accept from their "Car-Service Division" directions concerning car distribution, and the "Car-Service Division" as agent for the carriers accepts service of orders from Bureau of Service of the Commission.

existing equipment. Traffic was to be forwarded by the most available route irrespective of shippers' directions or the ownership of cars. Relocation of empty equipment was promoted by sending open-top coal-cars eastward and box cars westward, and the confused situation inherited from the Railroad Administration was adjusted. Terminal committees, following the practice of the war period, were organized at traffic centres, composed of railroad, shipping, and regulating interests, the duty of which was to keep gateways open and to advise as to requirements. As an outcome of this emergency organization the Commission plans to maintain service organizations at points where congestion is likely to occur, in order to develop local co-operation with the operating organizations of the roads.

Notwithstanding the urgent request of the carriers, the Commission declined to exercise its priority powers except with reference to the distribution of bituminous coal. Here the crisis was so acute that it took radical action, and in the case of the New England supply and that for the Northwest via the Lakes, it resurrected the pooling arrangements that had been employed by the war administration. Finally, in ways which do not publicly appear, the Commission through its Bureau of Service is now working to increase operating efficiency. It is in a position to exert a powerful influence in the years to come upon the efficient loading of cars and trains and the daily mileage made, and its oversight should be in the direction of greater co-operation of individual units and a closer weaving of these operating units into a nation-wide system.

It has already been stated that the Commission may, in time of emergency, require joint use of terminal facilities. But its power goes further. Whenever the Commission finds it to be practicable and in the public interest and not likely to impair the owning carrier's ability to handle its own business, it has power to require the use of the terminal by other carriers and to determine the compensation in case the carriers cannot agree.

Moreover, no carrier subject to the Act can now undertake an extension or a new line of road or acquire or operate such a road without first obtaining from the Commission a certificate of public convenience and necessity. Neither can a line be abandoned without the Commission's certificate. Notice of application must be filed with the Governor of each state concerned and the right of the state to be heard must be recognized. Also notice must be published for three consecutive weeks in a newspaper in each county through which the railroad operates. This is the extent of power reserved to the individual states. The certificate issued by the Commission is final.

2. *Accounting and Statistics*

It will be recalled that up to 1920 no regulations had been issued by the Commission prescribing specific depreciation rates, but that the carriers had been required to set up rates based upon their own experience, which they were prepared to justify. The new law imposes a specific mandate upon the Commission requiring it as soon as practicable to prescribe the classes of property for which depreciation charges are to be set up, and the rates to be used, and carriers are required to confine their depreciation charges to these classes of property and to these rates. The Commission has organized a special section in its office which is giving its time to working out the detailed requirements of this amendment. Its results should be of importance in the administration of the valuation section of the Act and in keeping the value of the railroads up to date.

The visitorial power of the Commission was strengthened in 1920 by authorizing it at all times to have access not only to "all accounts, records, and memoranda," but also to all "documents, papers, and correspondence now or hereafter existing." In 1915 the Louisville and Nashville Railroad had refused permission to examiners of the Commission to consult correspondence in its files which was believed to contain evidence that would show whether or not it had violated the Act. This refusal was sustained by the Supreme Court on the ground that the wording of the Act did not contemplate the inclusion of correspondence.[1] This seriously hampered the work of the Commission, as it is in the files of the carrier that "the most definite evidence of criminal intent is commonly to be found." In the same year, the Supreme Court had ruled that a mere "fishing expedition into the affairs of a stranger for the chance that something discreditable might turn up" is not permissible, but questions having a real bearing on the issue must be answered when within the Commission's jurisdiction.[2]

The broad and sweeping power of investigation now conferred is clearly justified if we concede that the carriers are public agencies pure and simple. It was this same Louisville and Nashville Railroad that refused in 1917 to answer questions concerning the expenditure of its funds for political purposes, and was compelled to do so by the Supreme Court. It was held in that case that in any political activities or efforts to suppress competition both of which were here involved, the public authority was justifiably interested in how the sums expended were charged in the accounts. This was a public matter which could not be withheld. Said the court: "If it be grasped thoroughly and kept in attention that they are public agents, we have at least the principle which should determine judgment in particular instances of regulation or investigation; and it is not far from true—it may be it is entirely true, as said by the Com-

[1] 236 U. S., 318.   [2] 237 U. S., 434.

mission—that 'there can be nothing private or confidential in the activities and expenditures of a carrier engaged in interstate commerce.' " [1]

As a comment on the propagandist activities of carriers which have become such a feature in recent years, and as an answer to the oft-heard query whether such activities are a proper burden on the rates paid by the public, the concluding words of this opinion are of interest: "Abstractly speaking, we are not disposed to say that a carrier may not attempt to mould or enlighten public opinion, but we are quite clear that its conduct and the expenditures of its funds are open to inquiry. If it may not rest inactive and suffer injustice, it may not, on the other hand, use its funds and its power in opposition to the policies of government"—whatever that may mean.

Regulations issued by the Bureau of Statistics requiring apportionment of expenses between passenger and freight service, which were suspended during the war period at the request of carriers, have been revived and amended and made effective as of January 1, 1920. The Commission is contemplating a still further step in cost accounting by way of a requirement for the separation of terminal costs from those of road or line service. If this can be satisfactorily accomplished it will mean a distinct step in advance toward the eventual shaping of a scientific rate structure based on the facts of operation. We have too long blundered along blindly, and have somehow managed to come out with the financial balance on the right side. But with the narrow margins of profit that must prevail, now that we have reached the intensive stage of railroading, and with the closer supervision of Government and the greater degree of accountability by the carrier to the public, there must be a more

[1] 245 U. S., 33, 47, 48 (1917).

scientific analysis of costs and a clearer justification of charges. Regulation cannot fail to be aided by it. The enforcement of such provisions in the law as the amendment to Section 4 providing that in cases of suspension of the distance principle the long-haul rate shall be reasonably compensatory would be assisted by some adequate analysis of costs of operation. One need not believe in the cost theory of rate making in order to advocate more scientific price fixing by our transportation agencies.

For these same reasons one must welcome the movement on the part of the Bureau of Statistics for the accumulation of commodity statistics that will actually show volume of traffic in the case of important commodities for different sections of the country and for different railroad systems. It is a curious fact that although financial and operating statistics have improved steadily, almost nothing has been done to develop commodity statistics, largely because the carriers have insisted that the expense would be prohibitive. Yet many of them accumulate the material for their own use. On December 1, 1919, a classification of commodities, consisting of seventy different items, was adopted by the Commission, and quarterly reports are now called for under this classification. Special experimental studies have been made showing additional information, such as the revenue from each class of commodities and the states of origin and destination. These studies may later be developed into current reports. Such material when currently available will be of inestimable value to the Commission in making rates. It will no longer be obliged to rely upon ex-parte material furnished by the litigants, but will possess in its own files information currently gathered upon which it may with reasonable confidence rely.

The Commission's statistical work was considerably extended by its inheritance of the system of reports developed by the statistical division of the Railroad Administration during the war, which carry into greater detail than before the statistical material having to do with the special units of operation such as train, car, and ton miles. Account should also be taken of the new classification of employees worked out co-operatively by the Commission and the Railroad Labor Board. The latter organization soon found its duties in prescribing wages and working conditions seriously hampered by lack of a uniform terminology or any clearly defined basis for the classification of employees. Accordingly, a classification was constructed on a functional basis which was made effective by the Interstate Commerce Commission, April 18, 1921, as a standard form for reporting all wage data. The use of standardized nomenclature makes possible more accurate comparisons with similar occupations outside. This task, brought to completion under pressure of labor controversies, realizes a long-felt need for more accurate wage data, and is another step in perfecting the statistical output of the Commission.

3. Cash Payment of Freight Bills

Section 3 was amended by requiring that no carrier after July 1, 1920, should relinquish freight at destination until all charges had been paid, except under regulations that the Commission might prescribe to assure prompt payment. The policy of cash payment for freight transportation was inaugurated during federal control under an order of the Director-General dated May 20, 1918. The evil of discrimination through the granting of credit to shippers had grown to serious proportions, large shippers often enjoying weeks and months of exemption in which to sell their goods and pay their transportation charges. Under competition there seemed to be no way of checking the evil. The voluntary action of the Federal Railroad Administration has now in effect been incorporated into law.

CHAPTER XXII

REGULATION OF WAGES AND WORKING CONDITIONS

THE most serious problem that the railroads inherited from the United States Railroad Administration was that which concerned their labor. Morale had broken down. If the individual railroad was to operate efficiently, the local discipline had speedily to be restored. Large numbers of employees were now members of unions who had before the war no such affiliations, and many unions were in existence where none at all had existed before. These labor organizations were immensely strengthened by the possession of agreements operating nationally which for reasons to be soon discussed did not terminate with the end of federal control. Finally, insistent and unsettled demands for wage increases had been passed on as a heritage to the carriers.

It will be necessary first to observe to what degree Congress assisted in the solution of this labor problem by providing adjustment machinery. The debates in Congress and the struggle between the proponents of the conflicting points of view furnish valuable reading for the student of labor literature. Many "solutions" were discussed, but only two that failed of enactment will be mentioned here. The first was the "anti-strike" provision of the Senate bill, which made it unlawful for any two or more officials or employees, for the purpose of maintaining or adjusting a dispute which could be submitted to the agencies provided by the Act, to enter into an agreement to hinder or prevent the operation of trains, and for any one to aid or abet in this action. Such illegality was declared to be a misdemeanor punishable by fine and imprisonment. But nothing was to prevent an individual from quitting his employment for any reason. This revolutionary proposal failed partly because of the bitter opposition of labor, not only railroad labor, but also the American Federation represented by Mr. Gompers, which declared it an enactment imposing involuntary servitude. But more than this, it gave an impression of sharp practice and unfairness. Labor had been drafted into the Government service as a war measure, had served patriotically, had refrained from extreme measures in seeking its ends, and had in fact accepted less in wages than it was entitled to. And this bill proposed, before labor should again be free of the shackles of Government control, to make it impossible for it to resort to the means which it had always felt free under private operation to employ. The proposal passed the Senate but failed in conference. An attempt to substitute for it in the Senate the Canadian plan, under which a strike should be illegal until sixty days after the decision of a wage tribunal, failed of passage by a tie vote.

In the House, the supporters of labor succeeded in having incorporated in the Esch Bill provisions which in substance perpetuated the adjustment machinery of the war period. There were to be three bipartisan adjustment boards, composed equally of employers and employees, with appeal to corresponding bipartisan committees on labor disputes. A majority vote was necessary for settlement. There was no enforcement machinery provided, reliance being placed on publicity. The public had no representation on the boards. It was a plan entirely consistent with the general development of labor policy. The goal was complete unionization of labor, followed by negotiation on a national scale between representatives of labor and capital. It certainly looked in the direction of the closed shop in the railroad business. The elimination of the neutral party representing the public was easily explained in the light of experience. Such arbitrations as had been conducted had not proved satisfactory to labor for reasons already discussed. Labor had no desire to crystallize this unfortunate experience into law. It is not without significance that the bill confirmed for the future all the orders and decisions of the Railroad Administration relating to wages, hours, and conditions of employment.

Out of the conflict of these two proposals appeared the labor provisions of the Act of 1920. They combined features of both measures. Compulsory arbitration was eliminated. Arbitration without power of enforcement was provided. The bipartisan boards of the House bill were rejected, but provision was made for voluntary adjustment boards.

The clauses of the Act of 1920 relating to labor open with the announcement that it is the duty of all carriers and their employees to adopt every available means to avoid interruption of operation which may result from any dispute. All disputes must be considered and, if possible, decided in conference between representatives of the two sides, and only if not so decided are they to be carried higher. Above this local conference, there is the board of labor adjustment, which may be established by agreement between a single carrier and its employees or organization of employees, or by a group of carriers, or by the carriers as a whole with corresponding employee groups. Such adjustment board is to have appellate jurisdiction over any dispute not settled upon the individual railroad that involves grievances, rules, and working conditions, but not wages. It takes jurisdiction upon the appeal of the representative of the carrier or the employee organization on the individual property, or the written petition of 100 unorganized employees, or upon its own motion, or it must accept jurisdiction at the request of the national

Labor Board, whenever this board is of the opinion that the dispute is likely substantially to interrupt commerce.

Finally, a Railroad Labor Board has been created with national jurisdiction. It has nine members, three representing labor, appointed by the President from a poll of six nominees offered by the employees, three representing the corporations similarly appointed, and three representing the public, appointed directly by the President. This board has jurisdiction over disputes involving grievances and working conditions that have not been settled by an adjustment board. In case no adjustment board is organized, the Labor Board receives the case directly on appeal from the individual railroad. Disputes not settled locally involving questions of wages go in all cases direct to the Labor Board, without the intermediation of any regional board, and the Labor Board may on its own motion take over the dispute if it is of the opinion that commerce is likely to be substantially interrupted. Moreover, any decision made on the individual railroad respecting wages may be suspended by the board, if it appears that the decision is likely to necessitate a substantial readjustment of wage rates.

As a guide to the adjustment of disputes, Congress laid down some general principles which have apparently been drawn from the literature of railroad arbitrations. Wages and working conditions are to be just and reasonable. As an aid in determining justness and reasonableness, the boards are to take into account, among other things, the following: wages paid for similar work in other industries, relation of wages to cost of living, hazard, training and skill, responsibility, regularity of employment, and inequalities that may have resulted from previous wage adjustments.

All decisions of the Labor Board must have the concurrence of a majority, and in case of wage disputes at least one of the public members must concur in the decision. Decisions are made public by transmittal to the President and to the Interstate Commerce Commission, and in such other ways as the board decides. If a decision is violated, the board may upon its own motion hear and determine the violation and make its decision public. Beyond this point its decisions have no sanction.

This was the organization which was to be put immediately to work upon the wage problem. The employees in large measure had awaited "with disciplined and patriotic patience" the reduction of living costs, and had submitted to the postponements of their demands, with the consequence that the new board received requests that dated back more than a year. At the suggestion of the President, representatives of carriers and employee organizations inaugurated conferences soon after the passage of the Transportation Act, and these continued until April 1, but all to no purpose. When the membership of the Railroad Labor Board was confirmed by the Senate on April 15, it was at once imposed with the burden of this wage controversy, involving all classes of labor, 2,000,000 men, and an area of national extent. Moreover, the necessity for speedy decision to allay discontent which was obvious on the surface, was made more imperative during the course of the negotiations by a letter from the President urging a prompt settlement. It was an accomplishment of no mean proportions to render a decision in two months. On July 20, 1921, increases were granted averaging 22 per cent over the wages of the Railroad Administration, and amounting in the aggregate, according to the estimate of the board, to about $600,000,000 per year. Back pay was granted to May 1.

It is not surprising to discover that the board was unable to find any formula for a just and reasonable wage. Many have tried before. No one has succeeded. "The determination of such wages," says the board, "is necessarily a matter of estimate and judgment." The seven conditions laid down by Congress as a basis were all taken into consideration. Hazard, skill, and responsibility were factors that were supported by the evidence of both employees and carriers. Railroad employment was found to be more regular and the character of work more desirable than similar employment outside. Inequalities in previous wage adjustments were a factor that could not be carefully investigated because of lack of time. As for cost of living, it could not be applied with any degree of exactitude to different parts of the country, because standardization of pay had proceeded so far and possessed such advantages that it was deemed inexpedient to disturb it. Yet cost of living was recognized as the principal ground for a general increase. It was found that the wages generally were substantially below those for similar work outside, and that the increase in cost of living had thrown real wages below the pre-war standard.

Of course cost of living is not a sound basis upon which to determine the reasonableness of wage rates. It begs the entire question. It merely indicates that an increase or a decrease is due and the probable extent thereof. Rising cost of living furnishes labor with an argument, falling cost of living puts the shoe on the other foot. But in any case it is seized upon for strategic purposes by one side or the other and settles nothing as to the fundamental justice of the basic wage.

This decision was rendered at a period of inflated prices and high costs of living, and was generally accepted and put into force. But a period of readjustment beginning in the fall, in which traffic fell off rapidly, threw the railroads into a serious financial condition. Increased rates which had been granted in August were of little avail when there was no traffic to which to apply them, and relief was sought in a reduction in expenses. Conferences were held by the individual roads with various classes of employees with reference to cuts in wages, in all of which failure to reach agreement resulted. The first dispute was filed by the New York Central in March 1921. Appreciating that this was to be followed by many others, the board consolidated the disputes into a single hearing and rendered a general decision, effective July 1, 1921.[1] It found that the cost of living had decreased since its decision of a year before, and that the scale of wages for similar work outside had declined. Influenced primarily by this situation, it reduced the wages approximately 12 per cent on the roads and for the classes involved. For this decision the chiefs of the four brotherhoods and the switchmen refused to accept responsibility. After a vain attempt to obtain the attitude of the railroads concerning further decreases, and concerning the abolition of rules and the elimination of punitive overtime, they arranged for a referendum vote on the question of giving the chiefs power to call a strike. A similar referendum was taken by the shop crafts. In every instance, the authority asked for was conferred by overwhelming majorities.[2]

As early as December 1920, six months after the increase in wages had been announced, the board felt called upon to warn both carriers and employees that violations of law had come to its knowledge. Carriers were coercing employees, refusing conferences and refus-

[1] Decision No. 147, June 1, 1921.

[2] On October 15, 1921, an order for a nation-wide strike was issued by the five big unions, to be followed later by a dozen others, and involving altogether 2,000,000 men. The roads of the country were divided into four groups. The call involving the first group of 97,000 miles was made effective on October 30, and the other calls were to follow in rapid succession. But action by the Labor Board through formal orders and by personal appeal, combined with an aroused and hostile public opinion, led to a withdrawal of the strike order at the last moment.

ing to refer disputes to the board, and organizations of employees were declining to refer disputes, and were submitting strike ballots to their membership. Special emphasis was laid by the board upon the primary procedure that the law required—the adoption by the parties of every available means *to avoid interruption of operation.* This meant conference on the individual road and in case of disagreement, reference of the dispute to the board, and then by implication, if not by express wording of the statute, abstention from any interruption to commerce pending the board's decision.

Two cases will illustrate the board's position. In the one, an organization of employees, after failure to decide their dispute with the carrier by conference, went on strike and made application at the same time for a decision by the Labor Board. The board declined to entertain the application because the employees were not acting in obedience to the law. They had not "exerted every reasonable effort and adopted every available means to avoid any interruption to the operation of the carriers."[1]

The other case is that of the Erie Railroad, which, because of its financial condition, reduced the compensation of certain classes of employees in January 1921, after an unsuccessful conference with some of the classes involved. This action was condemned by the board and held to be illegal.[2] The following quotation from the

[1] Decision No. 1, April 1920.
[2] Decision No. 91, U. S. Railroad Labor Board, March 2, 1921. The first case of this kind was that of the Atlanta, Birmingham and Atlantic, which announced decreases on February 1, 1921, of approximately 50 per cent from the rates fixed by the Labor Board the previous July. This road was in a precarious financial condition, and following the decision of the Labor Board on February 21 that it had violated the law, it promptly went into the hands of a receiver. The reduced wage rates were confirmed by Judge Sibley of the U. S. District Court, and a new legal question was thereby raised.

decision clearly expresses the fundamental purpose of the new labor legislation:

"This position, of course, renders nugatory and vain the elaborate and costly processes established by the Act and applied by this Board. It sweeps aside at the will of one party a decision arrived at after the presentation of evidence and argument by the many parties to the dispute, accepted by all and now obeyed by substantially all carriers. It justifies a disregard of the factors specified by Congress for the ascertainment of just and reasonable wages and substitutes for these factors the financial benefit of the carrier. If valid, the intent of Congress that conference, reasonableness and justice should be substituted for power, violence and disorder in the settlement of railroad labor disputes is utterly destroyed and legislation enacted after the most careful consideration rendered ridiculous and even fraudulent. If a carrier may arbitrarily reduce wages decided to be reasonable and set aside rules while a party to proceedings with regard to such rules, no reason appears why railroad employees may not announce an immediate intention of abandoning the service in concert unless demands for increased wages or more favorable working conditions are at once satisfied, provided a trend toward higher living costs shall have appeared or wage scales in similar industries shall have advanced. Such conduct is highly provocative of interruption to traffic and is not only not consistent with the Act, but is thereby clearly condemned and prohibited."

This position of the board is emphatically reiterated in an elaborate opinion in September 1921,[1] and may be summarized as follows. Public interest demands uninterrupted operation of transportation lines. Congress

[1] Decision No. 224 (Docket 426).

recognized this by making it the legal duty of all carriers and employees to exert every reasonable effort and adopt every available means to avoid interruption of operation. It ordered that all disputes *shall* be considered, and if possible decided in local conference. If not so decided, they *shall* be referred to the proper board for hearing and decision. The Labor Board is required to hear and decide *all* disputes not settled elsewhere.

The particular case here at issue was one in which the road had discharged a man because he belonged to a union, and the road had challenged the power of the Labor Board to interfere in a matter of contract between employer and employee. But the board stood firmly upon the mandate of Congress that it must decide *all* disputes that were likely to interrupt the operation of the carrier. This position is profoundly revolutionary, for it takes out of the hands of the individual carrier all control of its labor relations when they have reached a stage of disagreement that cannot be settled by conference.

Of course there is no method by which the board can enforce its decisions beyond that of invoking public condemnation. So far as any specific penalty is concerned, each carrier and each employee organization is at liberty to set at defiance the procedure laid down by the statute. The extent of the punishment is a solemn declaration by the Labor Board that they are violators of the law. But in the present state of labor controversy, when popular opinion is counted upon to such a degree, when organized propaganda is being employed continuously by both sides for "educational purposes," no railroad corporation and no reputable labor organization will lightly incur the odium consequent upon violation of law. Only acute financial straits and the long delays in reaching settlement have led any of the carriers to break over the barriers of law, and the cases are very few.

Employee violation has been the work of "outlaw" organizations, recently formed, without traditions or experience and lacking in wise leadership.

The issue upon which the struggle between the carriers and their employees largely concentrated was that which involved the retention or abandonment of the "national agreements." As already described, five of these agreements became effective between October 1919, and February 1920, three of them after the presidential proclamation announcing the return of the roads had been issued. They concerned shop crafts, maintenance-of-way employees, clerks, firemen, and signalmen. They applied nationally and universally certain working rules regardless of local conditions or previous custom or agreement. They concerned the length of day, starting and stopping time, payment for time not worked, methods of paying for overtime. They prohibited piece-work and substituted the time basis of payment wherever piece-work had been introduced. They restricted apprenticeship. They reclassified occupations on craft lines, abolishing many existing practices under which an employee might perform in the course of the day several different types of labor. That is to say, they made the rules apply to the crafts regardless of a man's location in a department, thus creating a division of jurisdiction and a conflict in working rules among employees engaged in the same general tasks. And, of course, all this increased seriously the cost of doing the work. Employees insisted that all the rules had been previously in effect on the individual roads. Some of them had been in force on some roads, but no considerable number on any one. Many roads had no agreements at all with any organizations except those in train service. The only considerable territory in which agreements such as are here being described had been in effect previously was the Southeast, and there only since 1917, when under threat of a strike and the pressure of war traffic, the roads conceded demands of the shop crafts which approximated those of the national agreement two years later.

Why, it may be asked, should this goal have been reached so suddenly during the period of federal control, when so little progress had been made theretofore? In the first place, the fact that the roads were nationalized and operated as a unit, and that negotiations concerning working conditions were being conducted almost wholly in Washington for the entire country, would provide a situation favorable to the development of the national agreement. Then it is not without significance that the Director of Labor in the Railroad Administration was the chief of the Brotherhood of Railroad Firemen and Enginemen. His official reports show no tendency to treat employee organizations with other than extreme consideration. Finally, the actual method of negotiation explains the character of the agreements themselves. When committees of the Railroad Administration, consisting in part of former railroad executives, had twice failed to agree with employee committees on a large number of the rules, the Director-General appointed a new committee from his official staff, consisting wholly of men whose former affiliations were with union labor, and they sat down in conference with representatives of the Railway Department of the American Federation of Labor. Agreements that emerged from this happy family conference were approved by the Railroad Administration and put formally into effect.[1]

The carriers, relying upon the specific wording of the contract, took the position that the national agreements terminated with the end of federal control, and they declined in their conferences with the employees in March 1920, to discuss them at all. Their continuance was one of the demands of the employees when the whole ques-

[1] Senate Committee Hearings (June 14, 1921), page 649.

tion of wages and working conditions got before the Labor Board. Although they believed them to be abrogated, the roads carried the agreements along after March 1 because they were obviously involved with the matter of wages, and the Transportation Act had provided against any reduction in wages before September 1.

In its decision of July 1920, the Labor Board, because of lack of time for consideration, deferred action on these agreements and continued them in force until further hearings could be conducted. It was the following April before decision upon them was rendered.[1] The issue was this: Shall the conditions of work be agreed upon in a national conference between representatives of carriers and employee organizations and uniformly and nationally applied, or shall they be drawn up on each road to meet the local situation? The organizations insisted that local conferences meant a waste of time with a multiplicity of controversies producing irritation and disturbance, and that these local conferences would be exposed to all the pressure of the Association of Railway Executives, thus creating a disparity of force that would produce discontent and probably would result in "traffic interruptions"—a polite name for strikes. In this argument they certainly underestimated the power of their own organizations to stand up against those of the railroads. They had had great success with their bipartisan boards during the war. The labor members, with no other interest than wage schedules, had become expert negotiators, and there is no question but that the labor side of the argument won the day in the majority of instances. This success could be continued and perpetuated, so it seemed, under a plan of collective bargaining on a national basis with union recognition.

The carriers maintained that the most satisfactory rules were those negotiated by the employees and officers

[1] Decision No. 119 (April 14, 1921).

who live under them, and that the rules should reflect the substantial differences existing in the demands of the service on different roads. They found national contracts incompatible with efficient and economical operation, and insisted that negotiation should at least begin with the local unit. They demonstrated that the existing system was enormously wasteful and expensive. In their publicity, they claimed that the restoration of local negotiation would mean a saving of at least $300,000,000 per year. However, their official spokesman before the Senate Committee, and the best authority on the subject, stated that his committee, after exhaustive investigation, had come to the conclusion that there was no possible way in which it could arrive at even an approximate estimate of what these rules had cost the railroads.[1] There were some executives, but probably not a dominating element, who looked with disfavor and alarm upon the growth of the labor organizations and to whom the main object in restoring local bargaining was to break down national unionism. The fear of "one big union" occasionally cropped out in the testimony. What national bargaining certainly did mean was that railroad officers must deal with national officers first, and in this demand it violated what should be a fundamental principle of labor negotiation. To quote from the report of President Wilson's Second Industrial Commission:

"Industrial problems vary not only with each industry but in each establishment. Therefore, the strategic place to begin battle with misunderstanding is within the industrial plant itself. Primarily the settlement must come from the bottom, not from the top."

This principle is peculiarly applicable to the railroad industry, because the geographical difficulties are so seri-

---

[1] Testimony of E. R. Whiter, asst. to vice-president in charge of personnel, Pennsylvania Railroad, who handled the case for the railroads before the Railroad Labor Board. Senate hearings June, 1921.

ous. Employees are scattered over a wide extent of territory and thrown largely on their own resources. If the spirit of personal loyalty to the individual operating organization is not present, a deadening effect on the entire organization rapidly develops, which it is impossible to check.

The board was unable to find that all the rules were just and reasonable for all carriers, and it therefore refused to extend the national agreements indefinitely. It found that certain rules were unduly burdensome and should be modified to meet local conditions. Others were of a general nature, and uniformity should be preserved. Accordingly, it ordered that the national agreements should terminate on July 1, 1921. Meanwhile, conferences should be held locally and the board should be informed of the outcome, whether agreement or disagreement, before July 1. Undue delay on the part of employees might lead the board to terminate the agreement with regard to this class of employees, and undue delay on the part of the carrier might lead to its extension. In cases of disagreement, the board would promulgate rules effective after July 1. As a guide in the promulgation of working agreements on each road, the board issued a set of principles with which it ordered that the new rules should be consistent.

In view of the fact that this is the first occasion upon which a fundamental labor code has been attempted in the railroad industry, it is sufficiently significant to warrant reproduction of the code in full.[1]

"1. An obligation rests upon management, upon each organization of employees and upon each employee to render honest, efficient and economical service to the carrier serving the public.

"2. The spirit of co-operation between management

---

[1] Decision No. 119, Exhibit B.

and employees being essential to efficient operation, both parties will so conduct themselves as to promote this spirit.

"3. Management having the responsibility for safe, efficient and economical operation, the rules will not be subversive of necessary discipline.

"4. The right of railway employees to organize for lawful objects shall not be denied, interfered with or obstructed.

"5. The right of such lawful organization to act toward lawful objects through representatives of its own choice, whether employees of a particular carrier or otherwise, shall be agreed to by management.

"6. No discrimination shall be practised by management as between members and non-members of organizations or as between members of different organizations, nor shall members of organizations discriminate against non-members or use other methods than lawful persuasion to secure their membership. Espionage by carriers on the legitimate activities of labor organizations or by labor organizations on the legitimate activities of carriers should not be practised.

"7. The right of employees to be consulted prior to a decision of management adversely affecting their wages or working conditions shall be agreed to by management. This right of participation shall be deemed adequately complied with if and when the representatives of a majority of the employees of each of the several classes directly affected shall have conferred with the management.

"8. No employee should be disciplined without a fair hearing by a designated officer of the carrier. Suspension in proper cases pending a hearing, which shall be prompt, shall not be deemed a violation of this principle. At a reasonable time prior to the hearing he is entitled to be apprised of the precise charge against him. He shall have reasonable opportunity to secure the presence of necessary witnesses and shall have the right to be there represented by a counsel of his choosing. If the judgment shall be in his favor, he shall be compensated for the wage loss, if any, suffered by him.

"9. Proper classification of employees and a reasonable definition of the work to be done by each class for which just and reasonable wages are to be paid is necessary, but shall not unduly impose uneconomical conditions upon the carriers.

"10. Regularity of hours or days during which the employee is to serve or hold himself in readiness to serve is desirable.

"11. The principle of seniority long applied to the railroad service is sound and should be adhered to. It should be so applied as not to cause undue impairment of the service.

"12. The Board approves the principle of the eighthour day, but believes it should be limited to work requiring practically continuous application during eight hours. For eight hours' pay eight hours' work should be performed by all railroad employees except engine and train service employees, regulated by the Adamson Act, who are paid generally on a mileage basis as well as on an hourly basis.

"13. The health and safety of employees should be reasonably protected.

"14. The carriers and the several crafts and classes of railroad employees have a substantial interest in the competency of apprentices or persons under training. Opportunity to learn any craft or occupation shall not be unduly restricted.

"15. The majority of any craft or class of employees shall have the right to determine what organization shall represent members of such craft or class. Such organization shall have the right to make an agreement which shall apply to all employees in such craft or class. No such agreement shall infringe, however, upon the right of employees not members of the organization representing the majority to present grievances either in person or by representatives of their own choice.

"16. Employees called or required to report for work, and reporting but not used, should be paid reasonable compensation therefor."

While at first glance it may seem that the board, in issuing this code, has gone beyond its prerogatives and has presumed to dictate in matters of internal management, yet, when it is recalled that it is a court of final appellate jurisdiction in matters of working rules as well as wages, the code becomes merely an announcement of the grounds upon which it will decide disputes before it.

It is not feasible to discuss here the principles enunciated by the board. It is sufficient to point out that, if they are all conscientiously incorporated into agreements on all the roads, a substantial advance will have been made in the strategic position of railroad labor. The right of labor to organize, the right to be represented by those of its own choice, whether employees of the carrier or not, the right to a hearing in case of discipline, the right to decide what organization shall represent a particular craft in negotiations, are all fundamental demands of labor. The last point, covered in paragraph 15, is particularly significant. It gives the majority of any craft, whether organized or not, the right to determine what organization shall represent it in negotiations, and the agreement thus perfected applies to all employees of the craft. Thus, while it is specifically provided that non-union members may present grievances either personally or by representatives of their own choice, the tendency of the principle is to create and recognize craft organization, and to provide that such organization shall deal for all members of the craft, whether or not they are members of the union. In behalf of management, the code demands eight hours of work in return for eight hours of pay. Further, it recognizes that discipline is necessary, and that there is a limit to the application of the seniority rule and the classification of employees.

Adjustment boards, regional or national, have not as yet been put into operation.[1] Labor, except for train-service employees who have had for many years their territorial scheme of negotiation, has spent its efforts in attempting to continue the national agreements and with them national bargaining. The general disposition of the carriers has been to oppose these regional or national adjustment boards unless representatives of the public were made members; in other words, unless mediation were converted into arbitration. To this the employees have refused to agree. The consequence has been that controversies over working rules, which the law obviously intended should be threshed out through the mediation process, have gone directly to the Labor Board along with wages, and have burdened it unduly with matters that should have been settled in conference.

Following upon the reference to the individual carriers and their employees of the problem of working agreements, an issue of far-reaching significance developed on the Pennsylvania road between the management and the members of two groups of organizations, those comprising the shop crafts and the clerks, freight-handlers, express and station employees. In arranging for the selection by ballot of representatives of the men who were to confer with the management in drawing up working rules, the railroad company provided a ballot which com-

---

[1] It is announced (September 1921) that the Baltimore and Ohio and the New York Central are contemplating a joint regional board for the settlement of disputes concerning working rules with the train-service and switchmen's organizations. This movement is likely to spread.

pelled each employee to vote for individuals and to confine his vote to employees of the Pennsylvania Railroad
in the class to which he belonged.   Moreover, the company organized the railroad into divisions, and limited
the employees' choice to a representative upon their own
division.   The organizations referred to held this action
of the carrier to be in conflict with the law and refused
to participate, and the issue reached the Labor Board.
This board held that the carrier was in the wrong in undertaking to assume control of the selection of those who
were to represent the employees, and also in dividing its
system into regions and requiring regional representatives, which might easily lead to gerrymandering.   Moreover, the carrier was held to be culpable in refusing to
permit employees to place the name of an organization
on the ticket, instead of the name of an individual.   The
Act recognized the existence of organizations of railroad
employees.   Men had built up these organizations at
their own expense, had put their most competent men
at the head of them, had accumulated valuable data and
information to be used in wage controversies.   If the
majority desired to take advantage of this organization,
they could not be denied.   And in any case, the placing
of the name of the organization on the ballot was equivalent to placing there the names of individuals, because
it was recognized that the officers of these organizations
would represent them in any conference.   Moreover, the
employee could not be restricted to voting for an employee of the Pennsylvania road.   He might choose any
one to represent him, which in the case of the unions
might mean one of the chief officials, who had no personal contact with the individual property.   On the other
hand, the employees could not require that the ballot contain only the name of the organization, because the statute
intended to give opportunity for non-union men freely
to express their choice.

The issue then was not a clear-cut one between the closed and open shop, for the Labor Board had expressly rejected the claim of the organization to control the election. On the other hand, the claim of the Pennsylvania of the right to organize the system in such fashion as to insure, so far as possible, individual employee voting with no specific recognition of the union was likewise rejected. It was to be an open unrestricted choice over the entire system of either individual employees or union representatives as the body of workmen decided.

The railroad made application to the Labor Board to vacate its decision on the ground that the board had exceeded its jurisdiction in prescribing principles to govern the making of agreements and in laying down the methods of election of the constituent members of a joint conference. The road claimed to be sustained in its position by 66 per cent of the employees affected by the rules governing working conditions. Its fundamental opposition to the decision of the board was that the road might be compelled to deal with national union officers instead of its own men, that the method discriminated in favor of the union and tended to compel the non-union men either to join the union or see their interests neglected, and that it violated the fundamental right of employer and employees to deal directly with each other in settling their own affairs. One is impressed as in all arguments of this character with the extreme solicitude of the management for the welfare of the non-union man. He is the lay figure over which the fight for the "open shop" is being fought. There are many reasons for believing that the issue on the Pennsylvania road is not local to that system, that the carriers as a whole are making this a test case, and that the future relation of labor to management in this industry is now at stake in much larger degree than the public realizes. In fact, the answer of the board, granting only in minor degree the request of the Pennsylvania system, and sharply criticising the road for proceeding in disobedience to its orders,[1] has apparently been received in a defiant manner by the carrier, which maintains that the board is acting beyond its jurisdiction. This resistance of carriers to the interference of the board with contract relations between them and their employees, when considered in connection with the nation-wide strike called by the labor-unions consequent upon the board's decision reducing wages and relieving the carriers of some of the burdensome provisions of the national agreements, does not promise well for the future of the Labor Board. It apparently has not yet gained the confidence of either side.

Generally speaking, the attempt by the Labor Board to obtain agreements negotiated locally as a substitute for the national agreements previously in force failed throughout the country. This was due to the fact that local representatives of the unions stood firm, under instructions from their national officers, for the continuance unmodified of the national agreements which the Labor Board had temporarily suspended. The board has now been compelled to resume jurisdiction, and to undertake the task of revising the agreements clause by clause, in order to fit them fairly to existing conditions. For the board has stated that the complaint of the carriers is sustained, and that the rules formerly in effect are in many respects burdensome, unreasonable, and unjust. The important conclusions thus far reached by the board include the recognition of the principle of the eight-hour day, and punitive pay for overtime work in the shops, also the policy of paying time and one-half on Sundays and holidays except for work which is absolutely essential for continuous operation. Another issue soon to be decided is that of piece-work. The men insisted in the national agreements upon the retention of the hourly basis

[1] Order in re Docket 404 (Sept. 1921); Decision No. 218 (July 1921).

of pay on the ground that piece-work constitutes a form of slavery, that it makes a living wage impossible, and that it prevents the exaction of time and one-half for overtime. Managements, on the other hand, insist that the better men prefer it, that a fair wage is guaranteed under it, that it develops efficiency and economy to a high degree, to the advantage of both men and management.[1]

One question which the Act does not settle is that of the relation of wages to rates, specifically the relation of the Labor Board to the Interstate Commerce Commission. It has frequently been asserted, and with some measure of justification, that the body that makes the rates should have control of the expenses, and particularly of that largest single item, the wage bill. The Commission is instructed to see that the railroads are honestly and efficiently managed, but its only direct connection with the wage situation is in the requirement that the Labor Board shall keep it informed by transmitting its decisions. To what extent does the Labor Board recognize the rate situation or the financial condition of the carriers in making its wage decisions? When the abolition of national agreements was demanded by the carriers they made much of their serious financial condition. The board recognized that while its authority was limited to fixing wages and working rules, it could not overlook the fact that rules affected operating expenditures, and that unreasonable rules imposed an undue burden on carrier and public. Nevertheless, it said that the general financial condition of the roads was a matter for the Commission and not for the board. This can only mean that the board, while necessarily taking cognizance of the

[1] On October 14, 1921, the Labor Board authorized the railroads to open negotiations with the unions for the restoration of piece-work, thus setting aside Rule 1 of the national agreement with the shop crafts.

general financial situation, will decline to accept testimony specifically demonstrating the financial condition of the carriers. Yet, in both the law itself and in its interpretation by the board, there is a recognition of the inseparability of rates and wages. Reference has already been made to the circumstances or conditions which the law says must be taken into account by the board in adjusting wages, such, for example, as skill, hazard, and responsibility. The statute requires the board to take these factors into account "among other relevant circumstances." In its second wage decision the board declared that "other relevant circumstances" included "the relation of railroad wages to the aggregate of transportation costs and requirements for betterments, together with the burden on the entire people of railroad transportation charges." Again, the statute provides that the Labor Board may suspend any decision on an individual road if it is "of the opinion that the decision involves such an increase in wages or salaries as will be likely to necessitate a substantial readjustment of the rates of any carrier," and shall hear and decide the case promptly.

It is evident, therefore, that the Labor Board cannot and does not decide wage questions without regard to their effect upon railroad revenue. But neither can the Commission fix rates regardless of the wage decisions of the Labor Board, for it is its duty to prescribe rates that under honest and efficient management will produce in net operating income certain results definitely specified by statute. These results cannot be attained if expenses, of which wages are the largest factor, are not fully taken into account. The close practical relationship of rates and wages necessarily prevails. The present situation is a travesty on justice, in which two federal agencies control essential factors in railroad income and expense, and in which neither is under statutory compulsion to take account of the rulings of the other. The Wage Board may prove to be a failure. In that case, wages as well as rates should be placed under the jurisdiction of the Commission. This might have been a wiser procedure in the beginning. But now that we have the Wage Board, it is entitled to a thorough test. Such a body provides a valuable laboratory for working out solutions of this complicated wage problem. Its prestige has been increased by its attitude toward the threatened strike. The Interstate Commerce Commission has abundant troubles of its own without taking on new ones of such proportions.

But an assumption of authority by the Commission over both rates and wages would not get rid of the difficulty of determining which should have prior consideration. It would merely get rid of the public scandal of having two official bodies at loggerheads. From the standpoint of economic theory there is no question but that wages must come first. There may be temporary emergencies, such as the present one created by a world-wide upheaval of industrial conditions, in which some compromise with fundamental principles is necessary,— when a deficit must be divided as equitably as possible between carrier, employer, and the public. But under normal conditions communities cannot expect to obtain railroad service unless they pay for it. Among the costs of furnishing this service, labor is the largest element. Labor must be paid the going rate for similar service outside if the railroads are to compete effectively with other capital in the labor market. The Interstate Commerce Commission must accept the determination of the Labor Board as one of the controlling elements in the fixing of rates. And, if the situation requires it, this must be made clear by a legislative mandate.

CHAPTER XXIII

REGULATION OF WATER TRAFFIC

UPON the termination of federal control all water-transportation facilities on inland canal and coastwise waterways, including boats, barges, and tugs that did not belong to railroad companies were to be transferred to the Secretary of War, who was to continue to operate them under the existing contracts and agreements. Further, he was authorized to construct terminal facilities on behalf of the Government that would promote traffic interchange, or to loan funds for construction to any state whose constitution prohibited ownership of terminal facilities by other than the state or a public body. Operation was to be subject to the Interstate Commerce Act and to the Shipping Act, exactly as though the facilities were privately owned.

Agitation soon arose for the removal of all Government craft from the New York Barge Canal. Representations were made officially to Congress by the New York Canal Board that the operation by federal barges resulted in unfair competition and in discrimination against privately owned barges, and that the presence of the federal government in the canal-transportation business was a detriment to the investment of private capital for the formation of freight-carrying companies, upon which depended the ultimate success of the canal. Government operation had begun there in September, 1918, but without adequate equipment. The peculiar characteristics of the situation were carefully investigated and a fleet of cargo and self-propelled barges was designed and constructed. However, not until late in 1919 were the cargo barges ready, and none of the others appeared until 1920, after federal control had ceased. By the end of the season of 1920, the Government was operating twenty self-propelled barges and seventy-two new cargo barges. The financial statement for 1920 did not reflect these improvements. The gross revenue for the nine months, January to September, was less than half a million dollars and the deficit $87,000. The average monthly operating ratio was 119 per cent. Yet the Secretary of War urged a continuance of the service for another year, which he felt confident would be long enough time to demonstrate the practicability and profitableness of a modern barge-transportation service.

But Congress refused to listen and provided for the withdrawal of the Government in March, 1921, from operation on the New York Barge Canal, and also for the prompt disposal of all facilities by sale, or temporarily by lease.[1] The money obtained from the sale of equipment was to be used in the development of inland transportation elsewhere, in accord with the policy declared by Congress in the Transportation Act of 1920.

This declaration[2] put Congress on record in favor of promoting water transportation and preserving it in full vigor. The Secretary of War was instructed to investigate types of boats, terminals,[3] and transfers, to advise concerning locations and plans, and in general to investigate the present capacity and efficiency of the various inland waterways. A thorough and honest investigation of our existing waterways with a view to a decision whether they are actually fulfilling any economic function and

---

[1] Joint resolution, February 27, 1921.   [2] Sec. 500.

[3] The investigation of terminal and transfer facilities on a more elaborate scale was ordered by Congress in the Merchant Marine Act of June 1920 (Sec. 8), and made the duty of the U. S. Shipping Board and the Secretary of War. It was provided that if after the investigation the board was of the opinion that the rates and regulations of the railroads were detrimental to the development of adequate transfer facilities between water and rail, it should submit its findings to the Interstate Commerce Commission for action under the law.

whether they *ever can* do so would be worth far more than it would cost. But the mandate issued by Congress does not lead one to hope for anything beyond the usual superficial and unscientific survey of our water facilities. The investigation must determine "whether such waterways are being utilized to the extent of their capacity," and "to what extent they are meeting the demands of traffic," and "to investigate any other matter that may tend to promote and encourage inland water transportation." When we recall what a boon the river and harbor bills have been to our congressmen, and when we follow the work and the reports of the United States engineers in their struggles to convert swamps and brooks and sand-bars into navigable streams that are to bring untold prosperity to the settlements alongside, we can gather little hope for a scientific study of water transportation from this latest noble pronouncement of the Congress of the United States.

The jurisdiction of the Interstate Commerce Commission over foreign commerce has been extended by requiring every water carrier of United States registry so engaged to file with the Commission a schedule showing ports of loading, sailing dates, and routes. Upon a shipper's application a railroad must request and the carrier must supply full statement as to rates for a specific sailing. Upon notice from the railroad that the rate has been accepted, the steamship must reserve the necessary space. Based upon the information obtained, the railroad is required to issue a through bill of lading to the port of destination, although its liability ceases upon delivery of the freight to the water carrier. It is specifically provided that such bill of lading does not constitute "an arrangement for continuous carriage or shipment," and therefore the Commission has no control over the water portion of the rate.

It is of interest to observe that the Act requires the

Commission to publish for the information of shippers throughout the country the substance of the schedules furnished by the water carriers relating to sailings and rates, "the intent being that each shipping community sufficiently important, from the standpoint of the export trade . . ., shall have opportunity to know the sailings and routes, and to ascertain the transportation charges of such vessels engaged in foreign commerce." [1]

The Shipping Act of 1916 [2] and the Merchant Marine Act of 1920 [3] confer upon the Shipping Board certain powers with respect to rates charged by water carriers that are similar in character to the powers exercised by the Interstate Commerce Commission over rail carriers. So far as these powers relate to water commerce between United States ports, and in some particulars in matters of foreign commerce, they actually conflict with the powers granted to the Commission. It is not worth while to go into the conflicts of jurisdiction which have been heedlessly created by this recent shipping legislation. A reading of the two statutes referred to will suggest the problem with which the two administrative agencies, the Shipping Board and the Interstate Commerce Commission, are now wrestling. Jurisdictional conflicts appear in connection with granting priority or embargoes on traffic moving in foreign commerce, in connection with rates on commodities for export, and with respect to through bills of lading, port regulations, delivery of freight for shipment, and other technical matters of operating procedure. Conferences between the two authorities have thus far been without result, and Congress may have to be called upon to straighten out the tangle of its own making.

Of still more serious portent, from the standpoint of the public welfare, is that we now have two agencies in

[1] Sec. 25 (3).   [2] 39 Stat. L., 728, Secs. 17 and 18.
[3] Pub. Acts No. 261, 66th Cong., 2d Sess.

existence, in the nature of rivals, each interested in developing its own type of transportation. This eagerness for traffic is more marked in the case of the Shipping Board, for the obvious reason that the United States is in the shipping business and is apparently desirous of making a record. By the Panama Canal Act, the railroad companies were obliged to divest themselves of all ownership in water lines through the canal. In transcontinental territory their ability to compete with the water lines depends directly upon the extent to which the Commission will allow them to depart from the distance principle and charge only the competitive rate to and from coast points. But in addition to this they must have assurance of continuity in this business sufficient to warrant making investment in the necessary facilities. But when the Commission takes up this problem, it is faced with a Shipping Board determined to make business for its ships and free to draw upon the United States Treasury to cover its deficits. As already insisted, the public should enjoy the full benefit of its investment in the Panama Canal. But is it not a short-sighted policy to use this waterway and Government shipping to break down a rail-transportation system upon which a vast territory is wholly dependent?

We started on the wrong tack in the Panama Canal Act. The edict separating rail and water line ownership with the purpose of making them compete, was but one more evidence of the persistent vitality of the competitive theory, the working results of which in transportation affairs are so completely at variance with hopes and expectations. What is needed is a scientific allocation of traffic between the two agencies, both of which should be under Commission control as to rates and practices. In other words, co-operation as discussed in the final chapter should be made a working principle in the management of our transportation agencies.

CHAPTER XXIV

THE FUTURE

IT is apparent to any one who has followed the history of the relations of Government to railroads as told in the preceding pages, that the so-called "railroad problem" has not yet been solved. We have advanced from step to step, steadily increasing the authority of the Government and enlarging the area of its exercise. But we have not reached the goal. The public is not at the present moment enjoying efficient transportation service at satisfactory rates, nor is there any assurance that the basis has been laid for the preservation even of such service as we had before the war. We are not convinced that capital is ready in a practical way to back this industry and provide it with the funds needed for its growth. What, then, must we look for in the future? We are obviously in a state of unstable equilibrium. Can we adjust our present structure by modifications here and there and thus stabilize it for a considerable time ahead, or must we resort to revolutionary methods and cast aside our present system for something fundamentally different? Upon this question opinion divides. It is not the purpose here to present these divergent points of view except incidentally, but rather to suggest a line of development which seems to promise for the years immediately ahead the most satisfactory outcome. "Solutions" of such a continuing problem as that of the railroads, which claim to dispose of all difficulties for all time and to usher in the millennium, need not detain us.

The line of development here suggested is based upon the acceptance of the following propositions:

1. The railroads of the country cannot be operated privately without earnings sufficiently generous to in-

sure a constant stream of new capital into the industry. This rate of return cannot be stated with accuracy, but it is probable that at present it must be as high as 6 per cent on the investment.

2. If 6 per cent cannot be earned, it follows that inasmuch as the railroads must be operated, Government aid will have to be sought. Government aid means taxation, and this means inevitably Government ownership, and probably Government operation. Government ownership would be a hazardous experiment; Government operation would be disastrous.

3. No assurance is possible that under existing conditions 6 per cent can be earned continuously at present rates. Higher rates are inadvisable and probably would be less productive; many rates are now too high. It follows, therefore, that the necessary earnings must be assured through savings in operating expense. This means in brief the development on a national scale of a programme of efficient and economical operation.

4. The results sought cannot be attained by any of the minor economies frequently suggested and practised. They must come through a nation-wide introduction of methods of co-operation.

These propositions require some further elucidation. The first one will command general acceptance in principle. No rate-making body has ever promulgated a schedule of rates without having in mind its effect upon the investment market. Even if it were practicable so to fix rates that the public would not only pay for transportation service but also provide a surplus to be devoted to the improvement of the plant, there would be no justice in such a procedure. The railroads must seek new capital in the capital market. But they must be able to show an attractive income account in order to get it. Surveying the investment market as it exists to-day and considering the opportunities for investment likely to arise in other fields of industry during the next decade, it is improbable that a rate of less than 6 per cent will prove attractive.

It is a common expression that private operation is now on trial, and that if it fails, Government ownership is inevitable. That this is an exact statement of the situation is somewhat doubtful. The hostility to Government ownership at the close of federal operation was too genuine and too deep-seated to warrant the conclusion that the country would soon resort to this alternative. However, the one factor that might produce such an outcome suddenly would be that of the failure of credit. New capital is absolutely essential to the very existence of the industry. If the Government alone can furnish it, ownership will follow. It should be recalled that the Government's financial interest in the industry at the present time is probably nearly a billion of dollars. In considering whether Government ownership is desirable, it should be borne in mind that there is no question of principle involved. There is nothing inherently wicked about Government ownership or operation. To call it "socialistic" does not condemn it, for we are enjoying to our universal satisfaction many "socialistic" activities of a similar sort, such as public postal facilities, water-supply, and public highways. The only question involved is one of expediency, which method will give the public the better service at the lower rates.

Government ownership disassociated from operation has many attractive features. It means above everything else unification of property in one agency, with all the possibilities that such an ownership gives in working out a unified system of administration. It means assured credit, and probably in the long run some, and possibly a considerable, saving in interest. But in view of the undesirability of federal operation, Government ownership would be justifiable only if the Government were able to effect satisfactory leases of the property for operating purposes. No one can say whether this would be possible, but it is clear that the operation of a Government property on a rental basis would remove much of the incentive to vigorous and efficient management that prevails under a régime where the owners are the managers.

As for Government operation, that suggestion should be resolutely laid one side until we have developed a public civic consciousness that will stand the strain. To-day we are ill fitted to undertake such a responsibility. In fact, there is no precedent anywhere. For no country that has tried it has the size of ours, or its diversity of industrial interests, in combination with the democratic form of Government. Canada has had it forced upon her as the result of reckless finance, but Canada would be rid of her burden if she could, and a study of the results of Government operation in that country would not encourage us to try it.

There are two serious objections to it, an economic and a political one. From the economic standpoint, we should unquestionably lose all the benefits that spring from private initiative, and we should realize all the deadening influences of bureaucracy. It is unreasonable to expect men of the caliber of our railroad executives to remain indefinitely as Government employees and, it may be added, at the salaries that the public is willing to pay. They gave their services without reserve to the Government during the war, but when peace was signed they stole away one by one as rapidly as possible. The opportunities for waste in the railroad business are enormous. Oversight of operations is difficult because of the geographical extent of the industry. Anything that might be saved in interest charges through Government ownership would be far more than offset by the enhancement of operating costs, and the country would lose that valuable asset, discussed elsewhere under competition in service, which has been called railroad statesmanship.

The political effects of Government ownership are too well realized to require any extended comment. We have had suggestions in recent years as to what this might mean. The passage of the Adamson Eight Hour Law in 1916 showed us what labor could do politically when it got the country by the throat. The filibuster which closed the session of Congress in March, 1919, and defeated all the appropriation bills, causing acute financial distress in the Railroad Administration, was a minor illustration of the way in which political motives may affect the interests of industries dependent upon the Government. The multitude of ways in which a pestiferous politics-minded Congress could interfere in the affairs of a great industry like our railroad system is appalling, and should cause the people to think twice before they place their very economic existence in jeopardy.

All this is not to imply that private operation as at present conducted is not subject to much criticism, and that much actual mismanagement does not exist. It is a relative matter. On the whole, and at least for the present, we should seek our solution through the agency of private ownership and operation and persist in our experiment with Government regulation. The solution of our immediate difficulties should come through the development under centralized guidance of a national programme of co-operation.

The project assumes two aspects; first, co-operation for savings in operating costs, which involves mainly technical engineering and industrial problems; and, second, co-operation among the different agencies of transportation, which is an economic and traffic problem. There is not at present sufficient authority lodged in the regulating body to accomplish these ends. Properly, the

Commission's authority has been confined in normal times to the oversight of the carriers. Only in emergencies is it authorized to take the place of the management or to require one carrier to share its property with another. How far should this private-property right be invaded in the interest of transportation as a whole? To what extent should co-operation be made compulsory? For it is clear that without the force of law it will not go fast or far.

One method provided in the new law is that of consolidation, which would go a considerable distance in promoting the programme of co-operation here advocated.[1] But consolidation is voluntary with the carriers, and there is no evidence that it is arousing any enthusiasm among them. In fact, it will probably get but a little way unless made compulsory. Moreover, it has many obstacles, legal and financial, and would take much time to complete even if made compulsory. Co-operation, while involving vast projects of wide extent, can be undertaken much more speedily and can proceed from the simpler to the more elaborate without any upset of existing structures.

Suggestions for economies in operation through the development of co-operative relationships between the

[1] In support of this contention is the statement of Professor Ripley in his explanation of the tentative plan for the consolidation of railroads, prepared at the request of the Interstate Commerce Commission: "One of the larger aspects, then, of this proposed consolidation plan is that it offers a third choice, in place either of completely unified regional ownership and operation with its lack of incentive, on the one hand, or of the economic wastes which are incident to helter-skelter competition between a heterogeneous congeries of more or less imperfectly developed properties, on the other. One alternative threatens stagnation; the other has driven our railroads to the verge of bankruptcy. May not a well-ordered consolidation programme offer a way out, without resorting to the ultimate expedient of Government ownership, from which, once adopted, there can be no withdrawal?"

roads have been numerous, but are too technical to be fully discussed here. A few of them may be mentioned.

Joint facilities and terminals.
Standardization in construction, inspection, and repair of equipment.
Purchase of fuel and supplies.
Fuel consumption.
Locomotive improvement—electrification.
Standardization of shop practice.
Standardization of traffic regulations, such as demurrage, reconsignment, and the like.

All of these do not require co-operation among carriers. Some of them would have to be worked out in detail on each property. But co-operation in the analysis of the problem and in experimentation would materially expedite solution, and would accelerate the introduction of the new methods once agreed upon, into the operations of each separate property.

The terminal problem is probably the one in which co-operative action will reap its greatest reward, including in this designation interchange and storage yards and all track facilities outside the main lines. The underlying difficulty with the introduction of co-operation is the same as in all the other problems, namely, the desire on the part of management to preserve the individuality of the system, and an eagerness, entirely commendable, to develop an *esprit de corps* on the road and a prestige for the organization with shippers and public, which results naturally in an indifference to the interests of adjoining carriers, if not to actual hostility. Organizations of carrier officers of one sort or another manage to agree reasonably well on policies affecting general legislation, or on plans for educational publicity, but so soon as the discussion touches on a matter vital to the operation of an individual railroad, they begin to fall apart. This was what made the work of the Railroads' War Board in 1917 difficult. It is responsible in a measure for the unhappy manner in which the carriers presented their labor problems before the Labor Board in 1921.

The public has permitted these terminal properties to develop without, until recently, taking any serious interest in their character and location, and large cities have been provided with separate and scattered terminal yards constructed on the theory that each railroad is an isolated undertaking having no relation to any other. The result is that consolidation of terminal properties becomes to-day a well-nigh insoluble problem because of its physical difficulties and its financial magnitude. The claim that any movement toward joint terminals would be illegal under the Anti-Trust Act has no basis in court decision, beyond the ruling that such terminals must not be organized with the purpose of preventing competition.[1] One of the best illustrations of the terminal situation is found in the application of the New York Central Railroad to the Commission for permission to acquire the Chicago Junction Railway,[2] which serves the stock-yards and adjoining industries, and which has been used by most of the lines entering Chicago for switching and interchange purposes. The New York Central desired exclusive possession in order to enlarge its terminal facilities and balance those of the Pennsylvania Railroad. Eight railroads intervened with the Commission to prevent this consummation on the ground that it would result in destroying the neutrality of the line and the free interchange of freight.[3] A strict recognition of the competitive principle would have permitted the New York Central to proceed, but is it in the inter-

[1] 224 U. S., 383 (1912).   [2] Finance Docket No. 1165 (1921).
[3] Senate Com. hearings, June 28, 1921, page 914.

est of the public as a whole that this railroad should monopolize the traffic of this enormously valuable industrial district, or that other roads should enter it on terms laid down by the New York Central Railroad?[1]

The same attitude of mind is seen in the construction of the huge modern efficient interchange yard for the make-up and despatch of trains. All the talent of the engineering and operating staffs is devoted to carrying these yards to the highest point of efficiency, but all with the thought of perfecting the operation of the individual carrier. Scarcely, if ever, is the proposition considered of building such yards conjointly with neighboring roads. It is a well-recognized principle that the necessity of breaking up trains en route is the greatest obstacle to smooth and rapid railroad operation. The ideal is to load a train at point of origin and run it through solidly to destination without any delay beyond what is necessary for inspection. Some notable results of this kind were achieved during federal operation when private interests were laid one side. There is no reason now except private individual railroad interest why this principle of operation should not be rapidly extended.

Many objections will of course be raised to this argument. For example, valuable terminals already in existence cannot be scrapped. It is unfair that the benefits of terminals should be enjoyed by roads that have not contributed to their development. The demands of shippers require that terminals should be distributed and not concentrated. But these arguments are not convincing. Terminals need not be located in one unified area; belt lines can provide the necessary relation-

---

[1] This spirit of competition frequently leads to excessive investment which the public must indirectly carry. Unused property purchased for the future is a competitive necessity. It is said that due to duplication 70 per cent of the train-track capacity in the Chicago terminals is unused.

ship. The significant thing is the standardization and
the integration of terminal properties conducted as administrative units instead of the present extreme individualistic competitive arrangement.

Competition has had the effect of offering service at
terminals at a cost in excess of the revenue received.
Yet carriers persist in this policy, many of them, apparently, being only vaguely aware of the actual situation.
We need thorough enlightenment on the subject of
terminal costs in order to establish a basis for scientific
rate making and one upon which sound competition with
other agencies can be constructed. At present little is
known of terminal costs in spite of the fact that since
the enactment of the original Act in 1887 carriers have
been required to file schedules of rates which should
state separately all terminal or other charges that the
Commission might require and "any rules or regulations which in any wise change, affect or determine any
part or the aggregate" of the rates.[1] Testimony has
been developed in various cases showing that trunk-
line carriers have expended more in terminal costs than
they received for the total haul of freight, thus actually
doing business at a deficit. Competition has driven the
roads remorselessly along until they are absorbing enormous amounts in special services which should be recovered from the shipper. The New York Harbor Case
in 1917 brought out in a striking fashion the rapid and
disturbing growth in terminal costs as compared with
those of the line haul. It pointed to the time not far
distant when carriers can no longer absorb these costs
into their hauling rates but must impose specific terminal
charges. In the Iron Ore Rate Cases[2] the Commission,
after prescribing maximum dock charges and requiring
the carriers at these lower lake ports to establish separate rates for switching and other services, stated that it

[1] Sec. 6 (1).   [2] 41 I. C. C., 181 (1916).

ought not to be necessary to tear a rate apart in order to determine what proportion was intended as compensation for each distinct service. A declaration by a carrier of inability to dissect the rate is an obstruction to effective regulation.

It is, therefore, a fact of importance that the statistical bureau of the Commission is at work on the problem of separating line and terminal costs. It is obviously absurd for the carriers to distribute all their earnings for statistical purposes upon ton-mile and car-mile bases, when in many cases so large a proportion of the cost to which proportionate earnings should be assigned is incurred in terminal service into which the element of distance and carriage does not enter.

Another problem of long standing is that of the efficient distribution of equipment. The existence of a shortage of cars in one section of the country coincident with a surplus in another is a visible evidence of the incompetency of our railroad service as a national agency. For years the matter has been under discussion and proposals have been made for the pooling of a certain proportion of the equipment under centralized management, to be used as a "flying squadron" that should meet the emergencies in various sections of the country. But always the plan has been defeated by the selfishness of some few of the carriers.

Purchase of fuel and supplies on a co-ordinated basis has obvious economies. The study of fuel consumption should be undertaken on a comprehensive scale through the co-operation of all the carriers. Experts insist that the surface of this question has hardly been scratched.

Sufficient has been said to illustrate the point. Savings on the scale necessary to put transportation service on a permanently solvent basis can only be undertaken by the carriers working on a national scale, and with an eye to the situation as a whole rather than to the effect upon the individual property. For this reason the proposals put forward by the Association of Owners of Railroad Securities in the spring of 1921 warrant careful public consideration. This association had already secured in the Sundry Civil Appropriations Act of June 5, 1920, an amendment providing for loans to railroads during the guarantee period (March to September, 1920), in which the Commission was given power to designate an agency as appropriate for the construction and sale or lease of equipment to carriers. Acting upon this authority, the Commission had designated the National Railway Service Corporation chartered in Maryland at the instance of the Association of Owners of Railroad Securities and serving without profit, as a central equipment agency. Aided by loans from the Government out of the $300,000,000 revolving fund provided for emergency purposes during this guarantee period, it had supplied equipment to railroads under terms of conditional sale or lease. The Commission had made loans up to 40 per cent of the value of the equipment and the Service Corporation had sold trust certificates for the remaining 60 per cent, largely to the members of the Association of Owners of Railroad Securities, that is, to the insurance companies and savings-banks. The total of certificates sold amounted on July 1, 1921, to $33,000,000.

In July 1921, the Association of Owners of Railroad Securities presented to the Senate Committee a most elaborate plan for the development of the co-operative principle, and testimony was offered by the members of its Board of Economics and Engineering,[1] consisting of eminent engineers who were analyzing the problem here under discussion. The proposals of this association involve the national incorporation of the service agency already described, with power not only to aid railroads by selling them equipment on the car trust plan, but

[1] Senate Committee hearings, June 22, 1921, page 797.

to build and own equipment and serve as a pool for the balancing of equipment needs in various parts of the country. The remainder of their proposals involve a somewhat cumbersome organization designed to study and develop and eventually put into effect co-operative economies of nation-wide scope, the whole scheme being headed up in the Interstate Commerce Commission, which is to have supervisory power. The particular plan is not of great significance for this discussion. The important thing is that it has been proposed and that the Interstate Commerce Committee of the Senate has it under consideration.

One other phase of the operating problem will need to be grappled in thoroughgoing fashion before satisfactory results will be forthcoming. That is the relation of labor to the industry. The railroad labor problem has this feature that distinguishes it from the issue in most other industries. It is a public occupation in which the sense of responsibility to the patrons must needs be keener than elsewhere. Otherwise the principles involved are not essentially different from those of the labor problem in general. But the solution of the problem is complicated by the character and organization of the business. The industry is of enormous size, decentralized into a large number of independent operating units with workers classified into a multitude of occupations. For years each railroad endeavored to settle its own labor problems without regard to settlements on other roads, and even with the development of national organizations of management and men, there was extraordinary diversity of policy among the different carriers. Federal control did much to unify and standardize relations, and the effort of the carriers since has been to rid themselves of these national agreements and restore the local relationship.

There is here present that conflict which is evident

throughout the labor world wherever a solution of the problem is being sought, the struggle for organization on a national scale on the one hand, and on the other the effort to preserve local negotiation and the co-operation of the individual workers in the solution of the problems of the individual plant. National organization has done much and will do more to improve the lot of the individual workman on the individual railroad. It has stood between him and the exploiting policy of a hostile management. Its efficacy and its right to be are recognized by the Labor Board in ruling that workers may choose as conferees in negotiations with management officers of their organizations who are not employees of the road concerned. But national organization has, in multitudes of cases, prevented co-operation between management and men on an individual property, because the national officers, fearful of the possible undermining influence of such procedure, have elected to direct all questions of policy from national headquarters.

National organization as a medium of negotiation becomes a cold business transaction robbed altogether of the human element. It inevitably means that the goodwill of the employer is to be expressed alone in the pay-envelope, which Mr. Gompers is reported to have approved as the policy of the American Federation of Labor. But the inevitable result is an armed truce. It does not mean co-operation or efficiency. It means war, and as little work for as large pay as possible.

On the other hand, a complete decentralization of industrial relations would be equally disastrous. We should be thrown back to the confusion of pre-union days. On some roads co-operation would be admirably developed, with ample recognition of labor in joint counsel. On other roads despotism would prevail, which might be successful as a policy so long as the tyrant was benevolent, but which would result in revolution when his arbi-

trary successor came upon the scene. Some managements would encourage unionism, some would tolerate
it, some would oppose it. From the standpoint of the
country as a whole, there would be no assurance that
labor would obtain justice, neither would there be any
considerable degree of co-operation between management and men.

The solution probably lies somewhere between. If
national union organization is to continue and receive
public support, it must show itself far more elastic than
it has been in the past. National agreements must
give room for a flexible adjustment to local needs, an
adjustment to be effected not by national officers but
by local conference. Moreover, the unions will have to
yield in the matter of individual participation in management. A persistence in the policy of refusing to permit
local participation in management for fear of undermining the union will eventually result in wrecking the
union itself. For only through local participation is
that spirit of loyalty to the industry to be restored which
has been destroyed during the last two decades, and
only through this spirit of loyalty is that efficiency to
be created which the public is rightfully demanding.

If the Railroad Labor Board is equal to its task, and,
conceiving the problem in its national aspect, is able to
evolve a labor code that will commend itself to both
sides, and if it is capable of establishing that nice adjustment between national organization essential to the
preservation of fundamental rights, on the one hand,
and local negotiation essential to the preservation of
operating efficiency, on the other, it will have performed
a service of extraordinary value to the industry and the
public. Labor must be given a larger share of interest
in the industry. Its sense of responsibility must not be
deadened by confining its relation to the pay-envelope,
the contents of which are arranged for by the negotia-

tion between organized and hostile groups. It was a mistake to eliminate from the Esch-Cummins Act the provision under which labor was to share in the excess earnings above 6 per cent, which now go to the carrier and the Government. Some profit-sharing provision of this nature should be operative, sufficiently direct in its effect to stimulate efficiency and develop morale in the working organization. But, more than this, management must look forward to the time not far distant when it must admit labor into the inner circles and give it a voice in management. There is much sound advice and wisdom to be gained from the more intelligent of the working force. Yet the advantage is not to the greatest degree to be found in the contributions that labor makes. Rather will it grow out of the fact that labor knows what is going on, appreciates the problems of management, and hence acquires confidence. This all works for conservatism in judgment, deliberateness in reaching critical decisions, and the development of a sense of responsibility. There is no greater source of savings to-day than is to be found in the development of the proprietorship spirit in the working force. This does not necessarily mean that employees must sit on the boards of directors. The result can be accomplished through other means; for example, through properly organized conference boards after the order of the Whitley Councils in England. The particular form of organization is not significant. What is required is that labor should feel that it is being given the opportunity to discuss and advise with reference to fundamental problems of management, and that none of the facts of the situation is being withheld.

Organized labor has not thus far shown the same sense of responsibility to the public that management has displayed, neither has it so clearly appreciated the public nature of the industry in which it is employed. Doubtless this is due to the fact that it has had to take the offensive in fighting its battles against an intrenched position, and that until its battle was won it had to concentrate on what seemed to be a wholly selfish objective. But if it is to win any continuous support from the public, it will have to make clearer than it has yet done that the public interest is not only not being disregarded, but that it is being given first place in the minds of the workers.

And this means that labor must prepare itself to abandon the strike and confine itself to arbitration as a means of adjusting labor controversies. It is fortunate that the proposal of this nature in the Cummins Bill failed to become law, for we are not yet fully prepared for it, and a premature trial of compulsory arbitration might have postponed its effective working for many years.

Every one recognizes the necessity for uninterrupted transportation. The utter dependence of the public upon transportation service gives it a legitimate interest in the causes of interruption and a justifiable ground for interference. There is no doubt that both capital and labor should be required to accept service in this industry subject to a limitation upon their freedom of action in the settlement of their disputes. But it is quite a different thing suddenly to incorporate the principle of compulsory arbitration into law, and impose it upon a group of employees just emerging from the restrictions of Government employment into which they were drafted for war purposes, a group long in service with many valuable seniority rights, and in large degree unfitted by age and service to seek an alternative employment. But the public should give warning in some unmistakable fashion that settlement of disputes in public-service industries must be accomplished by peaceful means, and that labor must prepare itself for a speedy realization of this programme. This involves the obligation on the part of the public to create a tribunal in which the administration of justice is assured. It involves the establishment by law of certain fundamental rights of labor, which might be called a labor code. A beginning has been made in the instructions laid down by Congress for the guidance of the Railroad Labor Board in the fixing of wages, considerations which the board is required to take into account when determining the reasonableness of wages and working conditions. And this encouraging beginning has been followed up by a more elaborate set of provisions drawn by the board itself. With the fundamental rights of labor assured, and with an informed and high-minded arbitration body in existence, there should be no more difficulty in adjusting labor disputes peaceably than there is in the settlement of ordinary cases at law. In the substitution of the modern law-court for the old trial by battle, we have an exact parallel to our existing problem. The substitution of an impartial tribunal for the strike is fully justified on the same broad grounds of public policy. With such a tribunal, the argument of involuntary servitude, whatever slight plausibility it may have had before, falls to the ground.

All this has related to the details of operation. But a problem of greater public interest, if not of greater importance, is that of the proper co-ordination of the different agencies of transportation. We have experimented with many types of transportation in the past and doubtless there will be many new types forthcoming. But at present there are but two agencies that perform any significant service other than railroads—certain types of water and highway transportation. We are here considering the subject in its larger aspects and with reference to the more substantial economies. Hence, we can disregard interurban electric transportation, which has confined itself in large degree to passenger service, a phase of transportation useful and necessary, but of relatively little interest to the railroads as a whole from the standpoint of net earnings. The interurbans might absorb all of the short-distance passenger transportation without seriously affecting the railroads of the country as a whole. And the interurbans are in their turn facing a competition from the individual automobile that threatens their eventual elimination.

For distances of 40 miles and less the motor-truck is at present in many parts of the country a serious competitor in freight traffic. In New England it threatens the very existence of the railroads. Its development has been extraordinary since the war, and only the obstacle of inadequate highways has prevented a still more phenomenal growth. That there must eventually be some sort of co-operation between motor-truck and railroad, and a tacit division of territory, seems fairly evident. But what is needed first of all is information as to costs of highway transportation properly assigned to their different categories, based upon a survey that is scientific and wholly uninfluenced by ulterior motives. At present our information relating to motor-truck transportation is confined to a few items of operating cost, furnished by some of the larger motor-truck transportation companies. Most of the information of this character emanates from concerns manufacturing either trucks or accessories, and their literature is largely directed to a beguiling of the public into the construction of improved highways upon which they can operate untrammelled and untaxed. Nothing whatever is said of the fundamental construction costs for right of way, which the public pays, nor of the enormous rate of depreciation on the plant, which likewise comes out of the public's pocket. Toward this increasing capital investment and depreciation expense the motor-truck contributes a trifling license fee, which falls far short of meeting its public obligation.

On the other hand, the railroads have acquired often at great expense their rights of way, and must maintain and improve them out of their earnings. To be sure, much land for right-of-way purposes was given the railroads, but under agreements by which they have at least in part returned the gift. Moreover, the public has profited through the development of the country to a far greater extent than the value of the lands given. That the motor-truck has a permanent place in the transportation system there seems to be little doubt. It serves a real need in its direct pick-up and delivery service. While its ton-mile costs for actual transportation are far in excess of the railroad costs, it avoids the heavy terminal expense, and even when imposed with capital charges for its fair proportion of highway construction and maintenance, it will furnish a superior service for short hauls. Its success in transportation for longer distances, 100 to 300 miles, is due rather to the inefficiency of its competitor than to its own fundamental superiority, combined, of course, with its exemption from nearly all legitimate charges. What is urgently needed is a survey that will furnish the public the facts upon which to construct a programme of scientific co-operation.

This same problem arises in the case of water transportation. The Panama Canal was constructed at public expense to furnish a through water route from coast to coast in competition with the railroads, and the policy is now being strongly urged of abolishing all canal tolls on coastwise shipping. Or, again, public money is expended in the improvement of the Ohio and lower Mississippi to increase the safety and promote the regularity of river transportation, and projects are urged at national expense for the construction of adequate transfer facilities in order to make water transportation more attractive. Legislation has from time to time been enacted in an effort to prevent the more efficient railroad from taking business away from the less efficient waterway. How far is the public justified from the social and economic standpoint in continuing its policy of subsidizing other forms of transportation?

The country is under no moral obligation to confine itself to railroad transportation and scorn all other, merely because it was first in the field and has made an irrevocable investment. Much of its business could not in any case be wrested from it. That which can be taken away, if drawn off by more efficient agencies, the railroads ought to lose. But what part can the public properly play in diverting this traffic? The answer is that it is justified in making the investment in a highway or a waterway to the extent that economic results warrant. If traffic responds appropriately the investment was worth while. But the public should see to it that it gets its return in lowered rates. Whether the motor-truck or the steamboat company is adequately taxed is a matter of public policy, but if it is not so taxed, this fact should be taken into account in the rates permitted to be charged by them. Which implies that these agencies should not be left uncontrolled on the theory that competition will give the public the lowest practicable price, but should be regulated as to their charges exactly as railroads are regulated. In other words, if the various agencies looked at from the public standpoint are placed under the control of a central authority, which assigns them their proper sphere in the co-operative scheme, and regulates their operation and their charges, much of the apparent discrimination against the railroad industry would disappear. The important point is that we need a policy, and one that is definite and constructive.

So far as water transportation is concerned, we as a people have spent our money recklessly and in utter disregard of sound business principles. We have proceeded on the theory that water transportation was obviously and always cheaper than rail, and if the water highway was once available, the people would have the railroads by the throat. Considerably over a hundred millions have been spent on the ditch known as the New York Barge Canal, which, toll free, is to furnish a cheap transportation to the people of New York State. But the only way in which the project can be made to exhibit any economic justification is by disregarding capital cost and the tax burden imposed on the people of the state. Enormous sums have been spent on the Ohio and the lower Mississippi by the United States Government. So far as these have to do with flood prevention they can be justified, but from the standpoint of transportation they have realized practically nothing. To be sure, there are many reasons to be assigned for this outcome, such as physical difficulties preventing the construction of satisfactory transfer facilities with rail, and, in some cases at least, destructive railroad rates. But when all is said, the fact remains that for this section the railroad is clearly the more efficient and cheaper agency and that the Government has spent its funds foolishly.

Even the Panama Canal, which broke a narrow barrier between great navigable bodies of water, the construction of which is clearly justified from the transportation standpoint, has thus far failed to realize the benefits in lowered transportation costs that were naturally to be expected. Shipping has been inadequate, and the boats available have been able to fill their holds at rates that were higher than a genuine competitive situation would have presupposed. However, this situation is doubtless only temporary, and we shall probably see in the immediate future an actual realization to the American people of their investment in this enterprise.

It is the observation of a railroad executive who has

long been a student of rail and water competition[1] that such competition is only temporary, that eventually one agency or the other takes the traffic according to its efficiency and ability successfully to handle, and the other retires from the business. He cites as instances to support his statement the coal business on the Great Lakes and coastwise from Virginia to New England, and the traffic between Southern cities and New York and Boston, and that on the Mississippi River. Whether this division of traffic will be as marked in the case of business from coast to coast through the Panama Canal remains to be seen. But certain it is that there must eventually be worked out, as already advocated in the case of highway transport, a programme of co-operation between water and rail that will give to the public the economic benefits to be derived from the presence of both. This involves not alone the determination whether transportation on inland canals, navigable rivers, and the Great Lakes is to be developed and, if so, to what extent, but it involves the solution of the terminal problem where transfer is made between rail and water. It is here that the good-natured tolerance of the American people has been grievously taken advantage of. At the ports, terminal facilities have come into the possession of the railroads by purchase or lease, and this possession has been used to compel exclusive shipment over the railroad lines and to effect exclusive traffic agreements with specific steamship companies. Ports have been split up into water-tight compartments by this railroad policy. No port unity has existed. In fact, the possession of monopoly privileges by a carrier has put that carrier into active opposition to all unification policies.[2] Car-

[1] President Markham, of the Illinois Central R. R. Co., before the National Rivers and Harbors Congress in Dec., 1920.

[2] An investigation has been authorized by the Interstate Commerce Commission of the port situation at South Atlantic and Gulf ports in its relation to rail carriers.

riers that serve several ports have centred their affection
upon one and have diverted traffic there, to the detriment of other ports and the injury of the service. Canals
may or may not have an economic justification, dependent upon their location and the nature of the service
they perform, but the public has little opportunity to
reach satisfactory conclusions when the canals are owned
by or leased to railroads that use them only when their
rail lines are congested. While physical difficulties have
been a deterrent to the development of co-operation of
rail carriers and river steamers, yet much more could
have been done toward the perfection of transfer facilities if the railroads had been interested in the development of this type of business. Only the pressure of public interest expressed through the regulating authorities
will secure that co-operation between rail and water
which has been so long delayed without adequate justification.[1]

[1] In this connection it is pertinent to quote the following from the
testimony of Director-General Hines before the subcommittee of the
House Committee on Appropriations, April 12, 1920. (Hearings, page
206.)

"Now, in general, in the past these inland waterways which have
been improved by the Government at very great expense have been
in the attitude of transportation systems without any feeders and
without any satisfactory opportunity to make arrangements for interchange traffic. I feel that since the Government has invested so much
in the improvement of the waterways through construction of locks,
dams, etc., and the deepening of channels, certainly an effort ought to
be made to see whether or not with proper interchange arrangements
established, so that on the one hand the waterways can feed the railroads and on the other hand the railroads can feed the waterways, it
will not develop to be a really practicable method of transporting certain sorts of traffic. My best judgment about that is that it will turn
out to be a desirable thing. It will vary as to different waterways.
Of course, the conditions are widely different. For example, the New
York State Barge Canal is subject to the condition that for a good part
of the year, when the demand for traffic is most insistent and when
transportation on the railroads is most difficult, the canal is frozen up
and is not available. On the other hand, the heaviest traffic is in the
fall months, in September, October, and November, when the canal is

This programme of co-operation, contemplating on the one hand the association of the carriers in far-reaching policies for efficient operation, and on the other a scientific allocation of the transportation work of the country among the agencies best fitted to perform it, is one that is essential to the future prosperity of the country. It must be taken in charge by some central agency upon which must be conferred adequate authority. The authority already possessed by the Interstate Commerce Commission and its familiarity with the problem based on long experience, suggests this body as the natural one to initiate a survey and construct a programme. But the Commission, if it is to be effective, must be protected

available, and there is a very great deal of heavy traffic that can move that way, and I have felt that it was well worthy of developing the experiment further to see whether that canal could not be successfully used for that traffic. The Warrior River in Alabama is very little interfered with by weather conditions and has a very large traffic southbound from the Alabama coal-fields, and I feel there is a very excellent prospect of that justifying itself.

"The Mississippi River, also, south of St. Louis is very little interfered with by weather conditions, and south of Cairo is interfered with still less, and it seems to me that that is a very important proposition that ought to be developed further with a reasonable prospect of its success. It is hard to tell what sorts of traffic can be most successfully carried, and I believe there will have to be a good deal of experimentation before anybody can settle down to certain lines of traffic that can be handled with the greatest degree of economy and satisfaction; but my general view is that as to these great waterways of the sorts I have referred to, there is a very strong probability that it will develop to be in the national interest and in the promotion of national economy to use them for transportation of certain classes of traffic. For one thing, I believe one great difficulty with railroad transportation has been that where the railroad traffic moves over a considerable distance, unless it is given preferred movement, like perishables or like these merchandise cars, the movement is rather uncertain, and you can count with a good deal more certainty on when a boat which leaves one end of a line on one day is going to reach the other end of it than you can when a car-load of traffic is going to reach destination, and it has occurred to me that that would be a distinct advantage with river movements as to some forms of traffic. On the whole, I feel that the experiment is well worth carrying forward and ought to be done with the expectation that it would be successful as to certain classes of traffic."

in its administrative independence. It must consist of men who are or may quickly become experts in this complex field, and they must feel free to take such steps as their expert judgment dictates. Moreover, their position is semijudicial in character, and their judgments and their anticipated decisions must no more be tampered with than are those of the Supreme Court. It is important to insist upon this position of independence, for there are many disturbing indications that the executive branch of the Government in Washington is conceiving it to be its duty to bring its powerful political influence to bear upon the Interstate Commerce Commission in the interest of policies held to be for the public welfare. Possibly as a consequence of our experience with federal operation, and also because of the Government's large financial stake in the industry, we have come to regard the Commission's relations to the roads and the Government's relation to the Commission in a different light than we did in 1916 and earlier. But it is a tendency that should be checked at the outset. It is a dangerous and undermining influence. If persisted in, it will wreck our great experiment in railroad regulation, which alone gives promise of offering in the distant future a clear road out of our difficulties.

APPENDIX I

BIBLIOGRAPHICAL NOTE

The sources of information for an exhaustive study of this period, 1910 to 1921, are to be found in official documents. In the first place, students should examine carefully the *Decisions of the Interstate Commerce Commission*, usually designated by the technical name of *Reports*. Volumes 18 to 57 cover the period discussed in this book. There is no other material at all comparable with this in its wealth of information concerning industrial, commercial, and transportation conditions in the United States. The rendering of a rate decision necessitates an analysis of the factors upon which a reasonable rate must be based, and this analysis is invaluable for the student of American industrial history. In addition to the *Decisions* of the Commission, the *Annual Reports* of the Commission to Congress and the annual volume, much delayed in publication, called *Statistics of Railways in the United States*, should be consulted.

There has been a plethora of congressional hearings during the decade, that have had to do with railroad affairs. They are worth reading because in most of them the railroad problem is under discussion in its broader aspects, and every phase of the problem and every point of view finds expression here at some time or other. The most important of these hearings are listed herewith:

Hearings before Joint Committee on Interstate and Foreign Commerce, 64th Cong., 1st Sess., Nov. 20, 1916, to Dec. 19, 1917.

Hearings before Senate Committee on Interstate Commerce, 65th Cong., 3d Sess., on Extension of Tenure of Government Control, January 3 to February 21, 1919.

Hearings before House Committee on Interstate and Foreign Commerce, 66th Cong., 1st Sess., July 15 to August 19, 1919.

Hearings before Senate Committee on Interstate Commerce, 67th Cong., 1st Sess., on Railroad Revenues and Expenses, May 10 to July 1, 1921.

Hearings before House Committee on Interstate and Foreign Commerce, 67th Cong., 1st Sess., on the Railroad Funding Bill, August, 1921.

Hearings before subcommittee of House Committee on Appropriations, 66th Cong., 2d Sess., on Appropriations for Federal Control, April 7, 1920.

The best source of material on the war administration of the railroads is to be found in the reports issued at various times by the Director-General, some comprehensive in scope and issued directly from his office, but the major portion the reports of his various divisions and of his regional directors. In addition, there have been published volumes containing the proclamations, general orders, circulars, and bulletins issued by the President and the Director-General and his subordinates.

For a presentation of the railroad point of view during the entire period, there is no better source than the files of the *Railway Age*. This periodical, edited with great ability by Samuel O. Dunn, while frankly an advocate of the railroads' cause, maintains the position of a friendly critic with decided success.

The Association of Railway Executives, which is sustained by nearly all the railroads of the country, issues from time to time statements and discussions that explain and defend the railroads' position. This publicity work has been in competent hands. Its statements of fact are to be accepted as a rule at their face value. Its arguments and opinions are frankly and necessarily partisan.

The Bureau of Railway Economics, established by the railroads in 1910, has earned a well-deserved reputation for scientific and accurate handling of statistical material. As a rule, it confines itself to statements of fact and refrains from partisan presentation. Its publications should be consulted in addition to those of the Interstate Commerce Commission, as it aims to interpret the official statistics and put them into a form more readily grasped by the non-technical reader.

APPENDIX II

TENTATIVE PLAN FOR RAILROAD CONSOLIDATION

The following scheme for the consolidation of the railroads of the United States "into a limited number of systems" has been promulgated by the Commission as a tentative plan,[1] in compliance with the mandate of the Transportation Act of 1920, Section 5 (4 and 5). The plan originally prepared at the request of the Commission by Professor William Z. Ripley, of Harvard University, has been somewhat altered by the Commission to minimize the dismemberment of existing lines. It has been made public for the purpose of eliciting "a full record upon which the plan to be ultimately adopted can rest."

SYSTEM No. 1.—NEW YORK CENTRAL

New York Central.
    Pittsburgh & Lake Erie.
    Rutland.
    Michigan Central.
        Chicago, Kalamazoo & Saginaw.
    Cleveland, Cincinnati, Chicago & St. Louis.
        Cincinnati Northern.
Western Maryland.
Fonda, Johnstown & Gloversville.
Lake Erie & Pittsburgh.
Central Indiana.
Pittsburgh, Chartiers & Youghiogheny.
Monongahela.
Boston & Maine.
Maine Central.
Bangor & Aroostook.
And all railway properties controlled by the above carriers through lease, stock ownership, or otherwise, except:

    Lake Erie & Western and Toledo & Ohio Central. } Both now controlled by New York Central.

    Zanesville & Western and Kanawha & Michigan. } Both now controlled by Toledo & Ohio Central.

[1] 63 I. C. C., 455.

Indiana Harbor Belt, now controlled by New York Central, 30 per cent; Michigan Central, 30 per cent; Chicago & North Western, 20 per cent; Chicago, Milwaukee & St. Paul, 20 per cent.

NOTE.—Prof. Ripley recommends the inclusion of the Western Maryland in system No. 5, Nickel Plate-Lehigh Valley.

Prof. Ripley makes no specific assignment of the Fonda, Johnstown & Gloversville.

The Lake Erie & Pittsburgh, Central Indiana, Pittsburgh, Chartiers & Youghiogheny, and Monongahela may be incorporated in either system No. 1 or No. 2. Prof. Ripley makes no specific assignment of these four roads, which are controlled jointly in the interest of the New York Central and the Pennsylvania.

The Boston & Maine, Maine Central, and Bangor & Aroostook may be included in system No. 7, New England, or system No. 7a, New England-Great Lakes. Prof. Ripley rejects the trunk-line treatment of the New England roads, but we present this alternative with a view to developing the situation upon hearing.

The Lake Erie & Western may be included in system No. 5, Nickel Plate-Lehigh Valley.

The Toledo & Ohio Central, Zanesville & Western, and Kanawha & Michigan may be included in system No. 9, Norfolk & Western.

The Indiana Harbor Belt is reserved for consideration in connection with terminal situations.

SYSTEM NO. 2.—PENNSYLVANIA

Pennsylvania.
> West Jersey & Seashore.
> Long Island.
> Baltimore, Chesapeake & Atlantic.
> Cumberland Valley.
> Maryland, Delaware & Virginia.
> New York, Philadelphia & Norfolk.

Pittsburgh, Cincinnati, Chicago & St. Louis.
> Waynesburg & Washington.

Grand Rapids & Indiana.
Cincinnati, Lebanon & Northern.
Ohio River & Western.
Louisville Bridge & Terminal.
Wheeling Terminal.
Toledo, Peoria & Western.
Lorain, Ashland & Southern.
Lake Erie & Pittsburgh.
Central Indiana.

Pittsburgh, Chartiers & Youghiogheny.

Monongahela.

And all other railway properties controlled by any of the above
carriers under lease, stock ownership, or otherwise, except the
Norfolk & Western and railway properties controlled by it,
which may be included in system No. 9, Norfolk & Western.

NOTES.—The Lorain, Ashland & Southern may be included in system No. 4, Erie, which owns one-half the stock, the Pennsylvania
owning the other half.

The Lake Erie & Pittsburgh, Central Indiana, Pittsburgh, Chartiers
& Youghiogheny, and Monongahela may be included in system No. 1,
New York Central, which controls one-half the stock, the Pennsyl-
vania controlling the other half.

SYSTEM NO. 3.—BALTIMORE & OHIO

Baltimore & Ohio.
>   Sandy Valley & Elkhorn.
>   Staten Island Rapid Transit.

Reading system, comprising the Philadelphia & Reading, Central
>   Railroad of New Jersey, and various others.

Cincinnati, Indianapolis & Western.

Chicago, Indianapolis & Louisville.

New York, New Haven & Hartford.
>   Central New England.

Lehigh & New England.

Lehigh & Hudson.

NOTES.—The Baltimore & Ohio Chicago Terminal is reserved for
consideration in connection with terminal situations.

The New York, New Haven & Hartford, Central New England,
Lehigh & New England, and Lehigh & Hudson may be included in
system No. 7, New England, or system No. 7a, New England-Great
Lakes.

SYSTEM NO. 4.—ERIE

Erie.
>   Chicago & Erie.
>   New Jersey & New York.
>   New York, Susquehanna & Western.

Delaware & Hudson.

Delaware, Lackawanna & Western.

Ulster & Delaware.

Bessemer & Lake Erie.

Buffalo & Susquehanna.

Pittsburg & Shawmut.
Pittsburg, Shawmut & Northern.
Lorain, Ashland & Southern.
Wabash lines east of the Missouri River.

NOTES.—Prof. Ripley recommends including the Lehigh Valley in this system; but in this tentative plan that carrier is proposed as a main stem for system No. 5, Nickel Plate-Lehigh Valley.

The Delaware & Hudson, Delaware, Lackawanna & Western, Ulster & Delaware, Pittsburg & Shawmut, and Pittsburg, Shawmut & Northern may be included in system No. 7a, New England-Great Lakes.

The Bessemer & Lake Erie may be included in system No. 5, Nickel Plate-Lehigh Valley.

The Lorain, Ashland & Southern may be included in system No. 2, Pennsylvania.

SYSTEM NO. 5.—NICKEL PLATE–LEHIGH VALLEY

Lehigh Valley.
New York, Chicago & St. Louis.
Toledo, St. Louis & Western.
Detroit & Toledo Shore Line.
Lake Erie & Western.
Wheeling & Lake Erie.
Pittsburgh & West Virginia.
Bessemer & Lake Erie.

NOTES.—Prof. Ripley recommends the Lackawanna as main stem in this system. In this tentative plan it is replaced for that purpose by the Lehigh Valley, and made available for either system No. 7a, New England-Great Lakes, or system No. 4, Erie. He also includes the Buffalo, Rochester & Pittsburgh and Wheeling & Lake Erie in this system.

The Bessemer & Lake Erie may be included in system No. 4, Erie.

SYSTEM NO. 6.—PERE MARQUETTE

Pere Marquette.
Detroit & Mackinac.
Ann Arbor.
Detroit, Toledo & Ironton.
Boyne City, Gaylord & Alpena.

NOTE.—The last-named road is a Class II road not specifically covered by Prof. Ripley's report.

System No. 7.—New England

New York, New Haven & Hartford.
    New York, Ontario & Western.
    Central New England.
Boston & Maine.
Maine Central.
Bangor & Aroostook.
Lehigh & Hudson River.
Lehigh & New England.

Notes.—Prof. Ripley recommends inclusion of the New York, Ontario & Western in system No. 4, Erie.

The Lehigh & Hudson River is not included in any system under Prof. Ripley's report, but is left as a "bridge line."

System No. 7A.—New England–Great Lakes

Same as system No. 7 with addition of the following, which otherwise with the exception of the Buffalo, Rochester & Pittsburgh may be included in system No. 4, Erie. That carrier may be included in system No. 5, Nickel Plate-Lehigh Valley.

Delaware & Hudson.
Ulster & Delaware.
Delaware, Lackawanna & Western.
Buffalo, Rochester & Pittsburgh.
Pittsburg & Shawmut.
Pittsburg, Shawmut & Northern.

Note.—The addition of these lines has not been recommended by Prof. Ripley.

System No. 8.—Chesapeake & Ohio

Chesapeake & Ohio.
    Hocking Valley.
Virginian.

Note.—Prof. Ripley recommends consolidation of the Virginian with the Norfolk & Western, Toledo & Ohio Central, and Kanawha & Michigan, in order to afford a western outlet for coal originating on the Virginian. This apparently would involve up-grade eastbound haul of westbound coal to the vicinity of Roanoke, unless there be new construction near Gauley Bridge, W. Va. The Virginian's present outlet to the west is via Deepwater, W. Va., and the Chesapeake & Ohio.

System No. 9.—Norfolk & Western

Norfolk & Western.
Toledo & Ohio Central.
    Zanesville & Western.
    Kanawha & Michigan.
    Kanawha & West Virginia.

Note.—From the Norfolk & Western is excepted the branch from Roanoke to Winston-Salem, which may be included in system No. 11, Atlantic Coast Line-Louisville & Nashville and the branch from Lynchburg to Durham which may be included in system No. 12, Illinois Central-Seaboard.

System No. 10.—Southern

Southern.
    Alabama Great Southern.
    Georgia, Southern & Florida.
    Mobile & Ohio.
    Southern Railway in Mississippi.
    Northern Alabama.
    Cincinnati, New Orleans & Texas Pacific.
New Orleans Great Northern.
Alabama & Vicksburg.

Note.—Prof. Ripley recommends inclusion of the Georgia Southern & Florida branch from Valdosta, Ga., to Palatka, Fla., in the Seaboard system.

System No. 11.—Atlantic Coast Line–Louisville & Nashville

Atlantic Coast Line.
    Atlanta & West Point.
    Charleston & Western Carolina.
    Louisville & Nashville.
        Nashville, Chattanooga & St. Louis.
        Louisville, Henderson & St. Louis.
Western Railway of Alabama.
Richmond, Fredericksburg & Potomac.
Norfolk Southern.
Atlanta, Birmingham & Atlantic.
Winston-Salem Southbound.
Roanoke to Winston-Salem branch of Norfolk & Western.
Florida East Coast.

Carolina, Clinchfield & Ohio.
Georgia & Florida.
Gulf, Mobile & Northern.
Mississippi Central.

NOTES.—Prof. Ripley recommends that the Richmond, Fredericks-burg & Potomac and Florida East Coast retain their present status without inclusion in any system.

The Carolina, Clinchfield & Ohio may be included in system No. 12, Illinois Central-Seaboard. Prof. Ripley recommends inclusion in system No. 10, Southern.

The Gulf, Mobile & Northern and Mississippi Central are not spe-cifically included in any system under Prof. Ripley's report.

SYSTEM NO. 12.—ILLINOIS CENTRAL–SEABOARD

Illinois Central.
  Yazoo & Mississippi Valley.
  Central of Georgia.
Seaboard Air Line.
Lynchburg, Va., to Durham, N. C., branch of Norfolk & Western.
Gulf & Ship Island.
Tennessee Central.
Carolina, Clinchfield & Ohio.

NOTES.—Prof. Ripley recommends that a separate system be built around the Seaboard Air Line.

The Gulf & Ship Island is not included in any system by Prof. Ripley.

The Carolina, Clinchfield & Ohio may be included in system No. 11, Atlantic Coast Line-Louisville & Nashville.

SYSTEM NO. 13.—UNION PACIFIC–NORTH WESTERN

Union Pacific.
  St. Joseph & Grand Island.
  Oregon Short Line.
  Oregon-Washington Railroad & Navigation Company.
  Los Angeles & Salt Lake.
Chicago & North Western.
  Chicago, St. Paul, Minneapolis & Omaha.
Lake Superior & Ishpeming.
Wabash lines west of the Missouri River.

NOTES.—Prof. Ripley recommends inclusion of the Central Pacific in this system.

The Lake Superior & Ishpeming is not specifically included in any system by Prof. Ripley.

SYSTEM NO. 14.—BURLINGTON–NORTHERN PACIFIC

Chicago, Burlington & Quincy.
Northern Pacific.
Chicago Great Western.
Minneapolis & St. Louis.
Spokane, Portland & Seattle.

NOTES.—From the Chicago, Burlington & Quincy are excepted the Colorado & Southern and Fort Worth & Denver City, which may be included in system No. 16, Santa Fe. Prof. Ripley recommends that they be included in system No. 19, Chicago-Missouri Pacific.

Prof. Ripley recommends extension of this system to the Pacific coast by including the Denver & Rio Grande and the Western Pacific. He also recommends redistribution of portions of the Minneapolis & St. Louis and Chicago Great Western.

The Spokane, Portland & Seattle may be included in system No. 15, Milwaukee-Great Northern.

SYSTEM NO. 15.—MILWAUKEE–GREAT NORTHERN

Chicago, Milwaukee & St. Paul.
Great Northern.
Chicago, Terre Haute & Southeastern.
Duluth & Iron Range.
Duluth, Missabe & Northern.
Green Bay & Western.
Spokane, Portland & Seattle.
Butte, Anaconda & Pacific.

NOTES.—The Green Bay & Western and Butte, Anaconda & Pacific are not included in any system under Prof. Ripley's report.

The Spokane, Portland & Seattle may be included in system No. 14, Burlington-Northern Pacific.

Prof. Ripley recommends that the eastern half of the Chicago & Eastern Illinois be included in this system.

SYSTEM NO. 16.—SANTA FE

Atchison, Topeka & Santa Fe.
    Gulf, Colorado & Santa Fe.
Colorado & Southern.
    Fort Worth & Denver City.
Denver & Rio Grande.
Western Pacific.
Utah Railway.
Northwestern Pacific.
Nevada Northern.

NOTES.—Prof. Ripley recommends inclusion of the Colorado & Southern and the Fort Worth & Denver City in the Missouri Pacific system. He also recommends inclusion of a part of the Gulf Coast Lines in the above system.

Prof. Ripley recommends that the Northwestern Pacific retain its present status.

The Nevada Northern is not specifically included in any system by Prof. Ripley. It may be included in system No. 17, Southern Pacific-Rock Island.

SYSTEM NO. 17.—SOUTHERN PACIFIC–ROCK ISLAND

Southern Pacific Company.
Nevada Northern.
Chicago, Rock Island & Pacific.
    Chicago, Rock Island & Gulf.
Arizona & New Mexico.
El Paso & Southwestern.
San Antonio & Aransas Pass.
Trinity & Brazos Valley.
Midland Valley.
Vicksburg, Shreveport & Pacific.
Chicago, Peoria & St. Louis.

NOTES.—The Nevada Northern may be included in system No. 16, Santa Fe.

The Arizona & New Mexico and Chicago, Peoria & St. Louis are not specifically included in any system by Prof. Ripley.

The Trinity & Brazos Valley may be included in system No. 18, Frisco-Katy-Cotton Belt. So recommended by Prof. Ripley.

Prof. Ripley recommends redistribution of portions of the carriers included by us in this system.

SYSTEM NO. 18.—FRISCO–KATY–COTTON BELT

St. Louis-San Francisco.
St. Louis Southwestern.
Louisiana Railway & Navigation Company.
Chicago & Alton.
Missouri, Kansas & Texas.
Trinity & Brazos Valley.
San Antonia, Uvalde & Gulf.

NOTES.—The Trinity & Brazos Valley may be included in system No. 17, Southern Pacific-Rock Island.

Prof. Ripley recommends inclusion of the San Antonio, Uvalde &

Gulf in either system No. 17, Southern Pacific-Rock Island, or in a Southwestern-Gulf system.

Prof. Ripley recommends redistribution of portions of the carriers included by us in this system.

SYSTEM No. 19.—CHICAGO–MISSOURI PACIFIC

Chicago & Eastern Illinois.
Missouri Pacific.
Kansas City Southern.
Kansas City, Mexico & Orient.
Kansas, Oklahoma & Gulf.
Texas & Pacific.
Fort Smith & Western.
Louisiana & Arkansas.
Gulf Coast Lines.
International & Great Northern.

NOTE.—Prof. Ripley recommends redistribution of portions of the carriers included by us in this system.

Certain lines such as the Minneapolis, St. Paul & Sault Ste. Marie, and the Central Vermont, which are controlled by Canadian carriers, have not been specially included in this tentative plan, because these lines form parts of through trans-continental Canadian systems in active competition with systems above set forth.

The carriers included in this tentative plan comprise most of the Class I steam railroads but very few of those in class II and Class III. Those not so included, whether industrial common carriers, terminal carriers, interurban electric railways operated as a part of general steam-railroad systems of transportation or engaged in the general transportation of freight, "short lines," or others, will be considered at the hearings to be hereafter assigned so that in the plan to be ultimately adopted provision can be made for their inclusion in the systems.

We have not specifically mentioned water carriers. Where these carriers are now controlled by carriers by rail they will be considered as being included tentatively in the systems in which the controlling rail carrier has been included.

INDEX

INDEX